T0340658

THE DIVIDED STATES OF AMERICA

The Divided

States of America

WHY FEDERALISM

DOESN'T WORK

DONALD F. KETTL

PRINCETON UNIVERSITY PRESS

PRINCETON & OXFORD

Published by Princeton University Press
41 William Street, Princeton, New Jersey 08540
6 Oxford Street, Woodstock, Oxfordshire OX20 1TR

press.princeton.edu

Library of Congress Cataloging-in-Publication Data

Names: Kettl, Donald F., author.
Title: The divided states of America : why federalism doesn't work / Donald F. Kettl.
Description: Princeton, New Jersey : Princeton University Press, 2020. | Includes bibliographical references and index.
Identifiers: LCCN 2019024582 (print) | LCCN 2019024583 (ebook) | ISBN 9780691182278 (hardback) | ISBN 9780691201054 (ebook)
Subjects: LCSH: Federal government—United States—History. | States' rights (American politics)—History. | Equality—Government policy—United States. | United States—Social policy.
Classification: LCC JK311 .K47 2020 (print) | LCC JK311 (ebook) | DDC 320.473/04–dc23
LC record available at https://lccn.loc.gov/2019024582
LC ebook record available at https://lccn.loc.gov/2019024583

British Library Cataloging-in-Publication Data is available

Editorial: Bridget Flannery-McCoy and Alena Chekanov
Production Editorial: Kathleen Cioffi
Text Design: Lorraine Doneker
Jacket Design: Layla Mac Rory
Production: Erin Suydam
Publicity: James Schneider and Kate Farquhar-Thomson
Copyeditor: Cynthia Buck

This book has been composed in Arno Pro

Printed on acid-free paper. ∞

Printed in the United States of America

10 9 8 7 6 5 4 3 2 1

CONTENTS

PREFACE

This book grew out of a concern that one of the most interesting, fundamental, and important institutions of American politics—federalism—has largely fallen from public view and scholarly debate. The nation's founders would surely be amazed to discover that one of their biggest and most important ideas, focused on how best to divide power between the federal government and the states, has gotten so little attention in the twenty-first century. Issues of federalism almost destroyed the effort to declare independence from George III. It nearly prevented the ratification of the Constitution following the victory over the Redcoats. And seventy years later, some of the biggest issues that the founders ducked at the beginning resurfaced in the Civil War and nearly ended the grand American experiment.

It would be hard to imagine anything in American politics more important. That makes it equally hard to conceive of why it could have vanished from public view and become no longer a subject of intense debate. Franklin D. Roosevelt rebalanced federal and state power as part of the New Deal and his efforts to battle the Great Depression. Dwight Eisenhower transformed federalism by creating the interstate highway system. In the 1960s, Lyndon B. Johnson made federalism initiatives the central part of his Great Society. Richard Nixon's sweeping domestic agenda was christened "the New Federalism." Ronald Reagan proposed a fundamental swap of federal and state responsibilities. But after the mid-1980s, there was little national attention to the truly fundamental issues of federalism. The White House Office of Intergovernmental Affairs, which once had been the center of the president's efforts to haggle over grand policy designs and big budget proposals, now increasingly dealt with state and local governments as one more constituent group to be managed. A truly great federal institution, the US Advisory Commission on

Intergovernmental Relations, was shuttered in 1996, in a budget-cutting move, because its work no longer seemed very important.

In the academic world, leading departments of political science and schools of public affairs once regularly offered courses in federalism, but those courses have become hard to find. A small handful of leading scholars continue to plow the fields, and *Publius: The Journal of Federalism* continues to publish important research papers. But it's hard to escape an essential conclusion: one of the most important and fundamental institutions on which the nation was built—indeed, James Madison's most essential invention—has slipped away from public debate and scholarly investigation.

This might make sense if federalism were no longer interesting or if it no longer mattered. But on the first point, Lin-Manuel Miranda demonstrated in his musical *Hamilton* not only that federalism remains interesting but that people will also pay enormous prices to listen to songs about it. A prime rule of every Broadway musical is to stage a boffo opening to the second act. In *Hamilton*, the second act gets rolling with "The Room Where It Happens," one of the show's best-known songs; it's about Alexander Hamilton's plan for the federal assumption of the state debt after the Revolution—in other words, it's about the balance of federal-state power. So there's strong evidence that federalism remains interesting.

Federalism also continues to matter—a lot. One of the most fundamental and wrenching issues of twenty-first-century America is the rising level of inequality. As the book argues, an important driver of differences, both within and between the states, is federalism. A host of federal policies designed to reduce inequality have been put into the hands of the states, and the result has been rising differences between the states in the way they design and manage federal programs. To a large—and growing—degree, the government that Americans get depends on where they live. To understand inequality, it's essential to understand its important roots in federalism. And dealing with the problems of inequality is going to take a strategy deeply rooted in federalism.

That makes federalism both fascinating and important. The truly essential invention to create the country in the eighteenth century provides the truly important insights to understand it in the twenty-first. This book embraces the broad sweep of American history, from before the founding of the republic to its more recently emerging issues, along with the strategies that would help rescue it. In the pages that follow, I tell the story of how we got to where we are, why it matters, and what we can do to uproot at least some of the forces of inequality through federalism. American democracy could not have gotten started without federalism, and it's going to be increasingly difficult to save it without federalism. Why and how is the story of this book.

In writing the book, I'm deeply indebted to Eric Crahan, who served as the project's intellectual godfather at Princeton University Press, and to Bridget Flannery-McCoy, whose unending string of editorial insights unquestionably made it a far stronger work. I'm grateful as well to Cynthia Buck, whose uncommonly skillful eye helped sharpen my prose.

The detailed suggestions from John J. DiIulio Jr. at the University of Pennsylvania and John D. Donahue at Harvard University provided simply invaluable insights that vastly improved the book. It's a measure of their great contributions that they will not recognize parts of the draft they read, which is now far stronger and better for their perceptive comments and suggestions.

Finally, my deep thanks go to my wife, Sue. She's been an unending source of love, support, ideas, and inspiration—the best partner anyone could ask on this or any project.

Donald F. Kettl
Austin, Texas
July 2019

THE DIVIDED STATES OF AMERICA

1

Madison's Balancing Act

The further the American Revolution recedes into history, the easier it is to miss just how close the United States of America came to being a divided collection of competing colonies under the punishing heel of an angry Britain. The nation's founders had first dared to declare their king a despot and then to challenge the most powerful army in the world to a war over turf. The odds of success seemed impossibly small, even if the red coats of the British troops made them conspicuous targets on the battlefield. A seven-year campaign, much bravery, a bit of luck, and the timely help of the French produced an unlikely victory. In September 1783, the promise of the Declaration finally led to the reality of independence.

But along with the triumph came a wrenching setback: the new nation's original plan to govern itself, the Articles of Confederation, simply failed to work. The states had been determined to prevent the new national sovereign from trampling on their liberty—having defeated the king, the last thing they wanted was another one—so the Articles intentionally created a very weak government. In their eagerness to prevent tyranny, its drafters overdid it. They created a United States of America not united enough to protect itself or its commerce. If the republic was to endure, this collection of divided states needed to be rescued from the fatal flaws of the Articles.

So, in 1787, the nation's leaders gathered in Independence Hall in Philadelphia to draft a new governing constitution. It was the same building where many of them had boldly voted to declare independence from Britain in 1776 and where they had drafted the Articles of Confederation in 1781. This time they knew they needed a more detailed constitution and a stronger national government. And they also knew they needed all the help they could get.

The founders struggled with a dilemma, one that has repeated itself many times since. The leaders of the states jealously guarded the separate identities that had emerged through the colonial times. They were proud, of course, of the new nation, but many were even prouder of the rich traditions of their own states. After all, the nation's short eleven-year history was a brief blip compared with the century and a half during which many of the colonies had prospered—and none of the proud states wanted to surrender their own interests to a new national identity. The agriculturally oriented South fiercely opposed having Northern merchants dictate policy, and the settlers who pushed west didn't want the big cities controlling their lives. Residents of small towns were always fearful of the reach of the large cities. The Articles of Confederation were so weak because the states were so strong, and state leaders wanted to keep it that way.

But the devotion to state power almost immediately clashed with the requirements of the new country. European powers coveted the vast, untapped wealth of the new continent. Tensions among the states threatened budding commerce, and the new nation lacked the most basic structures for making decisions. Even before Maryland became the last state to ratify the Articles in 1781, the document was obsolete.

So when the founders returned to Philadelphia in 1878 to draft the new constitution, they faced a profound dilemma. They needed to build a stronger national government without interfering with the states' expectations that they would keep their identities and their power. No other new nation had ever attempted to have its constituent parts create a strong national government without those parts deconstituting themselves in the process. The solution they came up with was federalism, American style. It had the great virtue of winning political support from the states, by maintaining their identity. It had the great challenge of creating a new ship of state, which had to navigate especially fierce and opposing currents. American federalism, in fact, has always been much less a fixed structure than a set of rules of combat. In the centuries since, the underlying tension between national unity and state power has never gone away. Neither have the great political battles that federalism precipitates.

That challenge has become both what defines the operating reality of American government and what differentiates American government from governments in the rest of the world. It is the field of battle on which the most important American political struggles have been fought. Through the years, these struggles have sometimes threatened the very principles that brought the founders to Philadelphia the first time to declare independence from the king.

When the founders met in 1787 to write the new constitution, James Madison led the debate. He was much younger than most of his colleagues, and he had a true genius for finding the bridge between opposing factions. As Joseph J. Ellis put it, Madison was "the acknowledged master of the inoffensive argument that just happened, time after time, to prove decisive." Madison "lived in the details," Ellis explained, "and worked his magic . . . with a more deft tactical proficiency than anyone else."[1]

His tactical brilliance, in fact, helped him cobble together the two greatest institutional inventions of the founders: separation of powers between executive, legislative, and judicial branches, which prevented the country's new president from becoming too kinglike; and federalism, which delicately balanced the powers of the national government with those of the states. Madison is perhaps best known for the first invention, but his second invention was the truly essential one, for without a plan to deal with the power of the states, the country could well have become fatally fragmented—and easy pickings for British, French, and Spanish governments eager to expand their power in the Americas. The invention of federalism allocated power between the federal government and the states in a way that gave the federal government enough strength to keep the country intact and accomplish national goals without making it so strong as to interfere with the self-government of the state and local governments. That was no mean feat.

(A quick aside: There's often much confusion around the terms "federal" and "federalism." In a formal sense, "federal" refers to a system of government in which power is allocated between the national government and its components, like the states. But in the United States, by long tradition, the national government is also referred to as the "federal government," so to keep with common usage, I'll use "federal" throughout the book to refer to the government run from the national capital. "Federalism" will refer to the American strategy for dividing power between the national government and the states.)

After they had drafted the Constitution, the founders knew just how fragile a system they had cobbled together. As they left Independence Hall on the last day of the constitutional deliberations, a lady is reputed to have asked Benjamin Franklin, "Well, Doctor, what have we got—a Republic or a Monarchy?" Franklin's reply: "A Republic, if you can keep it."[2] Keeping it ultimately depended on whether Madison's two great inventions worked. For more than two centuries, they did, if sometimes only barely, surviving partisan conflict, a civil war, and the rise and fall of multiple political parties. In the twenty-first century, however, the two institutions have become increasingly rickety, and so did the challenge of keeping the Constitution.

Madison made Congress the nation's first branch by putting it in Article I of the Constitution. But hyperpartisanship increasingly made Congress "the broken branch," as Thomas Mann and Norman Ornstein put it in 2006. Six years later, after congressional norms had broken down, budget stalemates had become routine, and Congress increasingly found it difficult to pass any legislation, they sadly concluded that "it's even worse than it looks."[3] Frictions between Congress and the presidency became deeply rooted, and writers began referring to the partisan split of what had been designed as a nonpartisan Supreme Court. All of these tensions fed a growing polarization that increased divisions in the nation. Madison's first great institution was in trouble.

His second great invention was in even worse shape, drifting into a deepening crisis that received relatively little attention. Tensions among the states over slavery had erupted in a civil war that almost ripped the nation apart, but in keeping it intact, the North's victory scarcely ended the battles over states' rights. The Supreme Court's 1954 decision in *Brown v. Education* launched a generation-long assault on segregation. A decade later, Lyndon B. Johnson's Great Society programs created the sweeping War on Poverty. There were, to be sure, large pockets of rearguard rebellion, but by the end of the 1960s there seemed to be an emerging national consensus on the importance of a strong national government focused squarely on reducing inequality among the nation's citizens—and among its states. The moment seemed to mark a profound truth about federalism: taking steps to reduce inequality in the United States relied on increasing federal power; putting more power into the hands of the states tended to increase inequality. That theme, in fact, has repeated itself constantly across the broad sweep of American history.

By *inequality*, I mean big differences among the states in policy outcomes that matter. We often look at inequality in income and wealth at the individual and family levels, and one of the biggest social and economic issues of American policy since the 1960s has been the growing concentration of wealth at the top of the income scale. But one of the most important drivers of this trend is the increasing inequality among the states. Some states are much wealthier than others, and their growing wealth makes it possible for them to provide better education, infrastructure, and health care to their citizens. Some states are far more aggressive in regulating the quality of the air and water, and that produces big differences in the quality of life among their citizens. Federalism was designed, of course, to allow—even encourage—policy differences among the states. But as we will see in the pages that follow, these differences, in creating growing inequality among the states, have made this a nation where the government that citizens get depends increasingly on where they live. That, in turn, is fueling political polarization in an already divided nation. There's profound irony here: the great invention that made it possible for the states to become united has ultimately become a sharp instrument for driving them apart.

In any system where different players make decisions, of course, they will inevitably make different decisions. That is inescapable—even desirable in fact, because citizens deeply value the right to set their own course and expect their decisions to be different from decisions made by other citizens elsewhere. At some point, however, deep, profound differences in the United States have created corrosive frictions, many stemming from issues of fairness: Is it fair that some citizens have much higher incomes than others? That some kids have much better schools than others? That some communities have much cleaner environments than others? How much equality is desirable—or possible—is, of course, a matter of political values. But the story of American federalism, especially since the 1970s, is a story of a growing divide among the states that has unleashed truly deep frictions among them. Do strong pollution controls in one state hurt its competitiveness with others? Does the poorer educational performance of some states make it harder for them to fuel economic growth? And perhaps most important, do the deep divisions among the states about the power of the federal government create very different patterns of health care, which profoundly affect the quality of life of their citizens?

The debates have been wide—and often wild. They have generated vast differences in how different states have approached national problems. These differences, in turn, have often created wide gaps in the outcomes of government. Madison's great invention of federalism, designed to bring the country together, has become one of the strongest forces driving it apart. In fact, when it comes to inequality in the United States, the federal government has been the great leveler and the state governments have been the great dividers. Federalism has always been a balancing act, but where the balance is found has constantly shifted. The debate about federalism is therefore a debate about how best to balance the respective roles of the federal and state governments. The result, as John Donahue points out, has been a remarkably "ambiguous division of authority" at the core of American federalism. Indeed, he reminds us, "the framers left ample room" for the nation's founding principles "to take effect in different ways to meet different conditions. And they inaugurated a permanent American argument over what version of federalism—at each particular time, in each particular set of circumstances—would be truest to the nation's bedrock values."[4] Federalism is about balancing authority, and one of the fundamental masterpieces of the American system is that the balance rests on such hazy laws and fuzzy values.

These differences multiply the sense that government is increasingly breaking the deal that citizens have with their government: they pay taxes and subject themselves to government's power in exchange for having the government produce the goods and services they want. But if they see some people seeming to get more from government than they deserve, that undermines their confidence in the basic social contract. Americans say that they like differences and want to live in diverse communities, but their behavior suggests otherwise: Americans increasingly prefer to live with people like themselves. That shift has aggravated the very tensions that Madison worried about.[5] In fact, one of Madison's biggest worries, as he explained in *Federalist 10*—one in the great collection of op-eds that made the case for the US Constitution—was that factions might pull the nation apart. The inescapable irony is that one of his greatest inventions, federalism, has helped to do just that.

Federalism has rich, textured roots in the country's first generations, but attention by scholars, analysts, and politicians to its central and important role in American political life has waned in the decades since the 1960s. In fact, federalism's biggest problems began increasing just as attention to it was shrinking. Johnson's Great Society programs in the 1960s promised a vigorous assault on inequality, and an emerging national consensus suggested that many of the deep, pernicious divides in the country had begun to heal. The Nixon administration in the 1970s had its own New Federalism programs, but they were designed to give state and local governments more flexibility in determining how best to accomplish the Great Society's aims. Civil rights seemed increasingly a universal principle, even though it was painfully obvious that, for many Americans, the problem was scarcely solved. But as an important driver of national debate, federalism drifted away from the center of attention. In fact, many opinion writers began speculating that federalism had died—that the debate over fixing the balance of state and federal power had largely ended with the rise of the federal government's power.[6]

As Mark Twain quipped about reports of his own passing, however, the report of federalism's death is grossly exaggerated. Federalism is far from dead, but like Madison's separation of powers, it has drifted into deep crisis. Unlike the separation of powers, however, its crisis has not been the subject of intense ongoing debate. Indeed, the more we have ignored federalism, the more it has drifted into crisis—perhaps *because* we have ignored it. Why have we ignored federalism? Because our attention has also drifted away from the big problem for which Madison's federalism was the uneasy, short-term, tactical solution: slavery and inequality.

Federalism, Slavery, and Inequality

Madison's biggest problem in 1787 was convincing the states to give up enough power to build a central government. There was growing realization across the states that this needed to be done, but when the war ended, so did the states' sense of urgency and unity. State leaders were proud people who cherished their traditions and differences, none of which they wanted to surrender in the interest of creating the federal government. They were wary of putting power in the federal government, and they didn't trust one another in making the decision about how to do it. The Southern states, in particular, anguished over whether the Northern states, with their larger population and commercial wealth, would enforce antislavery views on the South, at the cost of the region's traditions and economy.

Among the founders, Madison in fact was among the largest slave-owners, and unlike some other founders, he never freed the slaves he owned. He was, however, deeply torn on the issue. In an 1820 letter to Lafayette, he frankly acknowledged "the dreadful fruitfulness of the original sin of the African trade."[7] Even in recognizing "the evil, moral, political, and economical," of the practice, he also saw slavery as an important part of the country's economy, and that, he still maintained some years later, made it necessary to "yield to the necessity."[8] Madison was certainly a leader of deeply held principle, but he was even more fundamentally a pragmatist. It was the pragmatist in him that cobbled together federalism, finding a balance of federal and state power. It was also the pragmatist in him that found room in federalism to accommodate slavery.

Federalism was Madison's most important invention because slavery was the biggest problem he had to solve. It had nearly derailed Jefferson's Declaration. In his original draft, Jefferson indicted George III for his complicity in the slave trade:

> [H]e has waged cruel war against human nature itself, violating it's most sacred rights of life & liberty in the persons of a distant people who never offended him, captivating & carrying them into slavery in another hemisphere, or to incur miserable death in their transportation thither. . . . [D]etermined to keep open a market where MEN should be bought & sold, he has prostituted his negative for suppressing every legislative attempt to prohibit or to restrain this execrable commerce.[9]

Of course, there was profound irony in the harsh denunciation of a king who had not personally bought or sold slaves on the North American continent, in a document whose author had. Jefferson's arguments against slavery seemed heartfelt, but in the end it did not matter. South Carolina and Georgia refused to vote for independence unless the clause was removed. Years later, Jefferson suspected that the Northern shipping industry had also been quietly complicit in the pressure to remove the slavery clause from the Declaration because, he said, its leaders did not want to lose their piece of the molasses-to-rum-to-slaves business.[10] Whether or not Jefferson was right about the role of the Northern merchants in scuttling the antislavery language in the Declaration, he was right in pointing out that the economic interests around slavery were not limited just to Southern planters.

Jefferson faced a stark choice: remove the slavery clause or lose the vote for independence. He and his colleagues saw independence as the higher good, and they reasoned that they could return to the issue of slavery later, after winning the war—which was anything but a safe bet. For the proslavery members, it was a triumph of their own economic and political values. For the antislavery contingent in the Continental Congress, it was a sacrifice of one principle for another—of long-term values for a near-term necessity.

These battles resurfaced as soon as the founders debated the Constitution in Philadelphia, not so much as a matter of human rights but as a question of political balance. How was the Congress, created in Article I, to be organized? The larger states refused to accept the pattern set in the Articles of Confederation, which gave one vote to each state. The smaller states would not allow their voice to be diluted to apportion the Congress by population. This was one of Madison's biggest problems as he struggled with his draft.

Roger Sherman and Oliver Ellsworth from Connecticut suggested a compromise: unlike the government of the Articles, with just one house, Congress would have two, with two completely different plans for apportioning seats. Seats in the House of Representatives would be allocated by population, favoring the larger states, while each state would have two seats in the Senate, creating a counterbalance that favored the smaller states. But this neat solution created a second problem. If seats in the House of Representatives were allocated simply on the basis of population, that would favor the Southern states, given their large slave populations. These states surely would not allow the slaves to vote, and that would even further enhance the power of the slave-owners.

To crack the impasse, the members of the Constitutional Convention reached for the infamous compromise: slaves would count, but only as three-fifths of a person. This peculiar formulation produced a balance of seats in the House between the Northern and Southern states that each could accept, and it removed one of the biggest barriers to ratifying the Constitution. But just as with the amendments to the Declaration of Independence, political pragmatism came at the price of the nation's original sin of slavery. In *Federalist 54*, Madison frankly acknowledged the problem, but he argued that it was the best available solution to a problem that had otherwise stymied the founders.[11]

The compromise worked, but at the cost of a very long and dark shadow over the country's history. In a stunning 1987 speech, Supreme Court Justice Thurgood Marshall pointed back to the founders' fateful decision. At an event meant to celebrate the bicentennial of the US Constitution, Marshall, rather than deliver paeans to the nation's founders, made a blistering attack on them. He told his audience that he did not "find the wisdom, foresight, and sense of justice exhibited by the Framers particularly profound. To the contrary," he argued, "the government they devised was defective from the start, requiring several amendments, a civil war, and momentous social transformation to attain the system of constitutional government, and its respect for the individual freedoms and human rights, we hold as fundamental today."[12] The compromise made possible the short-term deal the founders needed, but the deeper problem ate like a cancer at the nation's soul.

Even this compromise was not enough to ensure the ratification of the Constitution. When state legislatures took up the question, the underlying issue of their power resurfaced. The Constitution was relatively explicit about the federal government's power and very clear about the limits on the state governments' power, leading the states to worry that they would be marginalized in this newly united country. The Articles of Confederation had demonstrated the risks that came with a state-centered government, but even with the painful evidence from the country's first decade, the states were unwilling to approve the federal government's new role without being much surer about their own.

That question frames one of the most fundamental debates about federalism. Is it a political convenience designed to allow the country's original sin to continue as the price of American democracy? If so, does that make the case for state power, because reducing it would have been politically impossible? Or are the states the best agents for restraining the federal government's size and promoting liberty? Is federalism, in short, a fig leaf to cover the nation's inability to deal with inequality, or a core principle to promote liberty? In these terms, federalism is anything but dead, because that question has been at the core of virtually every big domestic policy battle throughout American history, from the nation's first days to the present.

Prominent scholars studying the field have long been deeply split on the issue. On one side, the political scientist William Riker saw federalism in the 1960s as an unpleasant political bargain, created at the nation's founding to tiptoe around slavery without having to resolve it. Federalism, he said, was aimed at solving the founding's biggest short-term problems: keeping the union from fragmenting and protecting it from foreign attack. It was not, he believed, a core American democratic institution created to promote liberty by restraining the impulses of a powerful central government. Federalism, Riker argued, "may actually promote tyranny by its constant frustration of majorities" and "is an impediment to freedom." In fact, he contended in 1964, "if in the United States one disapproves of racism, one should disapprove of federalism."[13] He was truly worried about its pernicious effects, but he found one consolation: as an institution, federalism "does not have much effect on political life."[14] For Riker, federalism was an expedient tool to get the nation started, at the cost of feeding slavery. It was a tool, he concluded, for a time when the federal government needed to be stronger, but that time had long since passed.

At about the same time, Martha Derthick extensively championed federalism. A congenital Madisonian, she admitted that federalism—in allowing the resolution of disputes to be "left often to political and judicial dispute"—was both "complicated and unstable." Throughout her long career, however, she argued for leaving as many decisions as possible in local hands, because that created an important bulwark against an overreaching federal government. Federalism, Derthick believed, might be an uneasy foundation on which to base the quest for freedom in American democracy, but it was far better, she argued, than strengthening the federal government at the cost of local decisions, which she believed were far more likely to be responsive to citizens' views and much more likely to be managed effectively. Despite her many differences with Riker, Derthick did agree with him on one thing: that federalism had "undeniably atrophied over time."[15] But for Derthick, it nevertheless was a tool that provided a strong foundation for adapting broad goals to local norms, a tool that remained as lively and vital as it had been for Madison.

Derthick found comfort in Madison's search for the uneasy, pragmatic middle ground between those who sought to unify the country under a powerful federal government and those content to allow the states to spin it in many different directions. It was that search for a middle ground that Riker found unacceptable, because he feared that it paved the road to inequality, but Derthick found unavoidable; the alternative, she worried, would sacrifice liberty. What mattered, as Derthick pointed out, was that

> [f]ederalism both presumes and facilitates differences among the states. Assuming that the states are granted more freedom, will policy differences among them widen, or will their policies tend to converge? And if they grow farther apart, will this be tolerated, or will it be seen as prima facie evidence of injustice, requiring a national remedy and thus recentralization?[16]

Riker, in contrast, believed that federalism remained little more than a pretense that had justified the nation's original sin of slavery but that had evolved into an ongoing strategy that prevented the country from absolving it effectively.

The fundamental irony here is that, just as some writers were declaring federalism dead, it had become ever more important. Just as the vinegar and passion seemed to leak out of the battles over federalism, its stakes were growing: the focus on reducing inequality became more important than ever, on a far broader array of fronts. Just as academic attention to federalism diminished—every major university once had a course in federalism, but that is no longer the case—its implications for American democracy became far greater. That left journalists, analysts, and political scientists to concentrate on Madison's other great invention, the separation of powers, where the big issues have seemed anything but settled and fierce politics have threatened to shred governance at the national level. So as federalism became more important, there were few observers to chart its remarkable transformation or growing impact. Given federalism's vastly more complicated role, that intellectual irony is a political tragedy.

The Inescapable Tensions of Inequality

It became tempting to push federalism aside because, for much of its history, it had been closely identified with slavery and civil rights. But it would also become far more enmeshed in a far broader collection of issues.

First, consider the increase in inequality. The federal government waged the War on Poverty, but it scarcely won the campaign to reduce the country's vast divide between the rich and the poor. In the generation after the launch of the War on Poverty, income inequality in the United States increased substantially. In 1967, the top 5 percent of households received 17.2 percent of the nation's income. Fifty years later, in 2017, that share was 22.3 percent—more than the bottom 40 percent of households combined.[17] During that period, the states were occupied by a wide collection of issues that helped to feed this trend.

Second, income inequality across time got worse in *every* state, from 1969 to 2014. In some states, income inequality only got a bit worse: in Alaska and the two Dakotas, for instance, inequality increased at less than half of the national average. In contrast, inequality became much worse in five states—Rhode Island, Nevada, New Jersey, California, and Connecticut—where it increased at 50 percent more than the national average.[18] The states' own policies helped to increase the divides among them.

Third, income inequality *between* the states has worsened as well. According to 2017 data, income inequality was lowest in Utah, Alaska, Wyoming, and Iowa, with Utah 12 percent better than the national average. Illinois and Tennessee were at the national average. Meanwhile, New York, Louisiana, Connecticut, and California had the most unequal distribution of income, with New York 7 percent worse than the national average.[19] The states found themselves ill equipped to narrow these gaps.

Income inequality plagues every nation.[20] The United States, however, has the highest level of inequality among the world's leading industrialized nations. The country is getting richer, its average income is dropping, and more wealth is being held in fewer hands.[21] This part of the story is well known. However, much less well known but far more important is that income inequality *among* the states is growing. It is less well known because most analyses focus on the broad—and vital—national trends, and it is more important because the states are where an ever more important collection of policymakers and policy intermediaries both shape and implement national policy. It was one thing to allow the states flexibility to protect their pride, their traditions, and their values. But since the 1960s, their policy role has increasingly injected more inequality into the nation's policy system. That, in turn, has created more polarization and more friction, and it has made the United States a collection of states divided. This trend is vitally important to American democracy but has been largely hidden from view.

One result is that we have been getting much of the story wrong about the true balance of power in the United States. Federalism is scarcely dead; indeed, it has become ever more vital and consequential in far more unexpected ways. The states are becoming more important, not less so. They are increasingly going their own way, and their policy differences are increasingly driving the country apart. Madison's tactical genius prevented the union from disintegrating at the very start, but he also laid the foundation for deep divisions that have since come to plague the country's politics. The battle over the Obama administration's Affordable Care Act, for example, was largely portrayed as based in Washington. The important policy battles, however, have been fought within the states— in the decisions about whether to build their own health insurance exchanges, whether to expand the Medicaid coverage of their lower-income citizens, how to regulate health insurance, and what health insurance coverage ought to be provided to citizens. With so many important decisions at play, federalism is surely not dead, and it certainly has not atrophied. But the debate between Riker and Derthick over how best to pursue liberty was a very different one from today's struggle over how to define federalism.

Mann and Ornstein worried that the breakdown of the separation-of-powers invention at the federal level is "a formula for willful obstruction and policy irresolution."[22] But in many ways, the strains on Madison's other great tactical invention—federalism—are even worse. Federalism not only has corroded the separation of powers, as we shall see, but has also fed inequality in the nation, and that inequality has eroded trust in government. The grand American experiment might be able to survive a disease in one of Madison's inventions. It may well not be able to survive a cancer in them both.

The Roots of Inequality

To the extent that most people think about federalism at all, they assume that it is a relatively dry and outmoded concept, invented by the founders to explain the role of the states. In fact, however, it is remarkably vibrant, lively, and dynamic. As figure 1.1 shows, American federalism has advanced in American history through a series of generations, with each generation defined by a pendulum movement seeking balance: between some periods shaped primarily by a focus on boundaries, other periods defined by a search for legal standards, and still others characterized by bargaining. (The great political scientist Deil Wright identified the rising role of bargaining in his classic book on intergovernmental relations.[23])

In the First Generation of Federalism, the focus was on drawing a clear line between federal and state power and fixing that line in law. As we will see in the next chapter, the founders had a lively, sometimes raucous battle over drafting the Constitution, and creating that boundary was the last, big issue that they resolved, in the last amendment in the Bill of Rights; the Tenth Amendment explicitly gave to the states all powers not otherwise given to the federal government. That amendment created a line that favored the states, founded in law, and that is the source of what most people remember about federalism.

The apparent simplicity and clarity of the Tenth Amendment, however, began to dissolve as soon as the government began to govern. Pressures built up over just how far the states' power could stretch, especially over the issue of slavery. The clarity of law gave way to constant bargaining over the balance between the federal government and the states.

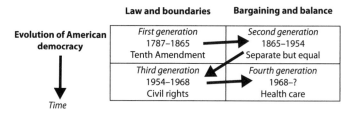

FIGURE 1.1. American federalism has been a constant search for balance.

That bargaining bent federalism until it nearly broke in the Civil War. The war, in turn, seemed to settle the issue of where the boundaries would be drawn—and who would draw them. But the North's apparently clear-cut victory, reinforced by the Fourteenth Amendment's guarantee of "equal protection of the laws," led instead to a new round of bargaining, dominated by the states. This Second Generation of Federalism became dominated by state-based actions to create "separate but equal" practices. Skating within a narrow interpretation of the law, these actions in fact reset the balance in favor of the states, some of which insisted on flaunting the protections that the Civil War seemed to have promised.

That ended with the Supreme Court's 1954 decision in *Brown v. Board of Education*, which led to the Third Generation of Federalism. That generation pulled policymaking back from the states into federal hands, through clear instruments of law that outlawed the discrimination and inequality that some states had advanced. President Lyndon B. Johnson's Great Society programs expanded *Brown* in a sweeping legislative campaign, with new legal guarantees of equal rights in voting, housing, and the workplace, along with the expansion of federal programs to deal with the legacy of segregation through the War on Poverty.

This Third Generation seemed to be the capstone of the long fight to end the inequality that had plagued American democracy since its beginning. In his famous "I Have a Dream" speech at the Lincoln Memorial in 1963, Martin Luther King Jr. had proclaimed, "Free at last, free at last, thank God almighty we are free at last." And indeed, for the first time in American history there seemed to be at least a general consensus about the quest for equality, the law's importance in defining it, and the federal government's preeminent role in promoting it and securing it. The balance seemed to have shifted, firmly and permanently, in favor of federal power.

But directly in the shadow of this Third Generation, a Fourth Generation emerged. Even though the federal government aggressively promoted equality through law, it also increasingly relied on the states as administrative agents for federal policies and reinforced their role as independent decision-makers. As the states exercised this power, the balance in the system shifted yet again, this time in favor of the states.

That shift, in turn, set the stage for federalism's important but often surreptitious role in driving the growing inequality in American life. As the states became more involved as administrative agents in more national policies, from the environment to education, health, and infrastructure, the scope of federalism broadened significantly. Over time federalism became interwoven in virtually every piece of domestic policy in the United States—and in many international issues like immigration as well. Not only did the scope of federalism increase, but big differences among the states also began emerging, slowly and often imperceptibly, as they gradually began moving down different roads, especially in health care. The result over time was a widening gap between the states in the policies they pursued, with the balance of power increasingly maintained by complex bargaining within an ever more complex intergovernmental system. As a result, the government that citizens got depended increasingly on where they lived.

Where does this lead? As the book's conclusion points out, the country could go down one of two roads, defined by the great traditions of ideas about federalism. Derthick's path would look to the power of the states to pull the country out of its accelerating drift toward ever-greater inequality. There is little in the country's history, however, to suggest that empowering the states would narrow the gulfs between them. On the other hand, the country could go down Riker's path, pushing federalism aside and relying more on the federal government. But there's little in US politics to suggest that the country is now ready—or is likely ever to be ready—to push the states aside as the price of greater federal power. Neither of these paths is likely to counter the increasingly dangerous trends toward greater inequality that the Fourth Generation of Federalism has helped feed.

What we need instead, as I argue at the book's conclusion, is a more fundamental rebalancing of federal and state power. American federalism is largely a Madisonian creation. What we most need is a more Hamiltonian strategy for making federalism work, a strategy focused far less on the boundaries of the states and far more on empowering them as agents of a broad, effective federal policy aimed squarely at reducing inequality. If the states' actions continue to feed inequality, they are likely to erode democracy and its institutions in a way that would undermine the very system that Madison worked so hard to create. If the states were enlisted by the federal government as instruments of coherent national actions devoted to reducing the inequality between and within the states—a Hamiltonian solution to the Madisonian dilemma—the prospects would improve. There could be no worse outcome than for the very inventions that helped build the nation to become the forces undermining it. On the other hand, there could be no better testimony to the founders' genius than to continue the process of reinvention that they so bravely began. A rebalancing in favor of Hamiltonian strategies is most likely to lead the way out of the problems of the Fourth Generation of Federalism.

Hamilton's Solution?

If Madison was a master tactician, Alexander Hamilton was the country's first great strategist. Like all the founders, he recognized the need for compromise, although he was so famously stiff-necked that compromise came much harder for him than for many of the other founders. His hard-headed approach to most things, in fact, led to the duel with Aaron Burr that cost him his life. When he did compromise, it was to sacrifice short-term goals (like the location of the nation's capital in a new town along the Potomac) in exchange for longer-term principles (like the federal government's assumption of the debt accumulated by the states during the Revolution). He always had his eyes on the long-term prize.

As Hamilton surveyed the gradual evolution of the newly semi-united states under the Articles of Confederation, he was gravely worried that competition among the states would pull the country apart. New York had created a tough duty on goods imported from the West Indies. The goods ended up in nearby Connecticut and New Jersey, but New York collected the income from the tariffs. Connecticut and New Jersey were furious that products sold in their states would enrich New Yorkers. Hamilton worried that this was just one example of the temptations that would lead the states to go their own ways, not only at one another's expense but also at the cost of the young nation's unity. If the states continued to create their own trade policies, they would not only erode their ability truly to be united but also become more and more unwilling to sacrifice for the nation's common good.[24] And Hamilton wanted the United States to be great.

Near the end of the Revolutionary War, Washington had laid out four principles that he believed would be required for the United States to achieve greatness: a strong federal government, which would bring the states together; repayment of the states' debts, which would establish the financial foundation of the new country; a strong army and navy, which would allow the country to defend itself; and harmony among the people, which would allow the country to find its common good. Though the list was Washington's, Hamilton, according to his biographer Ron Chernow, "would have written the identical list."[25] As the political analyst Michael Lind put it, "the United States was, and always should remain, a nation-state in which the states are clearly subordinated to a strong but not oppressive federal government."[26] Debate has raged for centuries over just how strongly opposed to states' rights—and the abolition of slavery—Hamilton was in practice.[27] But Hamilton was a leader of the abolition-ist cause in New York and pushed the antislavery cause to the point of intense friction with many of his fellow founders. Addressing inequality, Hamilton believed, required a federal government strong enough to deal with the centripetal forces of the states.

Hamilton might have been "more adept at meeting financial crises than mending political fences," as the historian Jacob Cooke put it, but there was no doubt that he had a powerful long-term vision for the country as a truly united collection of states.[28] He had no interest in creating institutions so powerful as to infringe on individual liberty—his essays in *The Federalist Papers* made that point—but neither did Hamilton want to license each state to push its own views down very different, conflicting roads.

In short, Hamilton would not have been surprised by today's rising inequality in the United States, or by the fact that the states had become the main drivers of it. That possibility was precisely what worried him most in the years after the Revolution. His instinct was to intervene to prevent such an outcome by rebalancing the powers of federalism toward the federal government and strengthening the role of the executive branch. That, of course, raises the familiar questions that have beset the country since its very start. Just how much federal intervention in state affairs are we willing to tolerate? And what would the cost be if the federal government chose not to intervene?

As we will see in the pages that follow, the balance between the federal government and the states—and between the states—has shifted over time. The inequalities that have crept into the American system are large and growing—and increasingly costly. We might not want to encourage more centralized power, but we might not be willing—or able—to tolerate substantially more inequality either. Madison and Hamilton—Derthick and Riker—have staked out the basic issues of the debate. We'll analyze these issues in the coming chapters and, even more important, explore ways to deal with the increasing problems of inequality that are growing out of the very system Madison designed to promote good government and enhance the power of America's citizens.

Federalism was thus *the* essential invention of the founders. The separation of powers set out to define how muscle would be exercised in the new country. But the invention of federalism was indispensable for determining whether there was even going to *be* a country—or whether the new states would melt into a ragged, unruly, and unworkable confederation that invited foreign invasion. Madison's biggest worry, as he explained in *Federalist 10*, was that "mischiefs of faction" would fester, shredding the sprawling new country's effort at unity before it could establish itself. Federalism was thus not only a plan to allow the states to keep their identity while creating a sense of national purpose. It was also the institution that the founders invented to safely vent the nation's perpetually simmering tensions before those frictions had a chance to destroy it.

The story of this book, however, is that deep fault lines of growing division have erupted in the very institution—federalism—that the founders had created to release the pressures of factions. Even though there seemed to be an emerging policy consensus in the 1960s for the federal government to guide the country toward greater equality, the fault lines of federalism have led since to growing pressures, increased polarization, and more inequality in the American polity. Not only is federalism not working as the founders had planned. It's also fueling the very forces that had caused them the greatest concern.

2

E Pluribus Unum

As the founders worked to build the new United States of America, they faced a difficult choice. Just what should be the balance between the states, which had created the nation, and the federal government, which was the spirit of the nation that the states had created? How united should the states be? The search for the answer defined the First Generation of Federalism in the American republic.

They found unlikely inspiration in an Englishman, Edward Cave. Cave decided in 1731 that the British needed a regular publication to bring together a wide range of interesting items, from parliamentary debates to Latin poems, along with a sprinkling of important data like the price of corn. No such publications existed at the time, so when he began compiling that information into a monthly periodical, he also had to decide what exactly to call it. He settled on "magazine," a name he borrowed from the French word for "storehouse," by Samuel Johnson's telling.[1] So began *The Gentleman's Magazine* (whose content he expected to be of little interest to ladies). It proved remarkably popular, lasting well into the twentieth century.

Cave recruited a large and influential stable of writers, including Samuel Johnson himself. For his own contributions, Cave took on the pseudonym Sylvanus Urban, a pun that captured the changes under way in English life: "sylvania" was the Latin word for forests, and "urban" was just beginning to catch on as a word for life in cities. His magazine was thus a blend of the great English traditions of forested land and the new urbanization squeezing out forests all across the country. For a motto, Cave chose "E pluribus unum"—a single volume assembled from many sources—which he proudly displayed on the magazine's cover.

The Gentlemen's Magazine found an audience among well-read Englishmen—and among American intellectuals like Franklin, John Adams, and Jefferson. In addition to adopting the Declaration of Independence on July 4, 1776, Congress passed a resolution calling for the creation of a great seal for the new nation. Not every great country had a declaration of its basic principles like the one Jefferson drafted, but no country could be great without a great seal, and every great seal needed a great motto. Congress gave the job of crafting both to Franklin, Adams, and Jefferson.

Great seals had deep roots. First used in times when few individuals could read or write, each king had his own seal and used it on important documents to signify that they had royal approval. Counterfeiting the seal was considered treason, since that would have been an effort to counterfeit the authority of the king. The Scots had had their own great seal since the time of Duncan II in 1093, and the English king's great seal dated back to the Norman conquest. When England, Scotland, and Wales officially joined together in 1707 to become the United Kingdom of Great Britain, the crown, needing a symbol of their unity, created a new great seal. (The British monarchy still has a great seal, safeguarded by the Lord Chancellor.)

So it was scarcely surprising that one of the first big steps of the newly united states was to commission a great seal, which not only would signal independence—the colonies would no longer be under George III's seal—but would also become a symbol of the new nation's unity and authority.

To help them decide what kind of seal the United States should have, the Franklin-Adams-Jefferson committee reviewed a large number of proposals. They sought inspiration from a 1759 painting based on the classic story of the "Judgment of Hercules," featuring the Roman hero flanked by the female images of Virtue and Vice. They also looked at biblical figures marking the wanderings of the children of Israel in the wilderness. They ended up with a proposal full of symbols representing the states, the Eye of Providence (which now appears on the back of the \$1 bill), and a pair of majestic figures.

Franklin, Adams, and Jefferson liked the sketch, but members of the Continental Congress were distinctly unimpressed. However, one element of their proposal did gain broad and enduring support: the motto "E Pluribus Unum."[2] It took until 1782 for Congress to finally agree on a very different design for the great seal. The seal, adorned with an eagle holding the motto on a scroll in its beak, remained popular. Franklin loved the motto, but he hated the eagle, a bird he said was "of bad moral Character," "a rank coward," and a scavenger "like those among men who live by sharping & robbing."[3] (Franklin was right: although the eagle is a majestic-looking creature that has been embraced by governments going back to the ancient Romans, it's also pathologically lazy, often happier scrounging for roadkill than swooping down to pluck fish from waterways.)

The motto stuck, though Franklin lost his battle against the eagle. Being Latin, the motto conveyed deeply historic, classical roots. Its connection with Cave's magazine signaled a link with literacy. And in recognizing the nation's diversity while emphasizing its unity, the motto captured the core of Madison's dilemma. But it also framed the nation's enduring question: How would the balance between a single federal government created from many states actually work? Would the one or the many win out? Would *unum* or *pluribus* triumph?

Franklin had anticipated this question many years earlier in his own magazine, the *Pennsylvania Gazette*. In 1754, he published the nation's first great political cartoon, which showed a snake cut into pieces and its segments labeled with the names of the states. "JOIN, or DIE" was the caption (see figure 2.1). It's not certain who drew the cartoon—Franklin himself usually gets the credit—but the cartoon's warning about a fragmented collection of states was clear. The problem, Franklin wrote in an accompanying column, was "the present disunited State of the British Colonies, and the extreme Difficulty of bringing so many different Governments and Assemblies to agree in any speedy and effectual Measures for our common defense and Security."[4] Without unity among the colonies, Franklin argued, they could never survive. His cartoon was a call, in short, for a truly united collection of states.

FIGURE 2.1. America's first great political cartoon calls for unity. *Source*: Benjamin Franklin, *Pennsylvania Gazette*, May 9, 1754. Courtesy of the Library of Congress, LC-USZ62-9701.

There were many ideas about what to name the new country, and "unity" was a constant theme. Franklin had suggested adopting a name already in common usage, the "United Colonies of North America," but "the UCNA" just didn't catch on. One popular revolutionary song, "On Independence," had a stanza that began, "May Heaven's blessings descend on our United States, And grant that the union may never abate."[5] Asking the blessings of Providence on our "United States" certainly worked better in song—and in spirit—than "our United Colonies," or "our United Colonies of North America." But the founders' choice of "United States of America" raised the country's most important founding question: just how truly united should the states of America be? Uniting together was a risky venture, but as Benjamin Franklin had warned his fellow founders at the signing of the Declaration in 1776: "We must all hang together, or most assuredly we shall all hang separately."[6]

From its very earliest days, the solution to that puzzle proved elusive. The quest to adopt the Declaration of Independence had almost fallen apart on the issue of slavery, and most of the nation's earliest political conflicts—and its most fundamental political symbols—rested funda-mentally on the question of the balance between national power and state authority. From its first days, the answer demanded tactical political com-promise as much as long-term strategic leadership.

Federalism itself was nothing new. The ancient Greeks, for example, governed using a version of federalism to help them deal with the wide differences among tribal states within a broader league. As Hans Beck and Peter Funke argue, "in the volatile interstate environment of Greece, fed-eralism was a creative response to the challenge of establishing regional unity, while at the same time preserving a degree of local autonomy." This is a formulation that Franklin, Adams, Jefferson, and Madison would have instantly recognized, in part because they themselves were steeped in an understanding of ancient Greece.[7] In the Middle Ages, there were endless tensions over the balance of power between kings and the local powers across their kingdoms headed by knights and dukes, often over questions of land and who controlled it. One of the oldest debates in government, in fact, centers on just how much authority a central government ought to have, how much power ought to rest with local governments, how to define the balance—and how to enforce it. That question was at the core of the classic struggles between Antony and Cleopatra and Rome, as well as the struggles that preoccupied medieval Europe.

Fatal Vices

The states had declared their independence. But how could they unite their militias into an army powerful enough to defeat the British, let alone run the new country? All of these big questions required producing an answer about just how united the states were going to be, and how much power the central government ought to have.

The founders' first effort at answering this puzzle had been the Arti-cles of Confederation, the version 1.0 of American democracy that proved to be a very leaky boat of governance. That document's Article II—an agreement to "certain articles of Confederation and perpetual Union between the States"—had made clear that "[e]ach state retains its sovereignty, freedom, and independence, and every power, jurisdiction, and right, which is not by this confederation, expressly delegated to the United States, in Congress assembled."[8] Article III noted, "The said states hereby severally enter into a firm league of friendship with each other."[9] They key point was this: the Declaration of Independence had not been a document framed by the people, but rather was "[t]he unanimous Declaration of the thirteen united States of America." The Articles followed on that foundation by creating a new government in which the states remained paramount—and the new national government had only the power that the states chose to give it.

But as I noted in chapter 1, many observers noted that the Articles were "obsolete when they were written and antiquated by . . . the last ratification"—by Maryland in 1781—even before the country won the war. The Articles operated with a Congress, but it functioned more as a clumsy collective manager than as a lawmaking body. As a system of governance, Congress under the Articles had such low prestige that it was often impossible to round up the nine states required to conduct business, even for something as fundamental as approving the Treaty of Paris, which ended the war with Britain. A special report looking into the problem began by noting that the founders had never imagined that just getting its officials to show up would be a problem. They had counted on their "firm reliance that the states could not be inattentive to a duty not only essential to the interests of each state, but likewise to a principle on which the federal government itself relies."[10] They turned out to be wrong.

When the Congress did manage to frame a policy under the Articles, it could not fund it, except by borrowing (assuming that anyone wanted to lend much money to the precarious new country) or by requesting funds from the states (which often had little interest in paying national bills). The national government could thus ask for anything—but it could not ensure the performance of anything.[11]

That was a major worry for Madison. In 1787, he wrote a fascinating essay about the Articles entitled "Vices of the Political System of the United States." Both during the Revolutionary War and in the years afterward, he argued, "the number and independent authority of the States" threatened to prove "fatal" to what the nation's founders had tried to achieve. After all, the British still had their outposts in Canada, and they had not taken defeat lightly (as they later demonstrated by burning Washington in 1812). The Spanish were pushing against the frontiers on the south and west, and some states were cutting their own deals with the Dutch. Under the Articles, Madison argued, the national government just wasn't strong enough to rule. The national body was not really a genuine government, he wrote, but rather "nothing more than a treaty of amity of commerce and of alliance" that left the states free to go their own way. The states, moreover, were increasingly tripping over one another with their own laws as they regulated commerce in their own ways. There was no common currency. The Articles of Confederation, in short, were a mess.

Nothing made that clearer than a rebellion led by Daniel Shays in 1786. Massachusetts farmers were in a serious economic crunch. The farmers had bought goods on credit, but when merchants asked for repayment, the farmers had no gold or currency to make good on the loans. When they couldn't make the payments, officials began arresting the farmers and foreclosing on their land. Shays, himself a farmer and a veteran of the Battle of Bunker Hill, organized some of the unhappy farmers, armed with guns and pitchforks, in a march on an arsenal in Springfield, Massachusetts, to capture more weapons. The militia finally put the rebellion down, but only after Shays and his followers had demonstrated just how weak the new nation was. If the nation couldn't manage its internal security, what hope would it have in defending the nation—or in promoting commerce? Alexander Hamilton and other Federalists seized on the revolt as an example of why the country needed a much stronger federal government if it was to survive, let alone thrive. In the eight years that the Articles of Confederation governed the new country, it was mostly a "Not Very United States of America."

The Articles of Confederation had indeed become an accumulation of fatal vices that, Madison argued, called into question "the fundamental principle of republican Government, that the majority who rule in such Governments, are the safest Guardians both of public Good and of private rights." To cure these vices, he wrote,

> The great desideratum in Government is such a modification of the Sovereignty as will render it sufficiently neutral between the different

interests and factions, to controul one part of the Society from invading the rights of another, and at the same time sufficiently controuled itself, from setting up an interest adverse to that of the whole Society.[12]

That is the nugget of Madison's quest: creating a government strong enough to protect liberty and freedom, but not so powerful as to become unaccountable. Virtually every important debate on the structure of American government—and the role of the states—flowed from this quest. In 1787, Madison and his colleagues knew that they did not want a government as strong as the king's powerful reach from England. Yet they had discovered that moving too far toward state power in the Articles was unworkable. Where, they wondered, should they set the balance?

When Madison and his colleagues gathered in Philadelphia to rethink governance—to devise a version 2.0 of American democracy—only two things were certain. One was that the Articles of Confederation had to be replaced. The other was that there was no consensus about what would replace it. In fact, there was little consensus even about how to carry on the debate. Rhode Island's leaders, deeply suspicious that the Constitutional Convention of 1787 would lead to a strong government, boycotted the meeting. Patrick Henry, who in 1775 had said that the choices were liberty or death, remained in Virginia because he "smelt a rat in Philadelphia, tending toward the monarchy."[13]

Madison's Great Inventions

Madison had experience in drafting constitutions—he had played a strong role in shaping Virginia's constitution and had already sketched out what the new national constitution ought to look like in a document that became known as the "Virginia Plan of Government." Compared with the Articles of Confederation, which built on the consent of the states, the new constitution, which famously began "We the People," set out on a different course. This time the source of power rested in citizens, and the document's goal was to create far stronger power in the national government. That power, in turn, rested on Madison's two great inventions: the separation of powers and federalism.

Madison is perhaps best known for the balance he helped craft among the executive, legislative, and judicial branches. If the federal government was to have more power, the founders were determined to limit its exercise. Thus, the Constitution made it possible for any two branches to check the other. The president could execute the laws, but only the laws that Congress passed, and the judiciary could review the actions of them both. Congress could pass the laws, but the president had to sign them, and the judiciary could judge their fit with broad principles. The judiciary thus had substantial power, but its structure was a creature of Congress and its members were appointed by the president. It was a clever invention of historic import, aimed at ensuring that the new United States would not face a tyrannical king.

The far tougher challenge was setting the balance between the federal government and the states. The Articles had established that the nation needed a strong federal government. But how could the nation lean enough toward federal power without infringing so much on the states' prerogatives as to undermine their support for the entire venture? The separation of powers might well be Madison's most famous invention, but federalism is his most essential one. Without finding an acceptable balance between federal and state power, the structure of power at the federal level simply would not have mattered.

The states were organizing forces in the Constitution: each state had two seats in the Senate, elected (at first) by the state legislatures, while seats in the House of Representatives were apportioned by population. The Constitution listed the things the states *could not* do, like entering into treaties and imposing tariffs. But in all its ringing rhetoric, there was no discussion about what affirmative role the states *should* play in setting policy. Some of the founders were puzzled—and worried. In Virginia's debate over ratifying the Constitution, Patrick Henry complained, "We are running we know not whither."[14] New York and Virginia were so unhappy with the draft of the Constitution that they pressed for a new constitutional convention, even though one of Virginia's favorite sons had been the father of much of it.[15] Scores of proposals surfaced to amend the

Constitution even before it was ratified. There seemed little chance that enough states would ratify the document without significant changes.

After a war that lasted more than eight years and cost more than 4,400 lives, Americans were not about to gamble their freedom on a new government that risked a new brand of tyranny. In fact, they were skittish about governmental power of any kind. On the other hand, Shays's rebellion had shown that a weak government could just as surely put that hard-won freedom at risk. How much government did Americans really want? Could putting more power in the states prevent federal officials from becoming so powerful as to threaten liberty? Without a strong federal government, could the states ever be truly united? These questions stood behind every important decision in Philadelphia.

At the core of the answers was a profound shift in the way Americans thought about themselves. In the Declaration of Independence, the states were paramount. It was the collection of "the Representatives of the united States of America, in General Congress, Assembled," who declared independence. In the Articles of Confederation, it was a confederation of states that ruled—and a loose one at that. But the Constitution began with the famous preamble "We the People." That was far more than rhetorical flourish. The preamble marked a sharp change from putting the states at the center of the government to enshrining the role of the people. But no one knew what "We the People" really meant, or what role the states had after that important shift had been made.

Framing the Role of the States

The Constitution won overwhelming approval from the delegates in Philadelphia, but before it could take effect it needed approval from nine of the states. Gaining that approval was anything but a sure thing, and Madison's opponents—a group of founders christened the "Anti-Federalists," who championed a much stronger balance of power in favor of the states—waged a big campaign to kill the document. To counter their efforts, Madison joined with two other leading Federalists, John Jay and Alexander Hamilton, to write and distribute a collection of eighty-five essays. Written from October 1787 to April 1788, the essays that came to be known as *The Federalist Papers* powerfully delineated what Madison and his colleagues had in mind when they sent the Constitution to the state capitals for ratification. Even today they make for lively reading.

For Madison, of course, one of the foremost problems was setting the balance of power between the federal government and the states. On the federal side of the scale, there was the necessity of ensuring national security and maintaining internal order. States could not be allowed to interfere with each other's commerce by, for example, establishing tariffs at state borders or preventing the free flow of citizens along the roads. The states were also forbidden from treating citizens of other states differently from their own. The Constitution's stronger framework had been designed to prevent the government from being frozen into inaction, but at the same time the founders were determined to ensure that the federal government did not trample on the prerogatives and traditions of the states. For instance, the federal government was not to dictate the operation of local schools, make decisions about new settlements, or determine citizens' choices about trade.

Most of all, the founders knew that efforts to interfere with the practice of slavery would scuttle any chance of ratifying the Constitution. The Southern states had insisted on deleting the slavery clause from the Declaration of Independence, and they would never vote for the Constitution if there was even a hint that the new federal government would interfere with the practice, which had been in place for generations. Preserving slavery was a matter of money—slaves were a form of wealth for slave-owners. It was also part of a tradition—many Southern planters saw slavery as part of their way of life. In addition, slavery was the ultimate emblem of state power—and the Southern states were not about to allow Northern abolitionists to dictate the terms of the union. And for Madison, who owned many slaves himself, slavery was also a personal issue.

The question of balancing federal and state power thus was a matter of enormous political sensitivity. The great European nations had never had to deal with such questions, because their governments had grown from systems set by medieval kings, whose power had gradually shifted over hundreds of years, rather than from a collection of colonies, whose power had to be transformed all at once. It was an unprecedented problem, and there was great urgency in solving it.

The founders drew on great European thinkers like John Locke and Jean-Jacques Rousseau, but none of these theorists had had to write a new constitution, let alone create a new government from scratch. They did, however, help Madison think through the issues. He started with a strategy that was both profoundly philosophical and eminently practical. The new nation was devoted to creating a democracy, but direct democracy—decision-making by the people—was, of course, impractical in a vast new country with more than three million residents. The alternative was to create a republic, where the citizens voted for representatives to govern on their behalf. The fundamental principle would be majority rule, of which Madison was a strong supporter. But he also argued, in *Federalist 10*, that majority rule carried an enormous threat: a majority might abuse the rights of the minority.

For Madison, one of the strongest cases for a powerful federal government was to prevent interest groups in the states from abusing the rights of their minorities. (Of course, Madison set aside the rights of the African American slaves, for such was the license that he believed that America's original sin gave its leaders.) The country needed a federal government strong enough to prevent these "mischiefs of faction," as he called them, in perhaps the most memorable phrase in *The Federalist Papers*. By "factions," Madison wrote,

> I understand a number of citizens, whether amounting to a majority or a minority of the whole, who are united and actuated by some common impulse of passion, or of interest, adversed to the rights of other citizens, or to the permanent and aggregate interests of the community.[16]

Factions, he argued, were inevitable, being "sown in the nature of man." The role of government was to prevent the very nature of man from creating tyranny against other citizens.

To cure the "mischiefs of faction," Madison suggested two possibilities. One was "removing its causes," but because the causes flowed from human nature itself, removing the causes was impossible. The other lay in a republican form of government. Elected representatives, he believed, were more likely to look out for the broad interests of the country than for their own narrow concerns. That was, of course, a big assumption, but Madison thought that establishing a republic was far better than allowing individuals to rule directly, a course that would inevitably lead to their pursuit of their own narrow self-interests. A republican government surely was not perfect. After all, the Articles of Confederation had been a form of republican government, but representatives in Congress under the Articles had represented the states, not the people. In the Constitution, of course, the states, not the people, elected members of the Senate, but the people directly elected the members of the House of Representatives, in proportion to the population. Madison emphasized the importance of this provision by making it Article I of the new Constitution. By requiring officials to stand for reelection, the public could replace those who did not measure up.

Opting for a republican form of government helped make the case for substantial power at the federal level. Putting big decisions at a higher level would dilute the role of factions. But how to prevent the federal government from threatening liberty? Madison believed that the states were a great bulwark against the encroachment of federal power. As he wrote in *Federalist 45*, "The State governments may be regarded as constituent and essential parts of the federal government; whilst the latter is nowise essential to the operation or organization of the former." In fact, he contended,

> The powers delegated by the proposed Constitution to the federal government are few and defined. Those which are to remain in the state governments are numerous and indefinite. The former will be exercised principally on external objects, as war, peace, negotiation, and foreign commerce. . . . The powers reserved to the several States will extend to all the objects which, in the ordinary course of affairs, concern the lives, liberties, and properties of the people, and the internal order, improvement, and prosperity of the State.

Then, to seal the argument, he continued, in *Federalist 46*:

> On summing up the considerations stated in this and the last paper, they seem to amount to the most convincing evidence that the powers proposed to be lodged in the federal government are as little formidable to those reserved to the individual States as they are indispensably necessary to accomplish the purposes of the Union; and that all those alarms which have been sounded of a mediated and consequently annihilation of the State governments must, on the most favorable interpretation, be ascribed to the chimerical fears of the authors of them.

The federal government had substantial power, to be sure, but its powers were only as great as needed, Madison argued, to secure the country's protection and prevent the mischiefs of faction. The states, he argued, had the real power over so many of the key elements of government. Those who contended otherwise were dreaming, he concluded, in an implicit put-down of the Anti-Federalists.

Madison recognized that he was trying to set a delicate balance, and he saw federalism as his best bet. The states were closer to the people, but putting too much power into the hands of the states could erode the freedom of minorities. The federal government could protect individual liberty, especially for minorities, better than smaller governments, but a too-strong federal government could itself threaten liberty. To work his way out of this dilemma, Madison framed a paradox: because smaller governments, being closer to the people, were more likely to be captured by narrow interests, only a larger and more powerful federal government could protect freedom—but in turn, only the states could restrain federal power. He argued:

> The smaller the society, the fewer probably will be the distinct parties and interests composing it; the fewer the distinct parties and interests, the more frequently will a majority be found of the same party; and the smaller the number of individuals composing a majority, and the smaller the compass within which they are placed, the more easily will they concert and execute their plans of oppression. Extend

the sphere, and you take in a greater variety of parties and interests; you make it less probable that a majority of the whole will have a common motive to invade the rights of other citizens; or if such a common motive exists, it will be more difficult for all who feel it to discover their own strength, and to act in unison with each other. Besides other impediments, it may be remarked that, where there is a consciousness of unjust or dishonorable purposes, communication is always checked by distrust in proportion to the number whose concurrence is necessary.

Factions might flare up in individual states, Madison concluded, but the federal government would prevent the spread of a more widespread conflagration. That, in fact, was his strongest argument for moving from the Articles of Confederation to the Constitution. In a 1787 letter to Jefferson, he contended that "private rights will be more secure under the Guardianship of the General Government than under the State Governments."[17]

Madison had constructed a remarkably complex argument, one based in the theories of the great Enlightenment thinkers and then given a pragmatic American twist. The separation of powers might well be Madison's best-known invention, but federalism was his most essential one. Without the case he made for setting the balance of federal and state power, there would have been no need to consider the separation of powers at the federal level because there might well have been no federal government.

Madison's case ran into significant headwinds, however, from a distinguished group of Anti-Federalists who included old hands like Virginia's Patrick Henry and George Mason, James Winthrop from Massachusetts, and Melancton Smith from New York. They were joined by ordinary citizens, especially farmers and new residents of the Western communities. They saw no point in replacing the British with a new government that could prove just as bad. One of the Anti-Federalists, writing under the pen name "Cato" (often identified as New York Governor George Clinton), argued in 1788 that "rulers in all governments will erect an interest separate from the ruled, which will have a tendency to enslave them."[18] For his part, Henry told Virginia's ratifying convention that taking power away from the states was "extremely pernicious, impolitic, and dangerous." The result, he said, would not be "a democracy, wherein the people retain all their rights securely."[19] For the Anti-Federalists, not only did the states represent tradition, but their power was also the essential foundation for democracy—a foundation that growing federal power could only erode.

The draft of the Constitution aggravated their worries because it contained almost nothing emphasizing the role or power of the states. That grand omission infuriated the Anti-Federalists, who campaigned in state capitals against ratifying the Constitution. The case for Madison's Constitution was this: the federal government could be strong enough to reduce the mischiefs of faction while the separation of powers would protect liberty. But Cato, Henry, and others countered that nothing could be more abhorrent to the pursuit of individual liberty than to pull government's power away from the people and the states into a federal government. That only made more important the problem of defining the role of the states. Could Americans ever accept a system that sought to balance federal and state powers if they did not have assurances about the actual role of the states? That became the biggest hurdle in the states' debates over the Constitution.

3

The Search for Unity

Many state officials were not big fans of Madison's Constitution, and hundreds of proposed amendments surfaced to correct the problems they saw. Madison whittled them down to twenty, and then a collection of a dozen amendments were packaged with the Constitution for an up-or-down vote in the states. The states refused to approve two of the amendments. One was a very complicated formula for allocating seats in the House of Representatives, which would have led to a House no smaller than 200 members and by the twenty-first century would have produced a House with more than 6,500 members. The other amendment voted down was preventing a change in the pay of members of Congress until after the next election; this proposal eventually became the Twenty-Seventh Amendment in 1992.

The remaining ten amendments became the famed Bill of Rights, one of the most important collections of principles about human dignity ever written. The last amendment in particular is noteworthy here. In contrast with the bold declarations of rights in the other amendments, the Tenth Amendment reads simply: "The powers not delegated to the United States by the Constitution, nor prohibited by it to the states, are reserved to the states respectively, or to the people." Compared with the truly giant statements—freedom of religion, speech, press, and peaceable assembly; the right to keep and bear arms; the protections against unreasonable searches and seizures, excessive bail, and double jeopardy; the right to a speedy trial by jury—the "reserved powers" clause of the Tenth

Amendment might seem pedestrian. Why go to the trouble of amending the Constitution—and why threaten not to ratify the Constitution—simply to state the obvious? The federal government, after all, had the powers enumerated in the Constitution. That the states had whatever powers were left seemed to go without saying.

But many state officials insisted that it be said. The Tenth Amendment, in fact, was the most important for many legislators in the states, who saw a dangerous specter of a federal government grown too big and too powerful. One prominent Anti-Federalist, calling himself "The Federal Farmer," contended that "men who govern, will, in doubtful cases, construe laws and constitutions most favorably for increasing their own powers."[1] If elected officials were likely to exercise power to enhance their own interests, then government needed tight controls on that power. Others pointed to the fact that the Articles of Confederation had an explicit clause reserving to the states any power not given to the federal government, and they worried that, without a similar clause in the new Constitution, it might be interpreted as an intent to expand federal power. Rather than take any chances, some state legislators insisted on the explicit statement: powers not given to the federal government were reserved to the states.

As Virginia's George Mason asked pointedly in 1788, "Is there any thing in this Constitution which secures to the states the powers which are said to be restrained?" The amendment, he said, would be useful "to remove our apprehensions."[2] In further debate in Virginia, Patrick Henry asked what the harm was in stating the obvious—that is, in simply "enumerat[ing] the rights which you are to enjoy." Madison had countered, "If an enumeration be made of our rights, will it not be implied that every thing omitted is given to the general government?"[3] The harm, Madison suggested, was that if the Bill of Rights listed some things but not others as being the province of the states, the federal government would have free rein to expand its power up to the point of the specific rights described. He worried about how to "tranquilize the minds of honest opposers without injuring the system."[4] Madison, in fact, at first had opposed the Bill of Rights. He thought that the amendments were unnecessary, and he worried that more verbiage would complicate the effort. He referred to the whole process as a "nauseous project," but he came to embrace it as a way of satisfying those who opposed ratification of the Constitution without weakening the government that the Constitution created.[5] A supreme tactician as always, he did not want to risk his work by opposing principles with which he fundamentally agreed, even if he believed that there was no need to spell them out.

Jefferson argued that the Bill of Rights was important to eliminate any ambiguity. In a letter to Madison, he argued, "Let me add that a bill of rights is what the people are entitled to against every government on earth, general or particular, and what no just government should refuse, or rest on inference."[6] In a letter to George Washington, Madison himself made a powerful case for clear boundaries:

> If a line can be drawn between the powers granted and the rights retained, it would seem to be the same thing whether the latter be secured by declaring that they shall not be abridged, or that the former shall not be extended. If no such line can be drawn, a declaration in either form would amount to nothing.[7]

As the debate over the Bill of Rights and the ratification of the Constitution neared its climax, it became increasingly clear that including the Tenth Amendment was the price of ratification. No one really opposed the principle, and not everyone thought enumerating them was necessary, but some states simply refused to ratify the Constitution unless they were included. The famous Bill of Right thus had its birth as a matter of practical necessity as well as fundamental norms. The states ratified the Constitution, including its Bill of Rights. The Bill of Rights included the Tenth Amendment, protecting the role of the states. Now the new government of the United States of America was in business.

The Tenth Amendment seemed so innocent because it was so clear, but its apparent clarity almost immediately evaporated. This was not so much because of dispute over whether the states had reserved powers. Rather, it was because the boundaries on the federal government's powers were anything but clear, as quickly became apparent in a battle over creating a national bank.

Alexander Hamilton had championed the bank as a way to stimulate commerce. He believed that the country's growth would be handicapped without a national currency and that, to create the currency, the United States needed a strong national bank. But that, of course, required more than just a strong federal government. Article I, Section 8, of the Constitution gave Congress the power "To coin Money, [and] regulate the Value thereof," but the idea of creating a new institution to govern the currency struck his opponents as a step much too far. Nothing sharpens a dispute like attaching money to it, and few issues had heightened the friction between the states and the new federal government more than the question of who would control the cash.

Hamilton previously had fought for federal assumption of the state debts that had accumulated during the Revolutionary War. In principle, the idea seemed simple, but as with everything else that mattered in the country's first years, the real dispute centered on how the plan would benefit different states. Southern farmers worried that the move would put inordinate power into the hands of big banks in the North, which they feared that Hamilton was trying to help.

But left to their own resources, most states had few prospects for paying off the old debts. If the economy remained hobbled by these debts, Hamilton worried that no one would be interested in lending money to the new country and that its growth would be hampered before it could get started. The nation was already struggling to conduct business with a chaotic currency. "Not worth a Continental" had become a bad joke during the Revolutionary War as the Continental dollar issued by the Continental Congress evaporated in value. Merchants dealt with local banks, each of which issued its own scrip, but that scrip often had little value outside its narrow region, making it hard to do business across state lines. It was the difficulty of borrowing and repaying debts without a currency to do it that had helped fuel Shays's rebellion.

In Hamilton's mind, creating a national bank seemed the eminently reasonable way to resolve these issues, and he convinced Congress to establish the First Bank of the United States in 1791. The bank was not only an instrument of national economic policy but also a commercial bank, making loans and seeking a profit. The bank proved financially successful, but that only fueled the worries that Northern financiers were reaping profits at the expense of Southern planters and rural farmers. They had never been happy with the creation of the bank, and when the bank's twenty-year charter expired in 1811, they worked to put it out of business. Hamilton, its biggest champion, had lost his life in a duel with Aaron Burr, so he was no longer around to defend it. The new state-chartered banks were happy to see their federal competition go away. Congress allowed the bank to die—but not for long.

The new era of good feeling that swept the country after the War of 1812, along with an expansion of national ambition, helped build the case for another try at a national bank. In 1817, Congress created the Second Bank of the United States, which branched out to two dozen offices around the country. The bank's critics continued, however, to campaign against what they saw as an unwise extension of federal power and a dangerous reach into private commerce.

Maryland, in particular, had never been happy with the idea of a national bank, which, its officials argued, the Constitution did not expressly give Congress the power to create. Therefore, state officials argued, the power to govern banking was reserved to the states under the Tenth Amendment. To make their point, Maryland tried to collect state tax on the operations of the Baltimore branch of the Second Bank of the United States. The branch's head, James William McCulloch, contended that Maryland was violating federal authority, and he refused to pay. Maryland took the Second Bank to court over payment of taxes and won, but McCulloch appealed to the US Supreme Court. There, represented by Daniel Webster, McCulloch was victorious.

Chief Justice John Marshall's decision in *McCulloch v. Maryland* became a landmark decision about federalism.[8] It was true, Marshall wrote, that the Constitution did not explicitly authorize the federal government to create a national bank. But he pointed out that Article I, Section 8, did give Congress the power "[t]o make all Laws which shall be necessary and proper" to carry out the responsibilities outlined in the Constitution. Moreover, the article, as I've noted, gave Congress the power to "regulate Commerce with foreign Nations, and among the several States," as well as "[t]o coin money" and "regulate the Value thereof." This "necessary and proper" clause was central, Marshall concluded. It "cannot be construed to restrain the powers of Congress" or "to impair the right of the legislature to exercise its best judgment." The people vote for Congress; Congress decides on behalf of the people which functions are "necessary and proper"; and if the Constitution does not expressly prohibit congressional action, then Congress's judgment about what truly is "necessary and proper" ought to rule.

Marshall therefore found that the Tenth Amendment did indeed reserve to the states all powers not given to the federal government. The federal government's powers, however, were those that the Congress decided were "necessary and proper" to exercise its role. Creating the national bank was constitutional because Congress had decided it was "necessary and proper," and Maryland had no right to interfere, not even by taxing its profits. This, of course, was precisely the nightmare that had worried critics of the new Constitution: that the federal government, once established, would decide what its power was, and that its decisions would erode the role of the states. The only protection against that erosion, they thought, was a clear boundary separating federal and state power.[9] They thought they had drawn such a boundary with the Tenth Amendment, but *McCulloch* showed that this was simply not the case.

With the Court's decision in *McCulloch*, the Tenth Amendment had become a clear declaration of federalism without a clear delineation of its meaning. Instead of clarifying the boundaries between the federal and state governments, it had created an arena for action and debate in which the critical battles over the balance of federal and state power would be fought. The boundaries would become no clearer in the centuries that followed. Federalism might have seemed, at first, to be a grand and bold statement of America's founding values, but in the country's very first decades it became a supremely American exercise in problem-solving. Federalism moved from a grand strategy in principle to a loose collection of tactics in practice. Those tactics, in turn, created a constantly shifting collection of boundaries founded more in pragmatism than in principle.

Federalism was indeed Madison's essential invention, without which the United States would never have come into being and without which it would quickly have spun apart. The Tenth Amendment might well have seemed the bright line defining just what American federalism would be. But it took just thirty years to make plain that neither federalism nor the Tenth Amendment were principles for defining roles and limiting government power. Rather, the amendment defined an arena for debate, action, and often dispute—in the halls of Congress, in the states, and often on the battlefields, ultimately in a civil war that almost destroyed the founders' dreams.

The Birth of Federal Grants

Before that epic struggle erupted, however, the federal government and the states were struggling with the growing pains of the expanding young country. Farmers needed to transport their crops to market, sometimes across state lines. Merchants needed to import goods from other states and nations into their shops. Citizens wanted a way to get around their new country. All of this required good roads, better harbors, and new canals—lifelines from the coast to the rapidly growing interior, and vice versa. Without an improved transportation system, the country's economy would stall. But who ought to pay for and build this infrastructure?

When it came to infrastructure, the Tenth Amendment appeared to have constructed an insurmountable wall. Building roads, bridges, ports, and schools seemed the very core of the state responsibilities from which the Tenth Amendment walled off the federal government. The state governments had the legal responsibility, but they didn't have the money. Moreover, most state governments saw little reason to cooperate with each other on fundamental infrastructure, even though it was becoming increasingly obvious that the growing country needed roads that connected one state to another.

The problem seemed to call for federal help, but even Alexander Hamilton, the strongest advocate for government's role in building a vibrant economy (and still alive as the issue first arose), couldn't see a way within the Constitution to get the job done. He worried, in fact, that it might be impossible to solve the problem short of passing a constitutional amendment. Previous efforts to raise federal taxes to pay for state infra-structure had stirred fierce resistance, including from a series of presi-dents. Madison opposed such expenditures, James Polk vetoed a series of bills, and Andrew Jackson fought to keep government and the private sector separate.

Albert Gallatin, who served as US secretary of the treasury in the Jef-ferson and Madison administrations, proposed a clever solution. The federal government couldn't order the states to build infrastructure, and constitutional barriers blocked it from doing the job itself. But, he sug-gested, the federal government could encourage a pragmatic partnership by providing the states with federal grants. The states would not have to accept them, and that would protect the Tenth Amendment. The admin-istrative energy would come from the states, so they would retain their sovereignty. The federal government could create a broad national plan, but the states could decide whether to take part in it (and give up the money if they did not). No state wanted to leave money on the table for things they wanted to do anyway. It was an offer that none of the states would want to refuse.

One problem, though: the federal government didn't have the money. The Louisiana Purchase, however, not only doubled the country's size but also provided a rare opportunity to raise a lot of money fast. As the federal government sold off the land for Ohio, Gallatin suggested hold-ing one-tenth of the proceeds to build roads, not just in Ohio but also from the seaboard to the interior. In one stroke, Congress invented federal grants.[10] The states got the new infrastructure they needed without hav-ing to pay for the projects themselves or being forced to take on the job. The federal government created incentives for the states to do what the federal government wanted done and to coordinate with each other in building the projects. And it all happened without raising taxes, trampling on the Tenth Amendment, or infringing on the broader sensitivities in the federal-state balance of power.

Gallatin's plan was a triumph of pragmatism in the Federalist–Anti-Federalist ideological battle. He had managed to tackle one of the coun-try's biggest problems without getting entangled in the kind of battle that led Hamilton to his deadly duel with Burr. He cracked the problem of the Tenth Amendment by sidestepping it, with a tactical solution that would become an enduring national strategy.

These grants took another step forward in the 1830s when the Jackson administration found itself with a government surplus. One option was to deposit the money in private banks—but that stirred the old fears of government capture by powerful corporations. Moreover, big federal deposits would inevitably flow more to some banks than others. Smaller, more rural banks feared that they would lose out in the deal. That option died a quick death.

The other option was to distribute the money to the states and allow them to spend it as they saw fit. That was politically attractive, but no one knew if it was constitutionally possible. To date, the country's biggest constitutional problem regarding the budget was how to deal with the enormous debt that the states had run up during the Revolutionary War. They simply hadn't anticipated how to manage the reverse problem. So, to avoid having the plan get stuck in endless court battles, federal officials decided not to give the states the cash outright. Instead, in an ingenious solution, they would make the states a loan of the cash, with the quiet understanding that federal government wouldn't ask for the money back.

With that clever policy footwork, they created in 1837 the first cash grants from the federal government to the states. The land grants had established the precedent that the federal government could induce the states to do things that it had decided needed to be done. (Congress used the same approach for the Morrill Land Grant Act in 1862 to create "land grant" colleges, from Texas A&M and Louisiana State University to the University of California at Berkeley and the University of Wisconsin; this new system of state universities was supported by federal funds generated, in turn, from the sale of public lands.) The distribution of the surplus established the precedent that grants could come in cash as well as land.

Federal grants became an important tool of federalism that helped the federal government navigate constitutional restrictions and financial restrictions without awakening the Anti-Federalist debates of the 1780s and 1790s about why they could not do it. The Tenth Amendment limited the federal government's power to tell the states what to do. But it said nothing about offers that the states were free to accept. Making deals too good to turn down, in turn, dramatically transformed federalism.

It is impossible to underestimate just how important these apparently small steps were to the evolution of federalism. The early debates were about determining the best way to set the balance between federal and state power. The Articles of Confederation leaned heavily toward the states. During the debates over the Constitution, the states worried that the draft went too far the other way, so they insisted on the Tenth Amendment, to make the boundaries clear. The early debates were therefore largely about broad strategy and fundamental principle.

In the first decades of the nineteenth century, politicians continued to revere the principles, but budding problems demanded solutions. The country needed—and wanted—to take big steps forward, from education to infrastructure. The states had no money and the federal government had no administrative capacity, so federal grants became an exquisitely pragmatic solution to the dilemma. A new approach to federalism emerged—and without any of the dramatic battles that had surrounded the constitutional debates and the Tenth Amendment.

The results were remarkable. New roads and harbors popped up, along with better schools and expanded trade. The Erie Canal connected the Great Lakes to the Hudson River and, from there, to the Atlantic Ocean, and that opened up the rapidly emerging West. The federal government helped set great ambitions for the new country, but it was the states that brought them to life. The early invention of federal grants established a foundation that proved enormously important in shaping federalism for generations to come.

But America's great original sin—the compromise over slavery that Justice Marshall said had made the country's founding ideas "defective from the start"—followed the nation on its steady road west. With every step toward expanding the country came fresh controversies about whether—and how much—slavery ought to be allowed to expand with it.

Lunging toward War

During the first half of the nineteenth century, the biggest questions of federalism revolved around decisions about admitting new states—and whether each new state would allow slavery. The three-fifths compromise in the Constitution and the Tenth Amendment had provided short-term solutions, but they only delayed the inevitable conflict. In fact, they might well have sharpened it by allowing these tensions to fester without being resolved. Every debate about admitting a new state centered on two questions: a moral one (should slavery be allowed to expand?) and a political one (how would bringing in a new state affect the balance of power in Congress?).

In 1820, Congress tried to cobble together a solution with the Missouri Compromise: a line was drawn on the map separating the new states into slave states and free states. When that compromise wobbled, other plans followed. The Compromise of 1850—which brought California into the union as a free state, gave the citizens in Utah and New Mexico the right to decide whether to prohibit slavery, and made it easier for Southern slave-owners to recover fugitive slaves—bought the country more time. The Kansas-Nebraska Act of 1854 rolled back the Missouri Compromise and reopened the battle over slavery in the land west of Missouri.

None of these deals stuck for long, and every effort only ignited new flash points. In 1852, Harriet Beecher Stowe's wildly popular novel *Uncle Tom's Cabin* appeared; it told the tale of Tom, who suffered for years in the "life among the lowly," as the book's subtitle put it. The book energized abolitionists and stoked the fires of Northerners eager to end slavery. In fact, Stowe's story gained extra support from John Brown's raid on a government arsenal in Harper's Ferry, Virginia (now West Virginia), a foray designed to create an armed revolt of slaves. Federal troops, under the overall command of a promising colonel named Robert E. Lee, stopped the attack, but it greatly worried Southerners, who feared that it was just the start of an armed effort to force an end to slavery and, in the process, destroy the economy of the South.

When Abraham Lincoln won the 1860 presidential election, many Southerners were sure that those days were coming and that a better organized campaign might well succeed. Franklin might have urged the states to "join, or die," but in the weeks after Lincoln's election, it became clear that some states were happier to see the Union die than to stay joined, if the cost was sacrificing slavery. Following on the old debates about a truly united collection of states in America, the Civil War was fought to decide whether the states could define what that meant. In the process, the fabric of the American republic frayed right up to the point of being permanently shredded.

The Constitution of the Confederate States clearly laid out the policy of the states that chose to secede from the Union: "[T]he institution of negro slavery, as it now exists in the Confederate States, shall be recognized and protected by Congress"—by the Confederate Congress, that is.[11] States joining the Confederacy had no choice about whether to adopt slavery; that was set in the document they embraced. South Carolina, the first state to secede, made its position clear in the declaration of its own independence when it pointed to "an increasing hostility on the part of the non-slaveholding States to the institution of slavery" and its concern that "belief that slavery is in the course of ultimate extinction."[12] Eleven Southern states decided to stand together to defend the practice of slavery and wrapped that argument in the mantle of states' rights.

The result was the bloodiest conflict ever fought on American soil. The war was, in many ways, the inevitable result of the uneasy compromise that the founders had made in the Declaration of Independence and the Constitution. To this day, debate continues over whether the Civil War was a battle of morals—over slavery—or of federalism—over states' rights. Any careful reading of the debates at the time, however, points squarely to slavery as the root cause, with states' rights used as an argument to defend it, although many people characterize the conflict differently. A 2011 Pew Research Center poll found that 48 percent of those surveyed believed that the Civil War was "mainly about states' rights," while 38 percent believed that it was "mainly about slavery." Younger Americans (under age thirty) were far more likely to say that the main cause of the Civil War was states' rights, compared with those over the age of sixty-five (by a margin of 60 percent to 34 percent). Southerners remain far more likely than Northerners to say that it is "appropriate for politicians today to praise Confederate leaders" (by a margin of 52 percent to 32 percent).[13] These disputes, in turn, have led to ongoing battles over whether it is appropriate to fly the Confederate flag from public buildings, to build its icons into state flags, and to have statues of Confederate generals in public parks. These battles have provided flash points for virulent debate and sometimes violent conflict over many generations, including the death of a woman in Charlottesville, Virginia, in 2017 during a protest involving neo-Nazis, members of the Ku Klux Klan, and white nationalists waving Confederate flags.

The Civil War made it clear that federalism was about much more than high principle. Because it was so engrained by then in the country's social and economic life and development, federalism provided a flash point for the deep tensions over slavery that the founders had decided to avoid. They had hoped that the passage of time would make it possible to resolve those tensions, but instead they sparked violence that almost tore the country apart, in a war whose outcome often seemed in doubt.

Moreover, the Civil War scarcely resolved these tensions over slavery. Rather, it transformed them in new and different ways that continued to challenge the nation's moral sense and even to spawn new violence as the nation sought to resolve the original sin that had plagued it since its beginning.

Separate but Equal

Lincoln's Emancipation Proclamation did not really end slavery, since it freed only slaves in territory that the North did not control. To make good on his promise, the North first had to win the war—and when it did, to define what the war's outcome truly meant. That challenge fell to the Fourteenth Amendment, ratified in 1868, which launched the Second Generation of Federalism in the United States.

The amendment was pathbreaking in asserting the fundamental equality of Americans, especially in its historic guarantee of "equal protection of the laws." The states were forbidden to "make or enforce any law which shall abridge the privileges or immunities" of any citizen. The "equal protection" clause did more than do away with the three-fifths rule: over time, it became one of the most sweeping declarations in the entire Constitution. It has driven a host of national policies, including reproductive rights, election recounts, gender discrimination, affirmative action, and, of course, civil rights.

After the guarantee of "equal protection of the laws," Section 5 of the amendment, in a phrase just as terse, says, "The Congress shall have power to enforce, by appropriate legislation, the provisions of this article." The federal government in general, and Congress in particular, had the power to draw the boundaries. The Fourteenth Amendment was thus very different from the Tenth. The Tenth Amendment arose from the quest to draw a clear limit on federal power. In fact, it turned out to be anything but—and it wasn't clear who was in charge of enforcing it. The boundaries set by the Fourteenth Amendment were a bit less sharp, but it made crystal-clear that Congress had the power to decide where that line would be.

The Fourteenth Amendment was breathtaking in its ambition. In its "equal protection of the law" phrase, it put a legal end to the debate that had entangled federal-state relations for seventy years. It also dramatically shifted the balance of power in favor of the federal government over the states. Where the Tenth Amendment, despite its simplicity, had allowed the debate about slavery and states' rights to simmer for decades, the Fourteenth Amendment straightforwardly defined rights and asserted who was in charge of protecting them. Congress, not the states, was in charge of ensuring that equal protection of everyone was now the law of the land. In an equally historic step, the amendment established the federal government's primacy over the states in a way that had never clearly emerged before in the country's history. It was, Sherrilyn Ifill, director of the NAACP Legal Defense and Educational Fund, said, a chance to "hit the reset button on American democracy."[14]

The amendment's protections, however, turned out to be unclear in practice. Does the "equal protection" clause require *equal procedures*, so that everyone gets the same fair shake? Or does it imply a process that produces *equal results*? If a state claims that a process is equal, can it truly be equal if different people benefit unequally? In short, just what does "equal" mean? And on what issues does it apply?

After the Civil War, the nation's leaders knew that these questions were tough and inevitable. However, one thing at the time seemed certain: the Fourteenth Amendment shifted the balance of intergovernmental power toward the federal government and away from the states—and away from the Southern states and toward the North. One of the great advantages of winning a war, after all, is that the winners can write the rules that govern the losers. As the next two generations of American history showed, however, it was one thing for the federal government to assert its dominance. It was quite another to define, establish, advance, and enforce it.

In fact, it took only a few years for the apparent clarity of the Fourteenth Amendment's promise of equal protection to dissolve, and no state was more important in this dissolution than Louisiana, through a series of court decisions. This debate, surprisingly, was fueled by butchers' tables.

New Orleans had become a major center of the animal processing business, and many of the butchers tossed the by-products, from blood and urine to entrails and manure, into the Mississippi River. This practice not only created an unpleasant mess but also caused outbreaks of diseases like cholera, which wreaked havoc with the digestive systems of people exposed to the water. The state legislature responded by granting a single company, the Crescent City Live-Stock Landing and Slaughter-House Company, the sole right to control and, it hoped, clean up the slaughtering business. Other slaughterhouses, however, fiercely complained that Crescent City's privileged role would hurt their businesses. The legislature, they contended, had deprived them of their property rights—their opportunity to make money—without due process of law. In short, they complained, they had been denied the equal protection of the law promised by the Fourteenth Amendment.

So, in an enormous irony, the first test of the amendment written to end slavery wasn't a slavery case at all. It was a case about a state's right to regulate commerce within its own borders, an issue that previously would not have involved the Constitution or the federal government. When the Supreme Court decided the case in 1873, by a narrow 5–4 vote, it held that the companies' rights had not been violated.[15] The federal government might have jurisdiction to ensure equal protection for freed slaves, the Court held, but it chose to read the Fourteenth Amendment narrowly, concluding that the states had jurisdiction over property rights. The amendment had seemed to be an opportunity to expand the federal government's reach. In the first major decision on the amendment, the Court ruled otherwise. It could have embraced a far more expansive reading of the amendment, but it chose to side with the autonomy of the states. And far more important, it created the foundation for allowing the states to decide for themselves just how strongly to protect citizens' rights.

In 1896, an even more important case reached the Court, with Louisiana at the center yet again. In 1890, the state had passed a "Separate Car Act" mandating the railroads provide "separate but equal" accommodations for African American and white passengers. Homer Adolph Plessy, a man of mixed race—seven-eighths Caucasian and one-eighth black— had boarded a train and taken a seat in a "whites only" car. When Plessy was told that he needed to move to a car for black passengers, he refused and was subsequently arrested. His case came before US District judge John Ferguson, who ruled against Plessy; on appeal, the US Supreme Court agreed.[16] How could that be possible, since the Separate Car Act clearly treated blacks and whites differently? The Court concluded that the Fourteenth Amendment guaranteed political equality for blacks, but that it did not guarantee them equal social outcomes.

In fact, the Court concluded, the case did not rest on any assumption that blacks were somehow unequal to whites. Any such argument, the Court ruled, was the product of the opinions of minorities themselves, not of Louisiana's law:

> We consider the underlying fallacy of the plaintiff's argument to consist in the assumption that the enforced separation of the two races stamps the colored race with a badge of inferiority. If this be so, it is not by reason of anything found in the act, but solely because the colored race chooses to put that construction upon it.

In *Plessy v. Ferguson*, therefore, the Court established a legal foundation for discrimination. It argued that the Louisiana law was consistent with the Fourteenth Amendment because it did not create legal inequality, from which blacks were protected, even though it legalized social inequality, which the Court said was not covered. The Court never explicitly held that creating "separate but equal" facilities was permissible. But since the majority of the Court pointed explicitly to the Separate Car Act and its provision for "equal but separate accommodations," the decision established the precedent that "separate but equal" facilities were, in fact, constitutional. In a profound paradox, the amendment that seemed to promise equality became the very instrument that, for the next sixty years, undermined it.

Moreover, the decision flipped the presumption that the federal government would have dominance over these issues. That, after all, had been the central issue of the Civil War, and the Fourteenth Amendment had explicitly given Congress, not the states, the power to enforce the amendment's protections. *Plessy*, however, established that the states, not the federal government, would define how the amendment actually worked. It established the notion of "separate but equal" facilities, and determining which facilities were separate but equal would remain a state decision until the Supreme Court's 1954 decision in *Brown v. Board of Education*.

The preeminence of the states in these issues of civil rights led to enormous variations across the country on an issue that the Fourteenth Amendment, in its plain language, said should be handled the same way in all states. "Separate but equal" allowed for segregation in local schools. It permitted enormous disparities in all aspects of daily life: in nursing care (Alabama protected white nurses from caring for black men); hair cutting (Georgia prohibited black barbers from cutting the hair of white women); circuses (Louisiana required separate ticket offices for black and white patrons); libraries (North Carolina mandated separate places for different races to read); fishing and boating (Oklahoma called for separate places for blacks and whites to enjoy the outdoors); lunch counters (South Carolina required separate facilities); movie theaters (Virginia required separate sections for blacks); baseball (Georgia prohibited amateur black and white teams from playing within two blocks of each other); and restrooms, drinking fountains, and restaurants—like a lunch counter in North Carolina that protesters later integrated through sit-ins.[17]

Plessy may have established "separate but equal" as policy, but in practice the facilities provided to blacks were invariably worse. "Travel in the segregated South for black people was humiliating," said the civil rights activist Diane Nash in a 2011 PBS documentary. One reason lay in the constant reminders of separate entrances, separate seats, and separate facilities for blacks. Another was the squalor of the facilities blacks were forced to use. "The very fact that there were separate facilities was to say to black people and white people that blacks were so subhuman and so inferior that we could not even use the public facilities that white people used."[18] Indeed, even the popularized name for the practice, the "Jim Crow" laws, was demeaning. Thomas Dartmouth Rice had been a well-known white entertainer in the years before the Civil War. In his minstrel shows, he portrayed a buffoonish character known as "Jim Crow" by putting on blackface and speaking in an exaggerated form of an African American idiom. His character became well known, and after the Civil War the caricaturized character became the symbol for the segregation policies that emerged.

In the nation's first century, some of the most important issues revolved around drawing boundaries between the federal government and the states. The states had insisted on the Tenth Amendment to make those boundaries clear, but the lines turned out to be anything but. The Fourteenth Amendment had been intended to end slavery and reinforce the importance of equal protection of the laws for all Americans, but many states found ways to circumvent the protections. Guarantees rooted in the law became instead opportunities for political pressure to adjust the balance, in ways that seemed to flaunt the language of the amendment. As a result, the states came to define what protection was truly equal, constraining the federal government's authority in the process, even though the Fourteenth Amendment had seemed to say exactly the reverse. This pattern endured for more than seventy years.

If the First Generation of Federalism had focused on drawing boundaries by framing them in law, the Second Generation would pursue state autonomy despite boundaries that the law seemed to make clear. It took a fateful 1954 decision by the US Supreme Court to transform the balance in American federalism.

4

Washington Rising

States' rights ruled social policy in America for eighty-five years, until 1954, with the Supreme Court's *Brown v. Board of Education* decision, which ended the "separate but equal" doctrine and spelled the end of state dominance in social policy. Before then, economic challenges—first the dramatic rise and transformation of urban America and then the Great Depression—had gradually shifted power from the states to Washington. The shift was subtle and unplanned, but nonetheless real. These intertwined threads created the foundation for the Third Generation of Federalism, but so too did the rise of local governments as important forces in federalism.

To this point of our story, the states have been the driving players in American federalism. But as the country grew after the Civil War, cities took on a more and more dominant role. The industrial age transformed the economy and fueled urban growth. From 1860 to 1900, for example, the number of agricultural jobs doubled, but the number of manufacturing jobs nearly quadrupled. In 1880, the nation hit an inflection point: for the first time in its history, non-agricultural employment surpassed jobs on the farms. By 1900, 40 percent of the nation's population lived in urban areas, compared with 20 percent in 1860 and 6 percent in 1800.[1] Fueling the nation's urbanization were waves of immigrants coming to the United States in search of new opportunities. Many of those opportunities were in urban areas, which increased the economic pressure on the nation's cities and the social pressure to integrate this new and very different population.

The working conditions for many of these new urban jobs were abysmal. Upton Sinclair's 1906 novel *The Jungle* brought national attention to horrendous settings in the meatpacking industry, and Jane Addams's penetrating 1910 book *Twenty Years at Hull-House* described the poor housing and limited opportunities for the people she cared for in the Hull-House shelter she founded in Chicago.[2] Besides immigrants, freed slaves also came to the cities, looking for jobs. Many of them ended up as workers in new factories, often with relatively low pay and poor working conditions. That led to the growth of urban slums where children often received a poor education and families suffered in crowded tenements. The nation had always had pockets of the rich and the poor, but aside from the scourge of slavery, it had never seen such big social problems in such concentrated areas.

The social problems cascaded into deeper urban economic problems. For the country's first 125 years, local governments had focused on basic services (such as education and public safety) and infrastructure (including roads and sewers). Local governments had never had to struggle with the type of deep social problems brought on by the industrial revolution, and they had neither the tax base nor the administrative capacity to attack these challenges. Indeed, the slums were not problems that fit Americans' sense of *governmental* problems. To the degree that society had an obligation to deal with them, Americans left the work to civic organizers like Jane Addams and nonprofit organizations like her Hull-House. But the capacity of these nonprofits was extremely limited, so it was inevitable that the spread of the slums created a new generation of urban poor who received little help from anyone.

The Rise of the Progressives

In response to these conditions, the Progressives built a robust movement in the last decades of the 1800s, arguing for a broader scope of government action and for a more professional government to accomplish it. Growing in the cities and states from the bottom up, the movement focused on improving government by rooting out corruption. The Progressives gave birth to the "muckrakers," a term that Theodore Roosevelt, alluding to *The*

Pilgrim's Progress, a 1678 novel, popularized in a 1906 speech. The book featured a character who could only look downward, intent on using his tool to rake dung. "The men with the muckrakes are often indispensable to the well-being of society," Roosevelt said.[3] Muckraking thus focused not only on busting the political machines but also on transforming the role of government itself. The focus on "the well-being of society" laid the foundation for a far broader definition of what government's role could— and should—be. Progressives elevated the plight of city dwellers to problems that demanded public attention, and they argued that this approach should begin with *governmental* attention.

In one of the most remarkably bipartisan reform movements in American history, the Progressives powerfully redefined government's role. Republican leaders like New York's Theodore Roosevelt and Wisconsin's Robert M. La Follette Sr., reformed their states. "Fighting Bob" La Follette, for example, led a broad-scale movement to regulate the railroads and reform the primary election system. He created home rule for local governments, which gave them far more power to set their own course; established a minimum wage for workers; won passage of a progressive income tax; and championed women's suffrage, the direct election of members of the US Senate, open primaries, and other electoral reforms. As governor of New York, Theodore Roosevelt fought for strong civil service laws to protect government from patronage and helped break the famous New York City Tammany Hall political machine through reforms of the police department. He became the best known of all the Progressives, with his 1912 presidential campaign in the Progressive "Bull Moose" Party—a moniker he picked up following an assassination attempt in 1912, shortly before he was scheduled for a campaign speech in Milwaukee. Despite suffering a gunshot wound, he still gave the speech. "You see, it takes more than that to kill a Bull Moose!" he told the crowd. Roosevelt collapsed soon after his address and was rushed to a hospital, where doctors patched him up. His close escape, however, only helped fuel his image—and the Progressive movement.

The Democrats had Nebraska's William Jennings Bryan, New York's Al Smith, and New Jersey's Woodrow Wilson, all of whom put their own brand on the Progressive movement. Bryan campaigned to reduce the power of big money in politics. Smith made great advances in improving the working conditions of factory workers, serving as a top official in a series of commissions investigating unsafe facilities. Following the tragic 1911 Triangle Shirtwaist Factory fire in New York City's Greenwich Village, a disaster that killed nearly 150 workers, mostly new immigrants, he brought safety inspectors into factories and led the campaign for a vast array of new laws to improve working conditions. Wilson left his faculty position at Princeton University to take on the political bosses in New York and used his success in that effort to fuel his presidential campaign.

The Progressives thus launched a most unusual movement, with powerful Republicans and Democrats making the case for a more expansive, more powerful, less corrupt government. Never before in American history—and only rarely since—has there been such a bipartisan effort to make government bigger and broaden its role. It was a bottom-up movement that spilled over to the federal government. National reformers pushed through the creation of the Department of Commerce in 1903 to stimulate business development; passed legislation establishing the Department of Labor in 1913 to protect workers; and established a series of regulatory agencies to protect citizens, like the Food and Drug Administration in 1906 and the Federal Trade Commission in 1914. The Progressives' imprint on the federal government was substantial, especially with expanding regulation of private businesses. But their work left unanswered the question of just how big government ought to be and, even more fundamental, where the balance of federal, state, and local power ought to rest.

At the close of the 1920s, everything would change. The crisis of the Great Depression dealt state and local governments a series of challenges that they simply couldn't meet and that the federal government concluded it had no choice but to address.

The Federalization of Governmental Action

The Great Depression was the most searing economic jolt in American history.[4] The aftershocks of the stock market collapse of 1929 would stretch on for years, with the market's value dropping 86 percent—the most painful bear market in history. It was 1954 before the market was back to pre-crash levels. Unemployment rose to 25 percent, incomes shrank by 40 percent, and more than 1 million families lost the farms that they had spent generations building. Industrial production dropped by almost half, and bank panics fueled further economic chaos. Bread lines and soup kitchens spread across many American cities. As one Chicago author from the period put it:

> We were almost, though not entirely, wiped out, like millions of other families. We saw the city at its worst. We saw Want and Despair walking the streets, and our friends, sensible, thrifty families, reduced to poverty. We saw the runs on the Big Loop banks—the Bank Holiday. One vivid, gruesome moment of those dark days we shall never forget. We saw a crowd of some fifty men fighting over a barrel of garbage which had been set outside the back door of a restaurant. American citizens fighting for scraps of food like animals![5]

As problems mounted, citizens turned first to the voluntary organizations that had been the engines of social policy for the previous generation. These nonprofits, however, were quickly overwhelmed by the sheer magnitude of the crisis. Citizens turned next to state governments, but they were in no better shape. W. Brooke Graves concluded that the Depression "made it unmistakably clear that the States were in a pitifully weak condition." State-chartered banks fell at a faster rate than those regulated by the federal government, and there were few state welfare programs to help citizens cope.

The Depression posed a big question about just how government ought to respond, which level of government ought to take on the job, and how to pay for the relief the nation so desperately needed. Except for wartime, the story for the previous century had been about the growth of local government as the increasingly urbanized population demanded education and basic infrastructure. Before America's entry into World War I, in fact, local governments accounted for about two-thirds of all government spending in the United States, and they were the center of action in American government. State governments, by contrast, were relatively small players in budgetary terms, responsible for just 10 percent of all government spending.[6] When the Depression hit, state and local governments had few resources with which to respond—state governments were small, and local governments devoted most of their budgets to basic services. Moreover, the Depression ate away at their revenue streams: receipts fell by more than one-fourth from 1929 to 1934. State and local governments were caught in an increasingly desperate squeeze—between citizens who were becoming more and more desperate and shrinking coffers with no cash to attack the problems.

State and local governments simply froze. The demands for local relief were far greater than anything they had ever attempted. Large groups of unemployed demonstrators descended on Harrisburg demanding action, but the Pennsylvania state legislature focused instead on legislating beer sales, fishing on Sunday, and baseball on Sunday.[7] An analyst at the time, William Elliott, argued that the constitutional system created a century and a half earlier, designed to solve a different set of problems, simply was not up to the challenges posed by the Depression.[8] Citizens looked to their state and local government leaders, but those leaders simply did not know what to do or how to pay for it. It became increasingly clear that the system of federalism that had survived the Civil War, if barely, might well not survive the economic crisis of the 1930s.

Citizens demanded that *someone* step in, somehow, and for Franklin D. Roosevelt, that someone was the federal government. The somehow was his New Deal, a sweeping suite of programs that transformed American governance in virtually every respect. Roosevelt sought aggressive new programs in part to shore up confidence. But the New Deal also was a restructuring and professionalization of government, in the spirit of the Progressive movement, and represented a fundamental change in government's role, with a massive infusion of government spending to stimulate the economy. Perhaps most importantly, this fundamental change in the federal government's role came with a far larger portfolio, which in turn, led to enormous changes in federalism.

As John Joseph Wallis and Wallace Oates have contended, "The New Deal meant much more than just a movement toward centralization of the public sector. It brought with it some fundamental and dramatic changes in the very character of American federalism, changes that would leave a permanent imprint on the intergovernmental system."[9] The federal government stepped in to do what state and local governments could not—or would not—do. In very short order, the pressure to respond to the Depression upended the Tenth Amendment and radically reset the balance of power among America's governments.

For Roosevelt and his team, the new programs represented less a sweeping transformative strategy than a series of pragmatic steps aimed at dealing with an overwhelming crisis: pumping out cash to help get people back to work, writing new rules to stabilize the banks, and building a safety net to keep the country from falling deeper into disaster. A broad collection of federal programs created new infrastructure, ranging from new roads, including Virginia's storied Skyline Drive, to impressive public buildings, like many city halls around the country. There was even money for painters and sculptors to decorate these facilities, which drove an influx of public investment in the arts. In San Antonio, the Works Projects Administration turned a waterway that periodically flooded the downtown into the city's iconic River Walk. San Francisco took advantage of federal money to build its aquatic park, and in New Orleans, the French Market, known to tourists for classic coffee and beignets, emerged from a deteriorated setting. Hoover Dam helped electrify Las Vegas. When it came to funding the programs through deficit spending, Roosevelt jumped fearlessly into the pool of red ink.

In short order, the New Dealers' efforts brought a dramatic change in federalism that the nation's founders never imagined. Before the Great Depression, local governments had dominated government life in America, except during wartime, when government spending grew before settling back to normal when peacetime returned. With the Great Depression, federal spending swelled with a broad sweep of federal programs to do what state and local governments could not. What started as a short-term, tactical emergency response became a new normal from which the federal government never retreated. More problems became government problems, especially in domestic policy, and more governmental problems became federal ones, despite the language of the Fourteenth Amendment. Driven by the Depression's enormous human catastrophe, government, for the first time, moved deeply into everything from housing to welfare—and the government leading the charge was the federal government.

Like so many of the changes wrought by the New Deal, most observers of American politics assumed that the changes in federalism would be temporary and that things would return to normal when the crisis had passed. But the crisis did not pass. Unemployment remained stubbornly high throughout the 1930s, and soon the looming crisis of a world war replaced the crisis of the Depression. The New Deal programs, in fact, marked a sharp turning point in governance. Federal spending began an upward trend that never diminished. State and local governments began their own period of growth, which blossomed especially after World War II. In fact, as Michael Schuyler points out, "The year 1940 was notable because it was the last time state and local government revenues and outlays were roughly on a par with those of the federal government."[10]

As was the case a century before, when the federal government explored strategies for expanding infrastructure programs, it discovered that federalism was not so much a principle as a tool. Many of the New Deal's initiatives were channeled through intergovernmental grants, with the federal government using state and, especially, local governments as administrative agents for the programs. There was little appetite for growing the federal bureaucracy even more, and with the need for fast action, there was little time to wait for constructing new federal agencies. It was quicker and easier to use state and local governments—and the strategy appeased those who were edgy about the expansion of federal power.

The Great Depression thus flipped the focus of policymaking and financial responsibility in the American system, from state and local governments to the federal government. It also transformed a substantial share of state and local administrative responsibility, as these governments took on a broader role as administrative agents for federal programs. In short, the Depression for the first time made the federal government the prime mover of domestic policy in the country. It proved to be a change with deep, lasting, and even revolutionary effects on American federalism.

The State-Local Balance

The New Deal also profoundly changed the balance between state and local governments. Local governments were willing, often eager partners in the New Deal programs, in part because state governments had been so slow and ineffective in responding to the pressures of the Great Depression. The growth of federal-local partnerships, however, created new political and constitutional challenges. Neither the Tenth Amendment nor anything else in the Constitution specified what role local governments ought to play in the American system. The founders knew that the nation would need local governments, but they simply assumed that state governments would sort out what local governments would do. In fact, the founders understood that the "reserved powers" clause of the Tenth Amendment included the power to create and structure the role of local governments. The revolution against Britain had its roots in the debates in local towns around the country, especially in New England town halls. Many of the most basic principles for holding public officials accountable, in fact, came from the towns.[11] Benjamin Franklin had created a local lending library and fire service in Philadelphia. The founders had great reverence for local self-government and for the services that local governments provided. But they also believed that the fundamental challenge was setting the balance between the federal government and the states, because meeting that challenge would enable the nation to endure.

With the great expansion of the government's scope of activity in the New Deal, however, two questions became far more important. In a bigger government, especially with so much of its activity aimed at putting Americans back to work in their communities, what should be the balance of power between state and local governments? And with so much federal money flooding into the cities, could—or should—the federal government do business directly with local governments? And if so, might that marginalize the role of the states?

The debate about the state-local balance had simmered for a long time after the country's founding. Given the Tenth Amendment, the presumption was that setting the balance was a state decision, but that balance in turn depended on just how much independence local governments ought to have. One of the most powerful answers came from Judge John Dillon of Iowa, who ruled in an 1865 state court case that local governments have only the powers granted by their state governments through their constitutions or laws. At the time, Dillon was perhaps the nation's most-respected expert on local government, so his judgment carried great weight. His logic was simple. State governments are the foundation of American democracy. They created the federal government—and the local governments as well. In a famous 1868 case that defined the precedent, he wrote:

> Municipal corporations owe their origin to, and derive their powers and rights wholly from, the legislature. It breathes into them the breath of life, without which they cannot exist. As it creates, so it may destroy. If it may destroy, it may abridge and control. . . . We know of no limitation on this right so far as the corporations themselves are concerned. They are, so to phrase it, the mere tenants at will of the Legislature.[12]

So, for Dillon, the answer was simple: as creatures of the states, local governments have only the power that the states choose to give them. As the New Deal grew, however, Dillon's Rule, as it had become known, raised new problems. Did local governments have the legal authority and standing to deal directly with the federal government, or were they limited to partnerships that the states had approved in advance?

Although the basic principle was that local governments were creatures of the states and had only the powers that the state governments chose to give them, some states allowed their local governments far more flexibility than others through what is known as "home rule": the power of citizens to rule their home, without needing advance approval on everything from the state. There was thus enormous variation during the Depression in the legal relationship of cities to their states, and that vastly complicated the federal government's policies in deciding how to work with local governments directly, and whether doing so was even legal. Many of the New Deal projects envisioned local action, but some states were unhappy that Washington was muscling into their territory, and even those who were happy to have Washington take the lead struggled to get their policy apparatus into gear. How could the federal government act quickly, sidestep roadblocks in state capitals, and enlist local governments?

Rather than have the federal government tell local governments what to do—and enmesh the federal government in a tangle with the states—the federal government reached back to the blueprint that had worked in the nineteenth century: the federal government could make grants available to local governments, this time in cash. State governments might grumble, but the problems were enormous and they had no capacity to fund solutions themselves. Local governments did not have to accept the grants, but many were very ready to do so; they saw their citizens' problems firsthand, and many of their states had been slow to recognize their problems and even slower to provide money to solve them. The result was a new federal-local alliance—a breed of governmental relationship that endured and expanded in the decades that followed.[13]

The historic roles of the federal and local governments thus reversed over the course of the New Deal.[14] Local governments had long been the dominant form of domestic government in the United States, especially in terms of spending. The New Deal changed that: now the federal government increasingly set the national agenda and provided grants to advance its policies. The state governments had long been the dominant political institution, having created both the federal government and their own state governments, but the economic crisis of the Depression—and the healthy supply of federal cash that sought to ease it—created a brand-new collection of powerful federal-local partnerships that forever changed federalism.

For much of the country's first 150 years, the Tenth Amendment was the defining statement about federalism. That changed—permanently—with the launch of the New Deal. The federal government had taken aggressive action on a broad front of policy areas previously dominated by the states. There were new federal-local partnerships. The states had been tried and found wanting in the challenges of the Depression, and their role had weakened. These forces combined to lead the US Supreme Court in 1941 to dismiss the old doctrine about the Tenth Amendment as "but a truism"—in the end, that doctrine had added little to the Constitution and provided no effective brake on the federal government's expanding role.[15] The stage was thus set for an even greater expansion of federal power into the realm of civil rights.

Segregation

The New Deal was the financial watershed of American federalism, but the Supreme Court's 1954 ruling on segregation, *Brown v. Board of Education*, was the transformative social decision of the twentieth century. It launched the Third Generation of Federalism in the United States through a profound shift in the balance of power.[16]

Brown capped the fundamental debate about equality that had been brewing since traders brought the first slaves to the colonies. The founders had sidestepped it in the Declaration of Independence and then again with the Constitution. They allowed the states to set policy until the Civil War, but even after the North's victory, states used the "separate but equal" doctrine to continue to feed the deep divisions of segregation. If the New Deal flipped the financial balance in the country to one dominated by the federal government, *Brown* asserted federal power in promoting social and economic equality among the nation's citizens. Justice Thurgood Marshall argued that the American republic was "defective from the start." Before he was named to the bench, he built a powerful base, as the lead attorney winning the *Brown* case, from which he and fellow reformers would seek to remedy that defect.

The case had emerged from a challenge to the school policy of Topeka, Kansas, which followed the principle that separate schools for black children were constitutionally acceptable. The practice was widespread at the time. Analysts estimated, in fact, that more than three-fourths of black students attended local schools with at least 90 percent black enrollment.[17] The lawyers for the plaintiffs argued that such "separate" schools were not—and never could be—"equal." They enlisted thirteen families to challenge the policy, and Oliver Brown, a railroad welder, would be the first plaintiff listed in the filing—and then for all history in the decision. Along with the other black families, he had tried to enroll his daughter, Linda, in an all-white Topeka elementary school, but he had been turned down. That, the plaintiffs contended, violated the Fourteenth

Amendment's "equal protection" clause. Racially segregated schools, they said, could never be equal.

The federal district court in Kansas did find that segregation had a "detrimental effect upon the colored children," and that it created "a sense of inferiority." In keeping with nearly a century of precedent that yielded policy primacy to the states, however, the district court refused to overturn Topeka's policy or the "separate but equal" doctrine.[18] The NAACP Legal Defense and Educational Fund, headed by Thurgood Marshall, challenged the district court's ruling and crafted an appeal to the US Supreme Court in a case that directly challenged *Plessy* and the "separate but equal" doctrine. Court observers believed that Chief Justice Fred Vinson would push to uphold *Plessy* and that the Court's decision would be split, at best. But just before the case was scheduled to be argued before the Court, Vinson died.

Naming a Supreme Court chief justice always ranks as one of a president's biggest decisions, but in this case, the decision turned out to be epic. President Dwight D. Eisenhower's choice was California Governor Earl Warren. He was a truly unusual figure in American politics: a Progressive who had run for governor in both the Republican and Democratic primaries, and who had won both of them. He strengthened the state's hospital and prison systems and led an expansion of the state's colleges and universities. Warren had toyed with running for president and then joined Thomas Dewey's 1948 presidential campaign as his vice presidential running mate. He launched a campaign for the Republican presidential nomination in 1952 but eventually threw his support to Eisenhower, who credited Warren with helping to put him over the top at the convention. When it came to choosing a successor to Vinson, therefore, Warren was a logical choice for Eisenhower, who named him to a Court deeply divided over the scope of federal power.

Warren was convinced of the importance of civil rights and was committed to overturning *Plessy*. But given the deep divisions on the issue, he didn't think simply overturning the earlier decision was enough—given the long and contentious history of the "separate but equal" policy, he believed that reversing *Plessy* needed a unanimous vote. With a political skill rarely seen on the Court, especially from a newcomer, he pulled together a 9–0 ruling to strike down *Plessy* and school segregation. His opinion had a powerful opening:

> Segregation of white and Negro children in the public schools of a State solely on the basis of race, pursuant to state laws permitting or requiring such segregation, denies to Negro children the equal protection of the laws guaranteed by the Fourteenth Amendment—even though the physical facilities and other "tangible" factors of white and Negro schools may be equal.

Warren concluded, "The 'separate but equal' doctrine adopted in *Plessy v. Ferguson* has no place in the field of public education." Few cases in the Court's history have had greater impact than *Brown*.

Saying so did not make it so, of course. *Brown* might have ended the legal justification for segregation, but it scarcely ended its practice. In the years that followed, rearguard segregationist movements continued, only to be met with growing violence in many urban centers. In 1963, Alabama Governor George Wallace stood in a university doorway in an effort to block the efforts of two black students to enroll at the University of Alabama. Arsonists burned down a school in Mississippi rather than allow it to be integrated. In the 1960s, rioting erupted in major American cities: the "long, hot summer" in Newark, Detroit, and Milwaukee in 1967 was followed by major riots in 1968 after Martin Luther King's assassination, in cities ranging from Washington and Chicago to Wilmington, Delaware, and York, Pennsylvania.

A national commission, headed by Ohio Governor Otto Kerner Jr., reached a blunt conclusion in 1968: "Our nation is moving toward two societies, one black, one white—separate and unequal." Judicial action alone, promulgated from federal courts down to local governments, could not erase the deep-seated patterns of inequality that had developed over generations. As the Kerner Report found, the roots of discrimination were deep: "Pervasive discrimination and segregation in employment, education and housing . . . have resulted in the continuing exclusion of great numbers of Negroes from the benefits of economic progress."[19] The issue of inequality had been joined—but it was scarcely surprising, given almost two hundred years of local segregation, that only strong federal action could uproot it.

Federal Preeminence

President Lyndon B. Johnson was convinced that the Court's ruling in *Brown* would never be enough to uproot such deep-seated segregation, and he set out to put muscle behind *Brown* with a blizzard of federal legislation under his Great Society banner. He might have seemed an unusual champion—an accidental president who hailed from the South—but both parts of this story helped motivate him. As the successor to John F. Kennedy, he was eager to carve out his own agenda, and as a Southerner, he believed that he had special political advantages he could use to advance the cause. And as the unquestioned "master of the Senate," as his biographer Robert Caro called him, he had the legislative skills to make it happen.[20]

Johnson pushed through a trio of civil rights laws—the Civil Rights Act in 1964, the Voting Rights Act in 1965, and the Fair Housing Act in 1968—to solidify the ruling in *Brown* and to strengthen the federal role in ending Jim Crow. He added Model Cities, a federal-local program to provide aid to troubled inner cities, and Medicaid and Medicare, to deliver health care to the poor and elderly; he also expanded welfare to create a more solid foundation for the poor.

In very short order, the federal government took an even more powerful role at the top of the federal system, through both regulatory and financial strategies aimed squarely at reducing inequality in society. Given the broad sweep of segregation throughout American history, the speed with which hundreds of years of policy crumbled in the short period from *Brown* in 1954 to Johnson's furious legislative assault in the late 1960s was truly remarkable.

The balance of power most certainly shifted toward federal dominance, but it was not a pattern of federal control. The federal government had shifted the boundaries around what was permissible, but the states retained a powerful role in carrying out policy. Their level of enthusiasm in embracing the new federal initiatives played a powerful role in shaping how much change they truly brought. Observers frequently pointed back to an 1832 decision by US Supreme Chief justice John Marshall, who had strongly rebuked the state of Georgia when it tried to push Cherokee tribes out of the state and harassed missionaries who were ministering to them. Marshall held that the Cherokee Nation was sovereign and that the state had no right to remove the tribe or badger those aiding it. President Andrew Jackson was widely quoted as having replied, "John Marshall has made his decision; now let him enforce it." (What he is reputed to actually have said is far less quotable: "The decision of the supreme court has fell still born, and they find that it cannot coerce Georgia to yield to its mandate."[21]) Having expanded its claim on power, the federal government needed to figure out how to make that power real.

Federal agencies had responsibility for enforcing federal policy against discrimination, but much of the work inevitably fell to state and local governments. As vast as the federal government's increase in power was, it still could not look deeply into the behavior of every school system or every housing development. The Justice Department was responsible for taking cases to court, but it could not possibly challenge every discriminatory practice that federal agencies found across the country. This constraint led the federal government to pick selected cases to prosecute and, with those cases, to leverage its power broadly without trying to enforce it everywhere.

The desegregation campaign spread from the South into the North and West, encountering battles over busing in Boston and court disputes in communities as wide-ranging as Louisville and Seattle. In the 1990s, much of the debate shifted to the exercise of local police power. Critics charged that racial discrimination lay at the core of Rodney King's brutal beating in 1991 by Los Angeles police, and in 2014 members of the Ferguson, Missouri, community charged that Michael Brown, an unarmed black teenager shot and killed by a police officer, had been the victim of a pattern of racially motivated police violence.

After the *Brown* decision, national attention to race—and especially to the actions of state and local governments that had prolonged discriminatory treatment—led to a powerful elevation of federal power. Local governments certainly had not been the only drivers of discrimination; slavery long predated the creation of the country. But for generations the flash points in the battle were the federal-state-local struggles over just where the lines on discrimination ought to be drawn—and who was responsible for drawing them. Federalism mattered not only because of the debate over what kinds of behavior should be seen as discriminatory, but also because of the debate over who ought to make that call, and how uniformly across the country that determination ought to be applied. Alexis de Tocqueville had celebrated the great diversity that the power of the states brought to the country. Civil rights proved a tough test of that proposition, since that great diversity had helped fuel patterns of discrimination across the nation.

The growing prominence of federal civil rights efforts thus not only marked a shift in the balance of power. It also sparked a shift in intergovernmental politics by elevating regulatory policy to a permanent place on the intergovernmental agenda. The federal government had set itself to work eliminating discrimination, but once it moved past the most blatant "separate but equal" practices, civil rights issues became far more subtle and pushed much deeper into the everyday operations of the most basic local services—including instantaneous decisions by, for example, police officers about just how much force they could use and whether their decisions demonstrated patterns of racial bias. Questions of federalism had moved far past boundary-drawing and into the most detailed and intimate decisions about local functions.

The Triumph of Federal Grants

From the 1950s through the 1970s, the federal government not only expanded its reach through civil rights policy but also vastly increased the role of federal grants—and accelerated the transition of these grants from a system based on wide distribution of money to one focused on redistribution, with money aimed at the nation's neediest.

As millions of veterans returned from World War II, there had been genuine worry about whether the nation's economy could absorb them. Would there be jobs for everyone? Would the economy be able to switch quickly from growth fueled by government spending on wartime production to sustainable growth in the private economy? Soon, however, the worries shifted: the vets stimulated a series of big booms, and the challenge became how to manage them. There was a baby boom as couples made up for lost time; a housing boom as larger families looked for room to spread out; a shopping boom as new families bought appliances and television sets; a school boom fueled by so many babies who needed education; and a college boom as returning veterans went back to school using their GI Bill tuition benefits. The defense industry, which at first seemed likely to shrink in the shadow of peace, boomed with the demands of the Cold War—to the point that Eisenhower himself warned about the "military-industrial complex." The Soviets' launch of satellites sparked yet another boom, both in military construction and in education, as national leaders worried about how to make sure the nation had the talent to keep up with the space race.

All of these booms required good transportation. A new generation of drivers with sleek cars needed better roads. So did the truckers carrying new consumer goods. Defense planners worried about how to shift troops and equipment quickly around the country in case of Soviet attack. In response, Eisenhower in 1956 proposed a vast network of highways to connect the country, but for this to work he had to solve the familiar federalism problem: How could the federal government get an interconnected national network built even though it didn't have the administrative machinery to do the job and couldn't force state and local governments, which were traditionally in charge of roads, to do so themselves?

The Eisenhower team came up with a two-part plan. First, the federal government would entice the states to build the roads by providing grants for 90 percent of the construction costs. No state would dare sit on the sidelines while its neighbors got fast new highways to carry sleek new cars, especially when the cost of getting into the game was just ten cents on the dollar. Second, to build political support for the federal grants, the administration christened the program as the National Interstate and Defense Highways Act. Wrapping the highway system in the cloak of defense helped make it bulletproof. The federal grants, in turn, made it far easier to secure the states' compliance with federal highway standards. During construction, big signs proudly noted the federal government's role—and the highways' support of national defense. Even though the federal government paid 90 percent of the construction costs, the states were responsible for the network within their borders. When citizens later complained about litter and potholes, the financing scheme gave federal officials a handy reply: the federal government might have paid for the roads, but the state governments owned them.

The defense portion of the story was certainly a handy tool for marshaling political support, but it wasn't complete artifice. The Defense Department's largest missiles, for example, had to be transported by roadway because they didn't fit on railcars. The missile transporters were huge and required a seventeen-foot clearance. So that missiles could be taken anywhere, a seventeen-foot clearance became the standard for bridges on the interstate system.[22] Federal requirements dictated state construction and design, but the states scarcely objected when the federal government was paying.

Despite the federal government's efforts to weave the roads into a system, the interstate system isn't completely seamless. For example, there has long been a choke point in central Pennsylvania, where I-70 has a clumsy connection with the Pennsylvania Turnpike. Drivers along the interstate are dumped onto a slow, winding, two-mile loop through the city streets of Breezewood, a town of 1,400 famous for its motels, gas stations, restaurants, and congestion—a tourist trap that local merchants have fought to retain.[23] Breezewood is notable for two things: for its decades-long battle to prevent a clean connection between the highways—all the better for local businesses—and for the fact that so few roadblocks like Breezewood disrupt the remarkable 46,876-mile interstate system.[24]

The interstate highway program revolutionized the relationship between the federal government and the states. It established that the federal government could—and would—advance national programs through the states by dangling federal cash. It established that the states could—and would—find the bait irresistible. And it demonstrated the federal government's power to create a transportation network linking the nation's cities in a way that the states never could have done. The connections, of course, were far more than just economic. The road network linked urban centers in a way that only science writers had previously imagined.

These grants clearly established the state and local governments as administrative agents of national policy defined by the federal government. All of the traditional constitutional, administrative, and political constraints of the Tenth Amendment remained in place, but the interstate highway program showed that when the federal government wanted to get something done, grants were the way—provided the incentives were large enough—to get the states to work on national priorities. In the process, the new intergovernmental system, created by federal grants in the 1930s but interrupted in the 1940s by World War II, became clearly rooted as a fundamental instrument of American domestic policy.

These programs, of course, sought to advance federal goals. But they had strong support from state and local governments, which quickly learned to use this new federal wealth to their advantage. Organizations like the Council of State Governments, the US Conference of Mayors, the National League of Cities, and the National Association of Counties soon became major lobbying organizations for more federal cash. The Hall of the States opened just a few blocks from the US Capitol as a base for state governments to lobby their members of Congress. The grant system not only provided federal leverage over state and local governments but also built a vehicle for creating state and local leverage over the feds.

Some members of Congress won a much bigger slice of this money for their own constituents. Pennsylvania's Bud Shuster, for example, was legendary in the 1980s and 1990s for steering projects to his central Pennsylvania congressional district, including the construction of the fifty-three-mile-long Bud Shuster Highway, whose signs reminded his constituents who had delivered the new road. He acquired so much power as chair of the House Transportation and Infrastructure Committee that he became, as the *Washington Post* reported, "one man on Capitol Hill whom no one wants to cross." Shuster proved so effective in steering projects toward his district, in fact, that he and his staff faced extensive ethics investigations.[25]

This vast expansion of federal grants stood in stark contrast to the national turmoil over civil rights. Civil rights policies forced state and local governments to make big changes, many of which were in deep conflict with hundreds of years of practice. The grant programs, on the other hand, were designed to help state and local governments do what they wanted to do but often could not afford to do on their own. No government wanted to leave money on the table, and no government wanted to have to explain why their neighbors got cash for new roads or bridges that they could not win for themselves. Moreover, the flow of cash helped counterbalance the coercion of civil rights policy. That fundamental difference—between regulatory policy for civil rights and distributive policy for the grants—marked a fundamental division in the underlying politics.[26] Together, regulatory and distributive policy fundamentally transformed federalism.

Through both the rise of regulation and the expansion of federal aid, the federal government became the dominant player in the intergovernmental system, whose transformation into the Third Generation of Federalism was based in law and greased by grants. This transformation occurred, of course, completely within the boundaries established by the Tenth Amendment, since no state or local government was ever *compelled* to accept the federal cash. But the result was a rebalancing of federal and state power in ways that the authors of the Tenth Amendment never could have imagined.

In a rousing defense of the new Constitution, Pennsylvania's James Wilson in 1787 had noted that there were those who worried that the document would "reduce the State governments to mere corporations, and eventually to annihilate them." Nothing, he said, could be further from the truth.[27] The combination of the New Deal and the Great Society certainly did not annihilate the states or turn them into "mere corporations," or wholly owned subsidiaries. But neither did these federal programs preserve the role of the states in the way that the founders had imagined. Federal programs reached ever more deeply into many areas that had once been the primary province of state and local governments, like education and transportation. They also created whole new intergovernmental policy areas, such as environmental and homeland security policy. Grant programs emerged for all of these functions.

These grant programs, moreover, helped grow government's size and reach. In his 1996 State of the Union Address, President Bill Clinton proclaimed that "the era of big government is over." The reality, however, was that the era of claims that the "era of big government is over" was over. Federal grants continued to grow and expand, even during Ronald Reagan's efforts to rein in the size and growth of government. The share of federal spending for grants steadily rose from just 1 percent of the federal budget in 1945 to 16 percent in 2000, where it reached a plateau for the next twenty years.[28] Meanwhile, federal grants came to account for almost one-quarter of state and local government spending—and almost one-third of state budgets, with some becoming even more dependent than that. By 2017, federal grants made up more than 40 percent of state budgets in Mississippi, Montana, and New Mexico.[29]

The period from *Brown* through the next several decades thus marked an enormous watershed in American federalism. In a remarkably short time, the federal government moved from being a relatively small player in domestic affairs to establishing a major role on the stage, both in setting policy and in paying the bills. It did not do so by brushing the states away but rather by enlisting the states—and their local governments—as agents of the national design. Other governments around the world, of course, were increasing the sweep of their own ambitions at the same time, but most of those governments were growing by increasing government spending while enhancing the size of the national government. The welfare state in most countries grew by increasing the size of the state. In the United States, however, the postwar government expanded primarily by increasing federal spending while fueling the actions of state and local governments.

It was scarcely a surprise that, as new problems emerged, American federalism would provide the framework for dealing with them. In the United States, however, the changes in federalism led to a distinctive growth in inequality, because more states had more power over the decisions shaping these policies—and that power, in turn, led to larger variations among the states. Inequality stimulated pernicious forces that fed the nation's growing political polarization. In *Federalist 10*, Madison had worried about the "mischiefs of faction." In the last decades of the twentieth century, factions proved especially mischievous indeed.

5

America's Struggle with Inequality

Toward the end of the twentieth century, the nation's great battles over inequality had certainly not been resolved. But, with the Great Society, a national consensus began to emerge, on several points: that inequality was unacceptable, that government had an important role in redressing it, that the federal government ought to take the lead, that state and local governments would be its instruments, and that progress was on the way. The rising role of the federal government, in particular, not only signaled a dramatic shift in the balance of power in federalism, but it also aimed squarely at seeking to unite a divided United States.

The promise of lowering inequality, however, has largely been unmet. In fact, since the launch of the Great Society, not only has inequality grown, but the growth of inequality has also been fed in significant part by the very features of American federalism that the Great Society sought to resolve. The "golden age" of federalism—the apparent consensus supporting federal policy to address inequalities—proved both short-lived and illusory. In fact, as the federal government's role increased, along with its bold rhetoric about a War on Poverty, differences among the states increased.

That would not have surprised some shrewd observers of America's first century. In his nineteenth-century exploration of American democracy, Tocqueville anticipated the problems that would blossom generations later:

In the case of men who have long enjoyed freedom before achieving equality, the feelings engendered by freedom conflict to some degree with the inclinations prompted by equality and, although central government increases its privileges, individuals never quite lose their feeling of independence.

In much of Europe, Tocqueville pointed out, "equality was introduced" and had already become a habit "long before freedom had entered their minds." In the United States, however, "it is freedom which is old and equality is comparatively young." The ideals flowed naturally from the English who first settled the new country: they had been deeply committed to liberties ranging from jury trials to freedom of the press. It was scarcely surprising, therefore, that they "imported these free institutions" to the new country and that "in their turn protected them from any encroachments of the state."[1] But neither was it surprising that the later embrace of the ideal so often proved more rhetorical than real. It became yet one more way in which federalism left its stamp on both policy and politics.

In the United States, the campaign for freedom came far easier than the pursuit of equality. Madison's strategy for attaining liberty allowed the nation's original sin, slavery, to fester through the uneasy balance of power that was hardwired into American federalism. Despite the promise of Great Society America, inequality continued to fester, an inescapable truth that defined the Fourth Generation of Federalism, even as the foundations for greater equality seemed to have emerged from *Brown*.

America on the Global Stage

Modern America is the most unequal of any rich nation. Among the world's most advanced economies, inequality in the United States is just below Mexico, Chile, and Turkey. The United States ranks just above Lithuania, Great Britain, and New Zealand. In fact, inequality in the United States is one and a half times higher than in the Slovak Republic, Slovenia, the Czech Republic, Iceland, Finland, Norway, Denmark, and Belgium.[2] The issue is so fundamentally—and strategically—important that even the Central Intelligence Agency has its own ranking of income inequality among 150 countries. On the CIA's global list, the United States comes in at number forty, just above Peru and Jamaica and just below Cameroon and Guyana.[3] Moreover, income inequality in the United States has been increasing over time. The Berkeley economist Emmanuel Saez found that, from 1993 to 2014, the income of the bottom 99 percent of the population grew 10.8 percent, after accounting for inflation. The income of the top 1 percent, by comparison, grew by 80 percent.[4] Over a longer period, from 1980 to 2014, the share of the income earned by the top 1 percent *increased* 125 percent. The bottom 50 percent saw their share of the total *drop* by 35 percent.

Analysts have sliced this problem in a host of ways, but the data all lead to the same conclusion. Income inequality in the United States ranks among the highest in the developed world—and it is growing. Although so many people, both in the United States and around the world, see America as the land of opportunity, it has also become the land of inequality on virtually every front, and the divide is growing. The great diversity of the country, which we have for so long held up as the driver of innovation and initiative, has turned into a driver of differences.

Income inequality is even more startling *within* the United States. There is inequality within cities. Take San Francisco, a city often seen as part of America's great technological revolution; income inequality there is on a par with the nation of Rwanda. And it is only ninth on the list of America's most unequal cities, with Boston coming in first and New Orleans second in a Brookings Institution study.[5]

There is also inequality within states. In New York, the top 1 percent of income earners make 45.4 times the average of the bottom 99 percent. In Connecticut, it is 42.6 times, followed by 40.6 times in Wyoming. At the other end of the inequality spectrum, the top 1 percent in Alaska make 13.2 times more than the bottom 99 percent, followed by 13.5 times in Hawaii and 13.9 times in Iowa. These are large differences, to be sure, but far less than in the states at the other end of the federalism spectrum. Nevertheless, even in the most equal American states, the richest 1 percent still earn more than 13 times more than everyone else.[6]

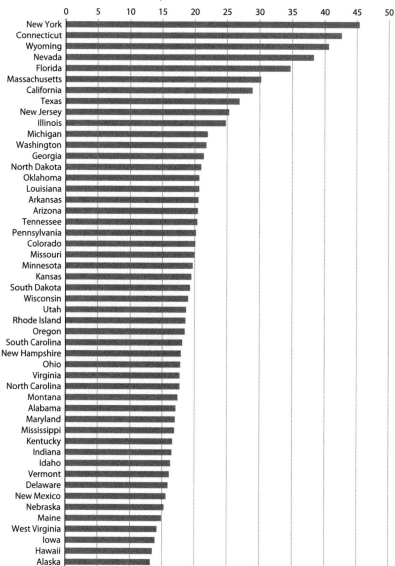

FIGURE 5.1. Income inequality is great among the states. *Source*: Estelle Sommeiller, Mark Price, and Ellis Wazeter, "Income Inequality in the US by State, Metropolitan Area, and County," Economic Policy Institute, June 16, 2016, https://www.epi.org/publication/income-inequality-in-the-us/.

Not only is there vast income inequality within states, but there is also enormous income inequality *between* them. Inequality is 3.4 times higher in New York than in Alaska. The Northeast is the most unequal region, at 31.9 percent, compared with 20.1 percent in the Midwest (see figure 5.1). As we have seen, income inequality within the United States is higher than in most advanced economies. But it may be even more disturbing that income inequality among the states is greater. It is very difficult therefore to attack inequality in America without dealing with the forces that drive inequality at the state level.

It is no surprise, therefore, that the poverty rate in the United States also varies enormously among the states. The lowest rate is in New Hampshire, where 6.9 percent of the population is below the poverty level. That is one-third the rate in Mississippi, where more than 20 percent of the population is below the poverty level (see figure 5.2).

Why does this matter? Over the years, America has become not only a melting pot of different peoples but also an amalgam of different ideas about opportunity and equality. As Barack Obama noted in a high-profile 2013 speech, "the premise that we're all created equal is the opening line in the American story. And while we don't promise equal outcomes, we have strived to deliver equal opportunity—the idea that success doesn't depend on being born into wealth or privilege, it depends on effort and merit." But since World War II, he contended, new technologies have made it easier to ship jobs out of the country, the wealthy have benefited from disproportionate tax cuts, and the debt burden for most Americans has increased. As a result, he concluded, "the basic bargain at the heart of our economy has frayed," a transformation that "challenges the very essence of who we are as a people." This, Obama concluded, is both a moral and a political issue. Rising inequality, he said, has produced greater distrust of institutions, of one another, and of democracy.[7] Obama's argument has framed the debate about inequality from the left.

But inequality has also been an issue from the right, even for Adam Smith, who saw great danger in inequality. He argued that the "disposition to admire, and almost to worship, the rich and the powerful, and to despise, or, at least, to neglect persons of poor and mean condition" leads to "the great and most universal cause of the corruption of our moral

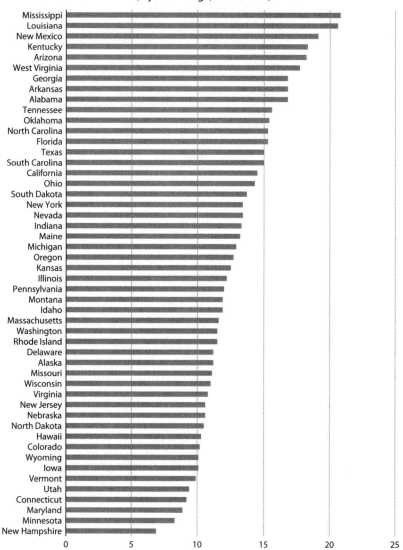

FIGURE 5.2. Poverty varies enormously between the states. *Source*: US Census Bureau, *Current Population Survey, 2014 to 2017 Annual Social and Economic Supplements*, September 2017, https://www.census.gov/data/tables/2017/demo/income-poverty/p60-259.html.

sentiments."[8] Inequality sows the seeds of moral misconduct among the rich and harms the welfare of the poor. It also tends to make people unhappier. The political scientist Dennis Rasmussen points out, "Happiness consists largely of tranquility, and there is little tranquility to be found in a life of toiling and striving to keep up with the Joneses."[9] Inequality might be the inevitable product of freedom as it comes to life in free-market competition, but it can also create unhappiness. And since happiness depends on health and access to health care depends on income, income inequality compounds the problem.

So from both the left and the right come strong reasons for worrying about inequality among the American states. Depending on one's perspective, it can create unfairness, undermine democracy, generate distrust, feed immorality, and generate gloom. There are lively, unresolved debates about just how large the consequences of inequality are and how much inequality society can tolerate without straining its fabric. But it is impossible to ignore the basic reality: inequality in the United States is higher than in almost any other major nation, it is growing, and the forces behind it have created a large, increasing, and negative effect on the American polity.

The roots of this inequality grow in the remarkable political diversity of the country. The very foundations of its remarkable political strength are also the wellsprings of its inequality. Americans have cherished the ability of their states to build very different policy strategies to match the very different policy problems that they face. But in spite of the rich and remarkable vitality in the country's diversity, there's no escaping the fact that the diversity of the states has also planted the seeds of income inequality, which have grown into a problem that is massive and pernicious.

A New Generation of Inequality

In 2017, a team of *Washington Post* photographers set out to discover the ideas that unite Americans. In many ways, their trip was a modern reinvention of Tocqueville's solo journey of American discovery in 1831. They identified six big concepts with remarkable resonance across the country: freedom, community and empathy, faith in the country, diversity, opportunity and drive, and a responsibility to engage. They also identified one idea dragging down the American spirit: a fear for the future rooted in the financial and personal insecurity that flowed from the 2008 economic crisis and the rise of terrorism. Collectively, these big ideas provide a remarkable bridge across a very diverse country, much as Tocqueville found in the nineteenth century.

A remarkably wide range of policy outcomes, however, have crept into the American system. In any system as vast as America's fifty states, outcomes are bound to vary greatly. The very purpose of American federalism was to allow local diversity to thrive, so evidence of different policy outcomes is evidence of federalism's success—to a point. But the government that Americans get, and what that government produces, varies significantly depending on where they live. Some of this variation, as we shall see, comes from the decisions of state policymakers. Others come from variations in the wealth of states; it is hard for states with less wealth to tax themselves enough to finance the investments that others are making. But the most important finding is this: there is wide variation among the states in how much they spend on services for their citizens—in part because some states *choose* to spend more money on some goods and services, and in part because some states simply cannot afford to do so because poverty within their borders is so much higher.

This is an important issue that goes far deeper than the obvious point that the fifty states across a vast country will make different policy decisions. Madison, after all, had anticipated differences among the states, but he expected that those differences would arise as a result of political factions. Riker was not surprised by the rise of differences, but he believed that they came from closet efforts to promote slavery. As the system matured and the shadow of slavery faded, he believed that the real impact of federalism would disappear as well. Derthick was not as concerned about local decisions, which she saw as the manifestations of a lively polity that provided a bulwark against the federal government's excessive power. But in twenty-first-century federalism, the states have increasingly formed clusters in which some states consistently provide different levels of services than others. The result has been a new generation of inequality. America's great debates about inequality once revolved around slavery, but the more modern manifestation presents a far broader front for the growth of inequality. Moreover, as inequality has spread, it no longer marks a difference between Northern and Southern states; the front is far larger and much more subtle. Inequality continues to embrace the nation's problems with race, but it has spread into far more issues as well.

Federalism, American-style, once provided a tactical accommodation to slavery that kept the states united in the nation's early days. It then became a strategy to accommodate the "separate but equal" doctrine, for regions not ready to embrace the full equality of their citizens. These deep racial forces have not faded away, but have been joined by the federalist accommodation of a new kind of inequality: a fabric of differences between the states that varies not only by race but also across the whole spectrum of citizenry. Black Americans—but also citizens of other racial origins and incomes—receive different levels of service across seven key indicators: poverty, health, infrastructure, environment, education, crime and corrections, and services for children.[10]

The states tend to cluster. States with relatively high rankings in poverty and health, for example, also tend to rank relatively high in programs for education and children. States that rank toward the bottom in several of these areas tend to rank low across the board. A relatively small handful of states—the "most-leading states"—have taken the most aggressive policy actions in launching new programs and investing in existing ones, and they rank highest across these indicators of performance. At the same time, a consistent collection of states—the "least-leading states"—cluster toward the bottom of the rankings (table 5.1).

No state ranks high across the board. Consider the top-ranked state, New Jersey, which has a high rank for environmental policy, services for children, crime and corrections, and education, but it tends to rank in the middle (number twenty-eight) for infrastructure because of its monumental problem of keeping its systems up to date. Minnesota, ranked second overall, does well in poverty, health, children, and education, but

TABLE 5.1. Policy Outcomes Vary Widely among the States

Fifteen most-leading states	Average rank	Fifteen least-leading states	Average rank
New Jersey	9.29	Texas	32.71
Minnesota	9.71	Georgia	33.43
Connecticut	10.14	Nevada	33.43
New Hampshire	10.71	Kentucky	33.57
Vermont	11.57	Tennessee	33.57
Massachusetts	11.86	Arizona	35.00
Maryland	13.57	South Carolina	37.00
Iowa	14.00	Alaska	38.00
Washington	14.00	West Virginia	40.43
New York	14.71	Oklahoma	40.71
Colorado	15.14	Alabama	41.14
Virginia	15.29	Mississippi	44.57
Utah	15.86	Arkansas	45.29
Rhode Island	16.86	New Mexico	46.29
North Dakota	17.14	Louisiana	46.43

Source: See note 10.

Note: Outcomes are measured across seven key indicators: poverty, health, infrastructure, environment, education, crime and corrections, and services for children.

has a middling record on environmental outcomes. Nevertheless, states with high rankings generally tend to rank high in all seven areas.

The clusters for states at the bottom of the rankings are much tighter. The lowest-ranked state, Louisiana, is low in every category, with no ranking higher than forty-first (for education). In fact, of the four lowest-ranked states (Mississippi, Alabama, New Mexico, and Louisiana), there are only two rankings not in the bottom ten: New Mexico ranks number thirty-six in health, and Mississippi number twenty-one in crime and corrections.

We certainly find in the twenty-first-century United States the kind of rich differences among the states that Madison foresaw, Riker worried about, and Derthick applauded. But the overall portrait is this: the quality of services that citizens receive varies widely; the variation depends on where they live; and some states tend to rank high in quality of services, while others tend to rank low. Federalism matters, and as a citizen, what you get depends on where you live.

How Does Federalism Matter?

How does it happen that quality of services for citizens varies so widely within the divided states of America? Some of these differences stem simply from the greater wealth of some states compared with others. Some states choose to spend their wealth differently. Poorer states struggle to provide the same level of services as richer states, while other states simply choose not to tax themselves as heavily to provide benefits to their citizens. The many different forms of inequality have become even more tightly bound to federalism, and that in turn has helped make the United States the most unequal wealthy nation.

Looking to other nations with federal systems, it is clear that there is something different about the United States. Four other highly developed nations have federal systems of government that share power between national and state governments—Australia, Canada, Germany, and Switzerland—and on a set of measures of income inequality, health outcomes, and educational performance, the United States ranks behind these other federal nations on every single indicator (see table 5.2). Among these five nations, the United States has much greater income inequality, a much higher number of infant deaths, and a substantially lower life expectancy, for both males and females. American literacy rates rank at the bottom among federally governed countries. The institution of federalism, in general, does not lead to such great inequality. It is the particular American version that is the source of the problem.

Now, of course, full equality in income, health, education, and many other areas of citizens' lives is impossible. No nation has ever achieved it. Nor might it be desirable. Few Americans would accept the big, powerful government that would be required to achieve full equality. In the middle of the nineteenth century, Tocqueville celebrated the American federal system, "which allows the Union to profit from the strength of a large republic and the security of a small one." Americans have celebrated this core principle with a devotion that a foreign visitor identified long, long ago. Indeed, one of the country's greatest strengths has always been its diversity and its ability to accommodate such widely ranging

TABLE 5.2. Income Inequality, Health Outcomes, and Educational Performance in Five Federal Systems

| | Income inequality | | Infant deaths per 1,000 live births | | Life expectancy at birth: Males (years) | | Life expectancy at birth: Females (years) | | Literacy | |
	Ratio of top 80% to bottom 20%	Rank	Number	Rank	Number	Rank	Number	Rank	Difference between adults with highly and poorly educated parents	Rank
Australia	5.7	21	3.6	16	80.3	8	84.4	9	29.95	6
Canada	5.2	19	4.8	12	—	—	—	—	36.26	14
Germany	4.4	13	3.3	12	78.8	20	83.6	19	54.03	31
Switzerland	4.6	17	3.9	19	81.1	2	85.4	6	—	—
United States	8.7	33	6.0	24	76.5	25	81.3	29	57.20	32

Sources: For income inequality, see OECD, "Income Inequality," https://data.oecd.org/inequality/income-inequality.htm, for data on thirty-five OECD countries in 2014, for the S80/S20 quintile share. For health inequality, US Department of Health and Human Services, Centers for Disease Control and Prevention, *Health, United States, 2016: With Chartbook on Long-Term Trends in Health*, https://www.cdc.gov/nchs/data/hus/hus16.pdf#015; see table 13 for data on infant deaths, which are for 2013, except for Canada, whose data come from 2012; see table 14 for data on life expectancy, which are for 2014, with no data for Canada. For literacy, Centre for Educational Research and Innovation, "Figure 1.1: Difference in Literacy Proficiency between Adults with Highly and Poorly Educated Parents," in *Educational Opportunity for All: Overcoming Inequality throughout the Life Course* (OECD Publishing, 2017), 18, https://doi.org/10.1787/9789264287457-en.

political views and policy results under a single flag, without shredding it. That has always been the genius of American federalism.

But it is increasingly clear that this genius extracts a great price.[11] Inequality in the United States—in family income and in what government produces for families—is large and growing, and much of it flows from the vast inequalities among the states. The core of these inequalities lies in health insurance.

In many ways, reducing inequality was the core of Lyndon B. Johnson's Great Society. The enduring core of the Great Society was Medicaid, the government's health care program for the poor. Much of the responsibility for administering that program, however, rests with the states. The ways in which they have carried out that responsibility have actually increased inequality. And this, in turn, has reinforced the Fourth Generation of Federalism—an era marked by increasing variation among the states, driven by the very different values they bring to the fundamental issue of health care, which is the important story we turn to in the next chapter.

6

Health, Unequal

When President Lyndon B. Johnson traveled to Independence, Missouri, in July 1965 to sign the bill creating the Medicare and Medicaid bills, he staged the ceremony at Harry S. Truman's presidential library and presented Truman with the very first Medicare card. The event was a triumph of Truman's vision. Just months into his administration in 1945, Truman had proposed a sweeping federal health insurance program. The program would be voluntary—citizens could choose to sign up for coverage in exchange for monthly premiums, and the federal government would cover the cost of care they received from doctors who signed up for the program. But the American Medical Association had launched a fierce counterattack, calling Truman's plan "socialized medicine" and saying that it was the brainchild of White House aides who were "followers of the Moscow party line."[1] The AMA's opposition had helped sink the proposal.

Johnson had revived the plan on the night of John F. Kennedy's assassination in Dallas. As his biographer Robert Caro tells it, Johnson could not sleep. He called three of his aides into his bedroom and started talking about the plans he had in mind, focusing even in his first hours in office on health reform as the foundation of his domestic agenda.[2] He wanted to push forward a revised version of Truman's plan, with a proposal that eventually became the bundle of Medicare (for the elderly) and Medicaid (for the poor). But knowing from the outset that they had to tackle the "socialized medicine" charge that had sunk

Truman's initiative, Johnson and his aides devised an especially novel strategy to do so. Medicare would be an insurance program, funded by premiums paid by taxpayers, much like Social Security. Medicaid would be an intergovernmental grant program in which the states would have primary administrative responsibility and would make their own choices about which coverage to add beyond a basic menu of benefits, with private insurance companies doing almost all of the administrative work.

Their strategy worked. Congress passed the program in 1965, and over time Medicaid evolved into the single most important intergovernmental program of the post–World War II era. By its fiftieth birthday, it had grown to almost 10 percent of all federal spending and accounted for 29 percent of all state spending.[3] For most states, Medicaid ranks among their fastest-growing expenses, increasing almost 50 percent from 1995 to 2017.[4] Medicaid does not provide health care directly. Rather, it is a health insurance program that provides grants to state governments to pay the costs of health care for lower-income individuals, with the actual health care provided by private and nonprofit health professionals, hospitals, and clinics. And it is not one program but fifty-one. Each state (plus the District of Columbia) covers a different menu of services.

Administration of the program is vastly complex, especially when compared with the social welfare programs in many other advanced democracies. When British children go to school, they are taught by teachers who are government employees. The same is true for American children (except those who attend private or parochial schools). When British people visit a medical clinic, except for a small percentage who choose to buy private health insurance, their health care workers are independent contractors who are paid by the government and are thus essentially government employees. This is not the case in the United States. With the exception of health care professionals working for the Department of Veterans Affairs and the Department of Defense, American health care providers are nongovernmental employees. They receive a large—and growing—share of their income, however, from the federal government, which covers the health care costs of one of every five Americans and spends one in every six dollars in the health care system.

That makes it exceptionally difficult to separate government-paid from private-paid health care in this country. In fact, the same health care provider might deliver precisely the same service to one individual whose care is covered by private insurance and another whose care is paid for by Medicaid. Medicaid pays half of the costs of nursing home care in the United States, and the program is the largest funder of long-term care in the country. Individuals on Medicaid visit doctors more often that those with privately funded health insurance, and Medicaid patients are just as happy with the care they get as those receiving care paid for by private insurance.[5] But sorting out the question of who pays which costs for which patients—and determining who is eligible for what kinds of care— is a vastly complex process that eats up a significant fraction of American health care costs.

From its launch, Medicaid has been caught in a policy dilemma. Johnson and his supporters wanted to expand health insurance coverage to poor Americans, their opponents saw that expansion as "socialized medicine," and the program emerged from an uneasy compromise between these radically different views. Those covered by Medicaid receive care at the same hospitals and clinics as other Americans, from the same health care providers, who often do not even know whether they are on Medicaid. This system prevented the growth of a large corps of government health care providers, as in Canada and the United Kingdom. The Centers for Medicare and Medicaid Services (CMS), the government bureaucracy managing the program, has always been kept deliberately tiny in a further effort to prevent the growth of a government health provider system. CMS manages about one-quarter of all federal spending (Medicaid, Medicare, and the Children's Health Insurance Program), but it has only about six thousand employees, or 0.2 percent of all federal workers. In contrast, the Harvard Medical School has twice as many individuals on its faculty, and the staff of the Mayo Clinic is about ten times the size of CMS. Private contractors do most of the work processing claims and making payments throughout the Medicaid system.

The program's governance thus depends on broad policy made in Washington, the more detailed spending decisions made in state capitals, state leverage over the financial intermediaries who administer the system, the health insurance companies that manage the paperwork and the payments, and health providers' relationships with everyone. The federal government sets the program's basic standards, and every state decides what other coverage to add on. Medicaid is an unwieldy contraption that no one would have consciously designed from scratch, but it is also the natural result of the effort to expand coverage without greatly expanding government—except its budget. As in so many other cases throughout American history, broad principles took on their real meaning through administrative solutions to the lack of health coverage—and pragmatism, managed through very different constellations of state politics, has reigned.

Medicaid thus is a federal program brought to life in the decisions of the states, a state-managed program with private contractors on the front administrative lines, a program that is different in every state and marked by immense administrative complexity—and a program that, as a result, has bred enormous variation and inequality. Medicaid is the very symbol of the Fourth Generation of Federalism, a generation that not only is characterized by federal policies in which the states have substantial decision-making authority but that feeds growing differences among the states. This version of federalism is the engine that has transformed the debate over inequality from one based primarily on race and slavery to one based on location and residence. The government that citizens get depends increasingly on where they live.

Medicaid's Peculiar Bargain

That inequality flows from the politics of the federal-state balance that emerged in the 1980s. The federal government defines who is eligible for health care, although states can expand coverage to other individuals, for other services, if they choose. The states thus have found themselves squeezed between individuals entitled to health care because of the federal standards, rising demands for broader health care coverage, growing health care costs they cannot control, and other state programs they cannot fund as a result. These pressures frame an enormous balance-of-power battle between the federal government and the states. Over time, as the states have exercised more and more control over the program, the balance of power has shifted increasingly to the states—and more disparities among them have emerged.

At first, the program's big battles focused on the debate between those who favored expanding health coverage and those who raised the specter of socialized medicine. In the first decade, however, the program's rapidly rising costs began to frighten both state officials and federal budget planners. The question came to a head in the Reagan administration. The governors heavily lobbied the president to "restore balance to the Federal system," as Georgia Governor George Busbee put it, by stopping the federal program's drain on state budgets. The Reagan White House, however, looked at a federal budget already squeezed by a deep recession, high inflation, oil shocks, sluggish growth, and tight monetary policy and proposed $1 billion in spending cuts and a cap on future federal contributions limited to the inflation rate, with the states responsible for funding the difference. The governors thought that this was a trap that would make them responsible for the really tough choices: reducing eligibility for the program, cutting benefits, managing the program more efficiently, digging deeper into their own already strained budgets—or all of the above. That, Utah Governor Scott Matheson told administration officials, was "unacceptable."[6]

Reagan came back with a two-pronged goal: to shrink the federal government's spending, and to use the debate to sort out the roles of the federal and state governments. In his 1982 State of the Union Address, he proposed an end to the super-complex structure that had grown up around the program by drawing new lines of responsibility. The federal government, he offered, would take over the full financial cost of Medicaid. The states, in exchange, would take over the full cost of food stamps, which provided nutrition assistance to the poor, and the main welfare program, Aid for Families with Dependent Children (AFDC). Then, in the program's second phase, the states would be responsible for more than forty additional federal programs, in exchange for revenues from a trust fund. The result, Reagan said, would be "a financially equal swap."[7] After generations of increasingly blurred boundaries, Reagan's proposal was a surprisingly elegant strategy to draw crisper lines between government functions and sort out just which level of government would be responsible for what.

But the governors smelled a rat. They were convinced that Reagan was presenting a plan that would leave them with big responsibilities for food stamps and welfare and not enough cash. They did not believe that the savings from Medicaid would amount to anywhere near an equal trade, and they did not trust the federal government to keep the deal. The governors' opposition ensured that Reagan's plan died a quick death—and it proved to be one of the biggest budgetary mistakes that the nation's governors ever made. From 1980 to 2016, federal spending for Medicaid grew four times faster than for all the other welfare programs. For their part, state governments in 2016 spent almost four times as much of their own money on Medicaid as on all other categories of welfare.[8] Had they taken the deal, the federal government would have been stuck with the costs of the fastest-growing program, Medicaid, and the governors would have had far more money to spend on other priorities, from education to highways. Besides the epic budgetary consequences, Reagan's proposal was also perhaps the last chance to rescue a shred of the Tenth Amendment's promise of clear lines of responsibility for the federal and state governments. Administering Medicaid, along with every other important intergovernmental initiative afterward, became an inescapable, ongoing battle of balancing federal and state roles in programs where neither had clear responsibility.

No single decision in America's history has so fundamentally changed state government finances. With rising health care costs and a growing elderly population, Medicaid has created a permanent squeeze on state budgets. It has forced state officials into increasingly difficult decisions about who ought to get how much care, while draining state revenues that could have been used for other programs, from higher education to transportation.

Not surprisingly, the rising demand of Medicaid spending on the states has created big differences in how states respond to that challenge. Consider Medicaid spending per recipient in the top fifteen most-leading states, compared with the fifteen least-leading states. (Here and throughout the book, I refer to the states with the highest outcomes on a host

TABLE 6.1. State Medicaid Spending per Recipient, 2015

	Average	Percentage of US average
Fifteen most-leading states	$7,063	123.1
Fifteen least-leading states	$5,433	94.7
US average	$5,736	

Source: Calculations by the author, based on Henry J. Kaiser Family Foundation, "Medicaid Spending per Enrollee: FY 2014," https://www.kff.org/medicaid/state-indicator/medicaid-spending-per-enrollee /?currentTimeframe=0&sortModel=%7B%22colId%22:%22Location%22,%22sort%22:%22asc%22%7D.

of policy measures as the "most-leading" states, and those at the other end of the spectrum as the "least-leading" states.) Those in the most-leading category spent far more than the national average for all states (see table 6.1), and 30 percent more per recipient, than the least-leading states. The inescapable conclusion is that the benefits that citizens receive, even in programs that are national entitlements like Medicaid, depend on where they live. The states make very different decisions in how they manage entitlements, and those decisions have big implications for their citizens.

The States and Obamacare

The big differences between the states in Medicaid spilled over to the decisions that states made in administering the Affordable Care Act (ACA), popularly known as "Obamacare." For Democrats, the 2010 program was the ultimate triumph of the campaign to expand the health insurance coverage that Truman started, Johnson advanced, and Bill Clinton tried but failed to persuade Congress to enact. Barack Obama used his electoral victory to convince Congress to pass a complex bill designed to provide universal health insurance, since yet again, truly universal health care was too far a reach.

Some Americans, of course, had health insurance through their employers. Older Americans received health insurance through Medicare, and poor Americans had coverage through Medicaid. The bill required anyone not covered through one of these programs to purchase health insurance through an online marketplace called an "exchange."

Individuals under a certain income floor would receive a federal subsidy to help cover their insurance. Obamacare also created incentives for the states to expand Medicaid coverage. The program's designers hoped that the tax penalty for not purchasing insurance would convince people to sign up for a policy. One way or another, the plan was for ensuring that all Americans had health care insurance. Obamacare also guaranteed that no one with a preexisting condition would be denied coverage, and it allowed Americans under the age of twenty-six to stay on their parents' plan. It was a program of extraordinary complexity, but Obama believed that it accomplished its two main goals: bringing all Americans into a health insurance program and doing so without creating a national health care system that, administration officials calculated, would guarantee that it would never pass.

Republicans fiercely attacked the program, labeling it a "government takeover of health care." For the Republicans, attacking the Affordable Care Act was not just a matter of principle. Having been stung by the 1935 passage of Social Security, which helped Democrats at the polls for almost three generations, the Republicans were also engaged in basic politics—they wanted to prevent the Democrats from getting another big political win. Independent fact-checking groups concluded that the ACA was neither "government-run" nor a "government takeover."[9] Private and nonprofit health care providers would continue to deliver care. Private insurers would offer their policies in what was intended to be an easy-to-use online marketplace. Government-funded "navigators" would help people find the best plan, and the subsidies would ensure that no one was priced out of insurance because they could not afford it. Obamacare surely lacked the clarity of the British National Health Service, or the straightforward government role in Canada's single-payer system. Many Democrats would have preferred a single-payer plan, with the government providing all health care as well as all health insurance, but they knew that could not pass. So, as was often the case, they reached for compromise through complexity, piling layers of coverage on top of each other and putting the states at the center.

One of the biggest challenges was creating the exchanges. The states were allowed but not required to create these exchanges, and citizens in any state that chose not to do so could use the federal government's exchange instead. Building an exchange was no easy chore. Some states, like Massachusetts, had experimented with them already, but there was precious little experience among the states in creating or sustaining them. For their part, marketing health plans through such exchanges was a whole new proposition for insurance companies. Many companies saw a vast new market they could tap into and priced their policies competitively to win business. Others were more nervous and stood back, but they realized that they risked losing business. The administration's own administrative fumbles in the program's first months undermined everyone's confidence, especially when the website the Obama administration created for the federal exchange crashed on its very first day, leaving many Americans unable to sign up for coverage.

The states were given several options. They could decide simply to allow their citizens to use the federal exchange, or they could build their own. State exchanges offered the chance for more experimentation and more state autonomy, but exchanges also posed substantial administrative challenges. The states ended up going down very different roads. Twelve of the fifteen most-leading states decided to create their own exchanges. In contrast, just five of the fifteen least-leading states decided to do so. The difference did not necessarily make one group of states better than the other. Many of the states that went their own way encountered very serious problems in creating and managing their new system. The states' decisions also revealed deep differences in how strongly they embraced policy innovation: some were eager to move policy initiatives forward, and others, quite simply, were not.

The same was true about state decisions about how to integrate Medicaid with Obamacare. The 2010 legislation required that any state participating in the Medicaid program expand its program to include individuals with higher incomes than in the past. The federal government would pay all the cost for the first three years, and then reduce its payment to 90 percent of the cost down the road. A collection of conservative states challenged this provision in the courts, however, and the US Supreme Court agreed with them. This Medicaid "mandate," the Court held, amounted to a coercive use of federal power, since the states had little real choice about whether to participate in the Medicaid program—the stakes for their citizens were simply too high. Decades of federal grant policy had grown on the principle that no state *had* to participate in a grant program—but the practical fact was that no state would choose to give up money that otherwise would flow to other states. The Court recognized the practical realities of the Medicaid program, and it held that Obamacare did not give the states a real choice about whether to participate in the program, that not giving them a real choice created federal coercion, and that, under the Constitution, such coercion was unconstitutional.[10]

Over the centuries, the Tenth Amendment had certainly receded in importance, but the states had never forgotten it. Its basic provisions remained clear: if the Constitution did not give the federal government explicit power over a particular policy issue, it could not mandate state action. When it came to expanding federal authority over the states, it was one thing to create inducements, through grant programs, that no state would want to refuse. It was another to coerce them into doing something that was not otherwise authorized in the Constitution. The Fourteenth Amendment had established the principle of equal protection, so there were grounds in 1954 to argue that "separate but equal" treatment was unconstitutional. But it was quite another to push the states toward increasing the eligibility of citizens for health insurance—and then, in a few years, forcing the states to pay for it. That, the Court ruled in a 5–4 decision, was unconstitutional.

The Court's decision gutted a key provision of Obamacare that was designed to ensure that the federal and state governments would take on the cost of paying for health insurance for Americans who earned income above the Medicaid limits but did not have enough money to pay for health insurance on their own. Removing the mandate thus left expansion of Medicaid as a state option, not a federal requirement. Many states chose sides, as the case was coming to the Court, by filing briefs either in favor or opposed to Medicaid expansion. Five of the fifteen most-leading states supported expansion, while just one of the fifteen least-leading states did.

When the Court struck down the provision, that left Medicaid expansion as a choice that each state had to make on its own. Which states chose to expand Medicaid? All fifteen of the most-leading states decided to do so. In contrast, seven of the fifteen least-leading states decided not to.

One of these states, Indiana, took its own route. Under Governor Mike Pence, who later became Trump's vice president, the state expanded the Medicaid program but used an option in the program to create the Healthy Indiana Plan (HIP) 2.0. The plan required those eligible for Medicaid to contribute to savings accounts in their name, and then use the savings account to pay for part of the bill when they received medical care. Individuals who failed to make the required payment would lose their health insurance. The goal, conservatives argued, was to promote "personal responsibility." Mike Pence said that the program was "intended to be a safety net that aligns incentives with human aspirations" by making sure that the program was not simply a handout. Liberal opponents contended that the program locked out individuals who otherwise would be eligible for care, and the Center on Budget and Policy Priorities called HIP 2.0 an overly complex program that created "barriers to care." After the first year of HIP 2.0, one-third of those eligible for the program were not covered because they had not made the required payment. Others were confused about the program and found themselves bumped to a lower-level plan.[11]

Among the most-leading states, Virginia launched its own version of Medicaid expansion in 2018. It was among the later states joining the program, and its Medicaid program traditionally had been among the least generous in the country. But months of very difficult debate eventually led to a bill from the General Assembly to expand Medicaid to residents who previously did not have health insurance. The Supreme Court had left states free to join Medicaid expansion, and Virginia chose to do so, as Obamacare had been originally designed: more individuals qualified for the program because the expansion boosted the income ceiling for eligibility; the federal government paid 90 percent of the cost of the expansion; the state budget covered the rest of the charges; and there was no Indiana-style requirement for individual contributions. Virginia's Medicaid expansion brought 400,000 state residents into the program and provided them with health insurance.

Variation by State

The opposing camps debated which approach was better. Obamacare advocates applauded Virginia's late embrace of the program. Other health care specialists pointed to Indiana's program as a prototype of Medicaid's future. Who was correct? In Obamacare's first months, the question was impossible to answer, because the shakeout period for such a vast, sprawling, and complex program was long and arduous.

But the more fundamental issue was that the states tended to form clusters, pursuing very different strategies, with different levels of administrative complexity and very different results. Although it might seem an obvious conclusion, Obamacare makes a very important point: the more the design and implementation of programs rests in state hands, the more different, in both tactics and outcomes, they are likely to be.

That skirmish line, in fact, set the stage for a fierce battle early in the Donald Trump administration. As a candidate, Trump had made an assault on Obamacare one of the signature parts of his campaign, and he pledged that Republicans would repeal and replace it. Shortly before inauguration day in 2017, President Trump tweeted out a warning: "People must remember that ObamaCare just doesn't work, and it is not affordable—116% increases (Arizona)." This was partially true. A twenty-seven-year-old in Arizona buying the midrange silver plan did face a 116 percent increase. But overall, Blue Cross Blue Shield of Arizona increased its rates by far less, 51 percent. In the Phoenix area, rates offered by Ambetter, another insurance company, increased 74.5 percent.[12] In the next year, however, the silver plan for a twenty-seven-year-old increased just one dollar, and the average cost for Arizona's plan settled at close to the national average. Moreover, these were not the increases that most people actually paid, because federal subsidies covered most of the cost.

In Arizona, the big premium swings came especially from big mistakes by insurers. Some companies lowballed their prices to gain market share. They signed up lots of people only to see their customers' costs end up far higher than expected. That drove some companies out of business. Some new companies jumped in to snap up the business but suffered the same fate. This churn in the industry scared many insurers out of the game, and in some parts of the state, like Pinal County in suburban Phoenix, no insurers wanted to write policies at all. Only one of the state's counties, Pima, ended up with more than one insurer for 2017, and that meant no competition at all for prices. The state's insurance markets eventually stabilized, but only after Arizona had become the poster child for Obamacare-gone-wrong. Experts in the field reminded critics that it took many years, and several rounds of administrative amendments, to get the far simpler Social Security program right.

In other cases, there were big differences in prices just across state borders. In 2019, for example, Affordable Care Act premiums for a silver plan in Milwaukee were $563, compared with $300 in Minneapolis. Rates in Minneapolis fell 8 percent, while they stayed about the same in Milwaukee. This might seem surprising because the populations are similar, as are the hospitals and health care costs of the two cities. The difference? Minnesota expanded Medicaid coverage as part of the ACA, and Wisconsin did not. States like Minnesota that have taken part in Medicaid expansion have tended to have lower premiums, and more of the uninsured have been brought into health insurance. Wisconsin had always had a well-managed health insurance system, so premiums there were still lower than in many states, including some that had decided to expand Medicaid. But the central point is important: with similar populations and health care systems, Minnesota, which expanded Medicaid, had lower premiums than Wisconsin, which did not.[13]

In the befuddling tug-of-war over who had it right, only two things were certain. One was that how much individuals paid depended on where they lived. The other was that this system was so complex, and increasingly so decentralized, that making sense of it to help the national debate became almost impossible. Almost half of all Americans, a Kaiser Family Foundation poll found, did not know the difference between Medicare's coverage for the elderly and Medicaid's support for the poor.[14] When asked about a counterproposal to replace Obamacare, "Medicare for all," three-fourths of all Americans liked the general idea of allowing people to buy health insurance through Medicare or Medicaid. When they began hearing the detailed arguments about the proposals, however, their support for the plan plummeted.[15] Details trumped broad principles.

To stay in good health, everyone needs good health care, and only the very rich can get good health care without insurance. Health, not surprisingly, is a hot-button issue for voters. Claims made through 140-character tweets are handy for people on all sides, but when those claims collide with the staggering complexity of managing the health insurance system, the rhetoric melts in the heat of mind-numbing complexity. Enormous variations have emerged from a system that, because of the administrative complexities of managing it, has become so complex that few people can understand it.

Inequality in Health Care

Such variation has fueled inequality in the availability and quality of health care, to the point that inequality in American health care is among the highest in the world. Compared with eight comparable countries (France, Australia, Japan, Sweden, Netherlands, Austria, Germany, and the United Kingdom), the United States has the highest death rate for conditions in which medical interventions could have made a difference—almost 40 percent higher. The United States significantly trails other major industrialized nations in potential years of life lost because of problems in health care, with a rate two-thirds higher. Hospital admissions for preventable diseases are much higher in the United States—68 percent higher for congestive heart failure and 37 percent higher for diabetes—and medical and medication errors are much higher in the United States as well. Health outcomes for some issues are as good or better in the United States than in other countries, including survival rates for heart attacks, postsurgical infections, and cancer. But, in general, the United States ranks lower than other major countries on a host of important measures—and Americans tend to wait longer to see a doctor when they need care.[16]

Americans themselves recognize the difference. In a 2017 global survey, respondents were asked, "How many people are there in [your country] who do not have access to the health care they need?" The United

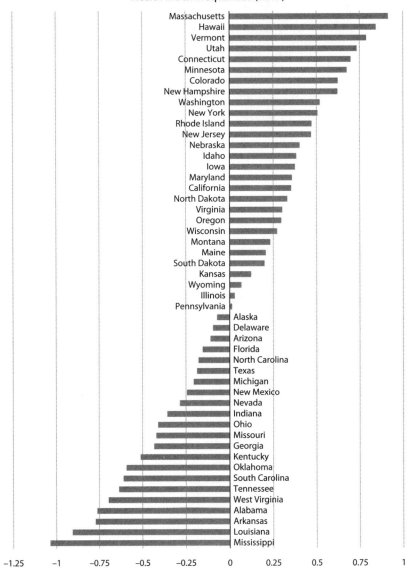

Health index inequalities (2017)

FIGURE 6.1. There are vast inequalities among the states in health. *Source*: United Health Foundation, *America's Health Rankings: 2017 Annual Report*, https://www.america shealthrankings.org/learn/reports/2017-annual-report/findings-state-rankings. A score of 0 is equivalent to the national average.

States ranked the lowest of the thirty-one nations surveyed, with 67 percent of respondents saying "many." That compares with 55 percent of Poles who answered "many," 53 percent of Filipinos, and 52 percent of Chileans. There were similar results when the survey explored citizens' perceptions of their own health. In general, citizens in most countries at the top of the income scale were far more likely to believe that they were in good health compared with those at the bottom. In the United States, the "good health" gap was the third-largest in the world, at nearly 26 percent. The United States was just behind Portugal (26.7 percent) and Chile (33.0 percent).[17]

Just as there are big differences in health care between the United States and the rest of the world, there are big healthcare differences among the American states. The United Health Foundation, a leading health policy organization, regularly produces "America's Health Rankings," and it shows substantial inequalities on a host of key indicators (themselves based on work by the World Health Organization).[18] As figure 6.1 shows, health index scores for the top five states—Massachusetts at the top, followed by Hawaii, Vermont, Utah, and Connecticut—were more than twice as high as for the bottom five states—Mississippi at the bottom, followed by Louisiana, Arkansas, Alabama, and West Virginia. These big inequalities spill over into a host of measures, from life expectancy and infant mortality to death rates from a variety of causes.

For example, life expectancy is highest in Hawaii (at 81.50 years) compared with Mississippi (where it is just 74.91 years). Infant mortality is twice as high in Mississippi as in Massachusetts, and there are eight times as many drug overdose deaths in West Virginia as in Nebraska. Death from cardiovascular disease is twice as high in Mississippi compared with Minnesota, and Utahans die from cancer at two-thirds the rate in Kentucky. The number of persons without health insurance is six times higher in Texas than in Minnesota. The differences among the states on a wide variety of issues dealing with health are, quite simply, startling and breathtaking.[19]

Health outcomes depend on access to health care, and access to health care, of course, typically begins with access to health insurance to pay for it. Differences among the states in the number of uninsured individuals, not surprisingly, leads to differences in health care outcomes. In 2016, the rates of uninsured Americans were three times higher in some states (Alaska and Texas, with rates higher than 14 percent) than others (5 percent in Vermont, Rhode Island, Pennsylvania, Oregon, Iowa, Hawaii, and the District of Columbia).[20]

At the core of all of these issues is income: for a host of reasons, Americans with less money tend to have poorer health than richer Americans. Those with higher incomes have better diets, better homes, better education, better living environments, and better access to health care.[21] These health care disparities persist, moreover, despite the fact that the United States spends 2.4 times as much on health care per capita as other major industrialized nations and almost twice as much as the industrialized nations' average on health care as a share of the economy.[22] In addition, the cost for providing health care varies widely by states as well. A 2016 study by the JPMorgan Chase & Co. Institute revealed that, in some states, families have to dig much deeper to pay for health care. In New Jersey and New York, for example, families spent 1.0 percent of their gross income on health care costs. In Louisiana and Oklahoma, in contrast, the burden was far higher, with families spending 1.7 percent.[23]

Medicaid was designed to close the health care gaps that poverty created. The states that have invested more in Medicaid have, in fact, closed the health care gap. States that spend more money per capita on Medicaid have better health outcomes. Medicaid coverage leads to better access to health care, more preventive screenings, fewer visits to the emergency room, and a lower death rate. Arizona, New York, and Maine all expanded the eligibility of their residents before the passage of Obamacare, and all produced a significant decrease in mortality rates.[24] States often make very different Medicaid choices, and these different choices produce very different outcomes. As a result, health care inequality has become hard-baked into American federalism, despite the 1960s-era program that Johnson hoped would vastly shrink the gap.

Since at least the time of the ancient Greeks, prominent thinkers have maintained that good health is essential for happiness. The Greek physician Herophilus argued, "To lose one's health renders science null, art inglorious, strength unavailing, wealth useless, and eloquence powerless."

In the United States, there has been little disagreement that good health matters, but there has been a huge debate about just how much responsibility the government has in delivering it—and how high and strong a floor the government ought to build underneath every American.

Public health was at the center of many nineteenth-century infrastructure projects. In London, John Snow made the startling discovery that a cholera outbreak was caused by microbes in infrastructure and that public investment in a better water system could stop the disease in its tracks.[25] Snow's work, coupled with the efforts of other cutting-edge public health workers, built the case that an increasingly industrialized, urbanized nation needed safe drinking water and effective sewage systems, and that this was an important local government responsibility. By 1900, forty of the nation's forty-five states (at that point) had created public health departments. That work was followed by efforts to control infectious diseases, like the great influenza epidemic of 1918, and vaccination campaigns to attack such scourges as polio, tetanus, diphtheria, and smallpox.[26] These efforts laid the foundation for the campaign, decades down the road, to expand government-funded health insurance in order to pay for the health care that many families could not afford on their own.[27]

But Americans deeply disagree about just how strong a role government should play in health care. It is hard to imagine anything that is more personal or more profoundly affects the fundamental questions of life and death, and it is impossible to imagine any area where citizens have a stronger opinion. When asked in a 2017 poll whether government has a role in ensuring that all Americans have health care coverage, 60 percent of Americans said yes, and 39 percent said no. If government does have a role, how should it work? One-third of Americans want a single federal government program, and one-fourth prefer a mixed public-private model. Partisan splits run deep. Among Democrats, support for a single-payer model was 52 percent, but among Republicans the number was just 12 percent.[28]

Americans have long been quite certain that they want good health care, uncertain that there is a strong government role in providing it, and deeply split on how government ought to play whatever role it has. Madison would recognize the biggest reason: a fear that a stronger governmental role over something so personal and fundamental might put individual liberty at risk. In 2005, the famed heart surgeon Michael DeBakey neatly framed the inherent tension in this view, which he characterized as "the need for accepting the desirability of some form of national health care, along with the willingness to pay for it, but avoiding its administration and total control by an ultimately rigid and unwieldy governmental or insurance industry bureaucracy."[29]

Rather than sort out these issues at the national level, as so many other industrialized nations did at the dawn of the post–World War II welfare state, the United States tended to set broad policies but transfer many responsibilities—both financial and administrative—to state governments. The result, not surprisingly, was a vast difference in health care—and health outcomes—among the states. Some of those differences grew from very different state finances: poorer states simply could not afford the same level of benefits as richer ones. But some of it grew as well from the very different judgments made in different states about just how much of a government role their citizens wanted in health care, and in a vast array of other functions. The result, in this Fourth Generation of Federalism, when states have played a larger role in shaping intergovernmental policy, has been a growing pattern of inequality. But compared with earlier generations, when differences were based primarily on race, this time the differences have grown out of basic differences in values across a far larger array of issues. The big issues of inequality have thus come to affect all citizens in this new generation of federalism.

7

E Pluribus Plura

The profound irony of the Fourth Generation of Federalism, which followed the golden age of Johnson's Great Society, was the emergence of federalism itself as one of the great drivers of inequality. The country produced not so much *e pluribus unum* ("from many one") as *e pluribus plura* ("from many, many").

Scholars and jurists alike have often celebrated federalism as the wellspring of liberty in the United States. In 2011, Justice Anthony Kennedy wrote succinctly, "Federalism secures the freedom of the individual."[1] That is the romantic notion of federalism. In the hard battles of American political life, however, federalism has always been a pragmatic instrument of compromise, a way of balancing the political interests of different states and the interests of the states against those of the federal government. When tough and divisive issues have arisen, America's leaders have often had two choices: try to find common ground, which has often proven elusive, or push the problem into the pot of American federalism, where it can boil and simmer, the states can capture wide differences in public views, and the interests of truly national policy can rise to the top. Federalism has also been an instrument of administrative decentralization, allowing the federal government to leverage its policy through state and local bureaucracies without having to concentrate too much power in national hands.

Finding a balance among all these cross-pressures was the central genius—both practical and political—of Madison's Constitution. But the rising inequality in American life, across a host of areas, challenges the genius of that solution and its enduring power. Major inequalities flow from the states' role in health policy, as we saw in the previous chapter. Similar challenges occur in a host of other policy areas as well.

Leaded Water

Like many of the manufacturing towns in the Midwest, Flint, Michigan, suffered badly from the 2008 economic collapse. Flint was once the home of the largest General Motors plant; for a time, "General Motors" and "Flint" were almost synonymous. Flint's manufacturing facilities produced spark plugs, filters, engines, and especially auto bodies in its iconic Fisher Body Division plant. But disruptions in the automobile industry had already destroyed many of the city's jobs. Manufacturing employment in Flint shrank from 46,000 workers in the mid-1990s to just over 12,000 in 2016. It was, one reporter said, "a hollow frame of a once affluent city."[2] Wages fell to half of the national average, a shift with racial overtones since half of the city was black and 40 percent of its residents were living below the poverty level. Other parts of the Rust Belt had taken big hits as well, but for Flint the one-two punch of industrial decline and the recession was staggering.

The loss of jobs and the resulting loss in income led to a crisis for the city's budget. The state concluded that Flint was in a financial emergency and that it had no plan to dig its way out, so Governor Rick Snyder appointed Ed Kurtz as emergency manager. Kurtz surveyed a wide array of options for cutting the city's budget and focused on the water system in particular. The city was buying its drinking water from the neighboring Detroit Water and Sewerage Department, but analysts in 2012 estimated that Flint could save $200 million over twenty-five years by drawing water instead from a different system, the Karegnondi Water Authority, and that is what Kurtz decided to do.

When the city council ratified the decision, the Detroit system announced that it would cut Flint off from its existing water system immediately, leaving Flint without a source of water until the connection with Karegnondi was ready. So the city decided to draw drinking water from the Flint River, which seemed an easy solution. The river had, after all, provided Flint's water until the 1960s.[3] When the city celebrated the switchover, Mayor Dayne Walling invited everyone to raise a glass of Flint's water. "It's regular, good, pure drinking water," he said, "and it's right in our backyard." Walling celebrated the change as a "monumental step forward in controlling the future of our community's most precious resource."[4]

In making the change, however, officials failed to take one important step: treating the water to limit corrosion of the city's ancient water pipes. As was the case in many American cities, Flint's pipes had been laid decades earlier. The old pipes were made of lead, and lead in the drinking water was dangerous, especially for children. Research had found that lead contamination, including lead additives in gasoline, lead in paint, and especially lead in drinking water, produced problems in cognitive development; in addition, once lead got into a child's blood, the damage was irreversible. The Detroit water system had treated its water with anticorrosives, but officials with the Michigan Department of Environment Quality (MDEQ), a state agency, told Flint officials that doing so was unnecessary. City officials believed that they had a bigger problem with acid in the water—a different issue—and that waiting a year to determine the right treatment was the best course. As the MDEQ spokesman Brad Wurfel put it,

> It's just a matter of getting it right. You know if I handed you a bag of chocolate chips and sack of flour and said "make chocolate chips cookies," we'd still need a recipe, right? And they need to get the results from that testing to understand how much of what to put in the water to address the water chemistry from the river which is different from the water chemistry in Lake Huron.[5]

Flint residents almost immediately began complaining that the water had an unpleasant smell and a bad color. Tests showed *E. coli* and other bacteria in the water, and the city boosted the chlorine it was adding. But worries were building that the Flint River water was corroding the city's pipes. For fear that contaminants would corrode its machinery, General Motors announced that it would stop using Flint River water. The state began buying bottled water for employees at its government offices, but the city continued to rely on the Flint River and insist that the system had no problem. But when complaints from one resident, Lee Anne Walters, led the city to test her water, the results showed lead content of 104 parts per billion (ppb). The Environmental Protection Agency's standard for safe drinking water is no more than 15 ppb, although research has shown that there is no safe level for lead in drinking water. Further tests found that Walters's child had developed lead poisoning.

Armed with the data, the EPA worried that the lack of treatment for corrosion was producing serious problems. An internal EPA memo expressed concern that neither the city nor the MDEQ were paying sufficient attention to lead levels.[6] Water experts recommended that the state test for corrosion in the water, but state officials preferred a wait-and-see strategy. As the Michigan spokesman Wurfel explained in an interview, the levels in the Walterses' home were an "outlier." He said, "Let me start here—anyone who is concerned about lead in the drinking water in Flint can relax."[7]

But complaints about unpleasant tastes and bad color in the water continued to flood in, spurring a research team from Virginia Tech to come to Flint and test the water in hundreds of homes. The team found serious levels of lead throughout the city.[8] Virginia Tech professor Marc Edwards, who led the study, said, "The levels that we have seen in Flint are some of the worst that I have seen in more than 25 years working in the field."[9] Yet the MDEQ dismissed that study too. Wurfel emailed a reporter:

> It's scientifically probable a research team that specializes in looking for lead in water could have found it in Flint when the city was on its old water supply. We won't know that, because they've only just arrived in town and quickly proven the theory they set out to prove, and while the state appreciates academic participation in this discussion, offering broad, dire public health advice based on some quick testing could be seen as fanning political flames irresponsibly. Residents of Flint concerned about the health of their community don't need more of that.[10]

The state maintained this posture even as evidence of health problems emerged. A local medical center found that almost twice as many children under the age of five had higher levels of lead in their blood after the switch, but the state's Department of Health and Human Services suggested that this was a result of seasonal changes, not the switch in the water supply.[11] When the city sent residents a lead advisory, state officials argued that critics were trying to score political points.[12] The governor's chief of staff, for example, told the governor in an email that "some in Flint are taking the very sensitive issue of children's exposure to lead and trying to turn it into a political football claiming the departments are underestimating the impacts on the population and particularly trying to shift responsibility to the state."[13]

Finally, the facts forced state officials to retreat from their insistence that there was no problem with the water and concede that the Flint River water was corrosive to the old pipes and that, without corrosion treatment, lead was leaching into the taps of city residents. Six months after they had proudly toasted the Flint River water, the city switched back to the Detroit water supply. Two months after that, the mayor declared a state of emergency. Governor Snyder and President Obama followed the next month by declaring their own states of emergency.

An independent task force later blamed state officials for their failure to test the water in advance and for failing to respond once problems emerged.[14] And the EPA's own internal analysis, conducted by the agency's inspector general, found that the MDEQ had failed to follow federal standards and that its delays had subjected Flint residents to "prolonged" exposure to lead. "Management weaknesses delayed [the] response to Flint water crisis," the EPA concluded.[15]

Years later, many Flint residents still did not trust the city's drinking water, even after the water system made big changes. No one truly knew how many kids had been affected in this city of more than 100,000. "It's known as a silent pediatric epidemic," one local pediatrician said. "It's something that we see years if not decades after exposure to lead."[16] Studies after the crisis found that lead levels had doubled among kids, and that the problems were especially serious in low-income neighborhoods, where lead water pipes were more prevalent.[17]

Fifteen state and local government officials were ultimately indicted on fifty-one criminal charges, both for what happened in Flint and for a related case in which evidence of a Legionnaires' disease outbreak had been hidden. Among those charged was the Michigan Health and Human Services director, the Michigan chief medical executive, the head of the MDEQ's drinking water unit, a DEQ water quality analyst, two of Flint's emergency managers, and Flint's public works superintendent.

The crisis was inevitably plagued by partisan bickering. The state's Republican governor was in a constant tussle with Flint's Democratic leaders. He had promised an economic turnaround, which included getting tough on cities that had driven themselves deeply into debt. Conservatives pointed to the city as an example of the incompetence of Democratic managers and evidence that the Democrats' approach to governance "poisons everything it controls," as a writer for the *National Review* put it.[18] Democrats fired back, with Rep. Elijah Cummings (D-MD) demanding in a House committee hearing, "I want everybody who's responsible for this fiasco to be held accountable." The hearing broke down into a blame game, with state officials saying that they were trying to give the local system time to work the kinks out of the transfer to a different water system and that the EPA had delayed in providing guidance about putting corrosion controls into place.[19]

It was a case of finger-pointing federalism. The EPA lead standards had been established in 1991 as part of the broader effort to improve the nation's drinking water. The goal was clear: to ensure that citizens were protected from dangerous levels of lead wherever they lived. But the EPA, of course, does not operate local water systems, so advancing the standard had to be an intergovernmental strategy. State governments oversaw local water authorities and had prime responsibility for overseeing federal guidelines. In Flint's case, the MDEQ was charged with ensuring that the city met federal standards, at the same time as the state was pressing the city to reduce the costs of its local government. The state was at once responsible for cutting water costs and guaranteeing compliance with the federal standard. The inescapable conflict led to state takeover of the key decisions and, ultimately, to the water crisis.

As a result of the crisis, Michigan regulators tightened lead exposure levels below even the federal standard, dropping them from 15 to 12 ppb. They also required water utilities to ensure that pipes were lead-free all the way to buildings, as some of the oldest pipes—those most prone to leaching lead—were between the street and foundations. Local governments wondered where the money would come from, since replacing the old pipes could potentially cost billions of dollars—and the areas where the problems were greatest tended to be the poorest. Having the local water utility pay for it would be easiest and cheapest, especially if it could work down a street and do all the work at once. However, the law typically prohibited public utilities from spending money for private purposes, and property owners usually owned the pipes running in from the street. Failure to replace these pipes would leave the biggest problems unresolved, especially in poorer neighborhoods. Replacing pipes would mean higher water bills for everyone. The city, already deeply in debt because of the economic collapse, had little money to fund the project, and its residents, already struggling as well, could not afford higher bills. The replacement project started but moved slowly—far more slowly than citizens wanted, especially knowing that kids who drank lead-containing water could never get it out of their system.

Flint's water problems are a twenty-first-century version of the debate that has been ongoing ever since the nation's founding. Pressure from the different interests in our federalist system produced those problems: the national consensus that drinking water ought to be safe everywhere, because no one wants to think twice about turning on the tap anywhere in the country; federal policy that sets national standards for lead in drinking water; and state administration, since the EPA has long arms but not a deep reach and must rely on state governments to oversee its standards in the thousands of local water districts around the country. Flint's water problems are also the product of local politics at play on the fundamental issues of who benefits, who pays—and who decides.

That last point is the one at the very core of the debate about the American system since Madison framed the fundamental dilemma. Just how united should the "United States of America" be? Madison's concern was that forcing a collection of states to be too united, through a powerful and concentrated national government, would create political conflict that would shred the country. Fostering healthy diversity, he believed, would help the nation endure, as long as there was enough central power to prevent factions from abusing minority interests. That was his central message from *Federalist 10*. And that is the understory for the Flint water crisis, where external intervention from Virginia Tech scientists and quiet pressure from the EPA pushed back on the problems that the leaded water inflicted on Flint's minority community.

The residents of Flint found themselves in a vicious crossfire of federalism. State officials stepped in to take over their local water system. The new water supply did not meet either federal or state standards. Federal officials set those standards, but state officials were primarily responsible for ensuring compliance with them. Local officials were unhappy, but they had neither the political clout nor the financial resources to push back. In the end, residents found themselves with contaminated water and no choice but to endure the slow, painful process of replacing the old pipes with new ones.

There is a clear national policy on lead in drinking water: do not expose citizens to unsafe water. The states, along with their local governments, have the primary role in ensuring that local governments meet that standard. But the more we allow diversity among the states in determining how that happens, the more we risk inequalities, with great potential for political conflict and personal harm. That is a fundamental cost of federalism in the United States.

Inequality in the Environment

In the 1960s and 1970s, rising national concern about the environment brought inescapable demands for governmental action. Rachel Carson's 1962 book *Silent Spring* had documented the effects of pesticides on the planet.[20] Los Angelenos struggled with smoggy air that made it impossible to see across town and caused respiratory distress. In Cleveland, an oil slick on the Cuyahoga River caught fire. Such pollution created big and inescapable images: photos of the toxic effects of DDT on wildlife; pictures of a burning river in the middle of Cleveland; or the comedian

Johnny Carson's recurring riffs about LA's air pollution, which local authorities called "unhealthy for sensitive persons"—"that means anyone with a nose," he joked.[21] One St. Louis resident complained that the city smelled "like an old-fashioned drugstore on fire."[22] In central Pennsylvania where I grew up, we regularly joked about a local creek as "the inky stinky Codorus."

Reducing pollution had become a national priority. But, as was the case with Medicare and Medicaid, *how* to go about it was the troublesome question. Industry was truly worried about the costs and about the prospect of answering to federal environmental police. Attacks on the "job-killing EPA," a phrase often credited to Republican uber-strategist and super-linguist Frank Luntz, became a conservative standard. But Nixon had no interest in creating a mega-environmental police force; sharing responsibility with the states seemed the easiest road. State governments took on the administrative burdens of administering federal standards. Federal grants enabled the states to cover their administrative costs. Even with new regulations in place, opponents were appeased—they recognized that devolving part of the job to the states would create a second front on which they could forestall aggressive implementation.

Environmental regulation, even when it comes to national standards, is a surprisingly intergovernmental process. The EPA is responsible for the administration of federal regulations, but it does most of its work through its ten regional offices. The regional offices delegate much of their work to the states, and the states, in turn, often work with local governments and private companies. Because this complex system of authority was in place for oversight of Flint's water, it was almost impossible in the end to determine who was truly in charge of what. When federal standards are applied on a national scale, it's little surprise that the results vary widely, given the big differences among the regions of the country in how they oversee the states and how the states have taken up these responsibilities.[23]

As part of their long-term analysis of data about environmental performance in the United States, Daniel Fiorino and Riordan Frost have created the state Air, Climate, and Energy (ACE) index. The index builds on three bodies of data, normalized by the size of a state's gross economic product: carbon emissions, air pollution, and energy efficiency.[24]

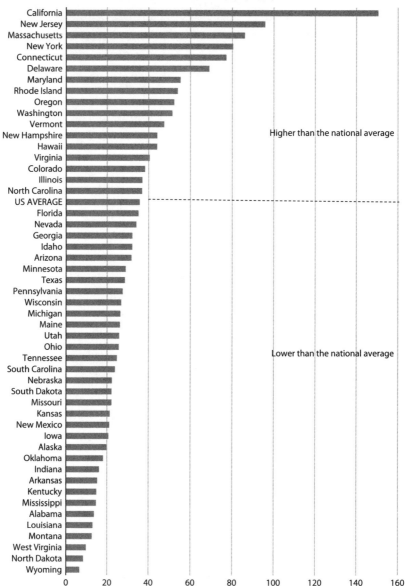

FIGURE 7.1. State environmental quality scores vary enormously. *Source*: Riordan Frost and Daniel Fiorino, "The State Air, Climate, and Energy (ACE) Index: A Tool for Research and Policy" (draft), 2018; Frost and Fiorino, email with the author, March 3, 2018.

California had the highest ACE index in 2014, followed by New Jersey, Massachusetts, New York, and Connecticut. California's score is twenty-three times higher than the state with the lowest index, Wyoming, which is joined by North Dakota, West Virginia, Montana, and Louisiana as the bottom five states. Most states are below the national average ACE index score (see figure 7.1).

There are significant differences among the states in environmental performance, but there have also been big shifts among the states over time. Since 2000, some states, led by New Jersey, Delaware, Massachusetts, California, and New York, have made major improvements (as measured in the 2014 ACE index). Other states not only have lagged behind but have also actually lost ground, with Rhode Island and Alaska falling the most, followed by Arizona, Missouri, and Colorado. In fact, the average change over this fifteen-year period was a four-point improvement—but there's a fifty-point spread between the state with the greatest improvement (New Jersey) and the state with the greatest loss (Rhode Island), as figure 7.2 shows.

These shifts have led to a major debate. As the role of the states has increased in environmental policy, some states have raced either to the top (with tougher environmental enforcement to produce a cleaner environment) or toward the bottom (with more attention to relaxing environmental standards to promote industrial development). Many states have enthusiastically embraced the development of renewable energy, which could help fuel substantial environmental progress.[25] But since the rise of federal delegation of environmental management to the states, others have forgone environmental concerns in favor of increased property values and reduced tax rates. Responsibility for environmental management has offered these states an opportunity, as an article from the Brookings Institution put it, to "race to the bottom line."[26]

The debate about whether federal reliance on the states has increased environmental inequality remains unresolved. In part, there is no way to know what environmental improvements would have emerged had the federal government maintained all enforcement power. Just as has been the case on virtually every major domestic policy issue, it has been a politically easier case for the federal government to define policy but share administrative responsibility with the states. But perhaps more

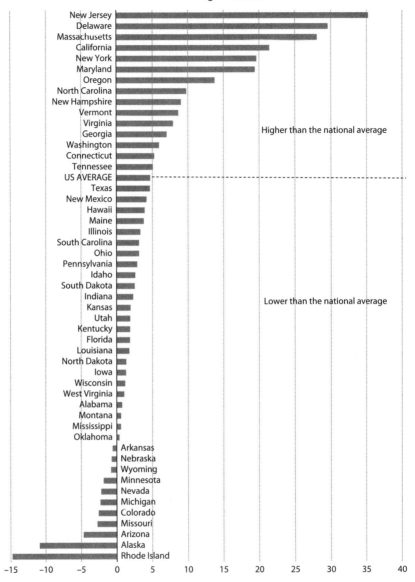

FIGURE 7.2. There have been big changes in environmental performance over time. *Source*: Frost and Fiorino, "The State Air, Climate, and Energy (ACE) Index."

important, the bigger issue is that federal reliance on the states has led to greater disparity *among* the states on environmental performance.

Inequality in Infrastructure

Few public services are more fundamental than transportation, as the founders discovered in the nation's first decades. When the Revolutionary Army finally sent the Redcoats packing and the British trade embargoes and tariffs ended, the new country eagerly turned to growing the economy. There were vast riches inland, and rich farmlands that produced grains and cotton. There were big cities along the coast that had eager customers, and big seaports were eager to ship the goods. But none of this could happen without a system of roads to connect them. The states had little money—so little money, in fact, that most of them were unable to pay off their loans for fighting the Revolutionary War. That problem, in fact, was the foundation of Hamilton's famous bargain with Jefferson and Madison over federal assumption of the states' debt.

Private companies stepped in to construct toll roads—more than 1,200 miles of them between 1800 and 1821. But the private toll roads soon began to fail, and the states had little choice but to take them over. Merchants, meanwhile, insisted on a better system of roadways, since no one wanted to carry wagonloads of goods only to reach the end of a private road or a state boundary and not be able to go farther. They also insisted on better construction. Early highways were plank roads, built from wood and raised above the surrounding land to prevent wagons from getting stuck in the mud. But the plank roads were a nuisance. The ride was rough, and the roads, made of wood, sometimes actually caught fire.[27] Bumpy, smoldering highways were no foundation for an ambitious country, so the states looked to the federal government for help in expanding the new nation's system of roadways.

The land grant program that emerged after Ohio was admitted to the union provided part of the answer. It produced the famous Cumberland Road, which ran from Cumberland, Maryland, to the Ohio River. Portions of this highway later became known as the National Road and, a long time later, as US Route 40—the "Main Street of America"—which ultimately stretched from Atlantic City, New Jersey, to San Francisco, California.[28]

The case for the National Road was simple: the private sector could not reliably build and maintain what the nation needed to feed its commerce. The states, unable on their own to afford to build the roads, turned to the federal government. The federal grant system grew and matured, eventually into the interstate highway system. From this pragmatic partnership came vast infrastructure—and great variation. Consider, for example, the condition of the nation's bridges. In 2016, the Federal Highway Administration deemed 56,000 highway bridges—9 percent of all bridges in the United States—as "deficient." (A "deficient" bridge is one with a serious defect of some kind, in its deck or supporting structure. A bridge labeled "deficient" is not in imminent danger of collapse—but it does need intensive maintenance, and soon.) The 2016 scores showed a big improvement from 1992: the number of deficient bridges had fallen by more than half. But that decrease masked differences between the states. In 1992, the average rate of deficient bridges was eight times the rate found in the bottom five states. In 2015, the rate was ten times. All of the states had improved, but the gap between them had grown.[29]

These numbers frame a recurring story in American federalism's Fourth Generation. In transportation and a wide variety of policy areas, there are substantial, sometimes enormous, differences among the states. Over time these differences have tended to increase. The highest-performing states tend to stay high; the lowest-performing states tend to sink—and sink lower. Inequality has grown not so much from the best getting better but from the lowest getting worse. And that is the story for educational policy as well.

Inequality in Education and Prisons

The founders believed deeply in the importance of a sound education. They were, for the most part, a well-educated group, and they created colleges throughout the colonies to ensure that the nation's future leaders would have sound training as well. Many began as seminaries, like Harvard in 1636, while others were officially nonsectarian, like the University of Pennsylvania, founded in 1740. After the Revolution, education became an important part of the country's expansion, and as we have seen, federal land grants established the principle of supporting local education. The strategy was both basic and profound: as W. Brooke Graves put it, "one of the basic purposes of federalism is that the superior resources of the central government shall be used to initiate and support national programs, largely administered by the political subdivisions."[30] It was the foundation of the system that, half a century later, led Tocqueville to celebrate "the strength of a large republic and the security of a small one," as we saw earlier. Profound pragmatism rests at the core of American democracy—and education policy as well.

But this pragmatism has also fed deep inequality in the nation's education system. In an OECD survey that compared educational performance for adults who had at least one parent with an advanced education to that of adults without a parent with a secondary education, the United States ranked thirty-second of thirty-three countries. A Pearson survey, supported by *The Economist*, put the United States eleventh in cognitive skills and twentieth in educational attainment, compared with other nations.[31]

That inequality spills over to great disparity in educational performance, both within and between the states. In 2016, two economists, Melissa Kearney and Phillip Levine, found that more than one-fourth of high school students in Louisiana, Mississippi, Georgia, and the District of Columbia failed to graduate in four years. That differs sharply from Vermont, Wisconsin, North Dakota, and Nebraska, where the rate is just 10 percent. What accounts for this sharp difference? Kearney and Levine found that the greater the income inequality gap between the rich and the poor in a state, the greater the dropout rate. The level of educational attainment depended on the level of income inequality.[32]

A broad survey of educational attainment and quality of education compiled by the website WalletHub revealed similar findings. The site

TABLE 7.1. Ranking of States by Educational Performance, 2018

Overall rank	State	Total score	Educational attainment rank	Quality of education rank
1	Massachusetts	81.92	1	1
2	Maryland	76.54	3	2
3	Connecticut	71.9	4	9
4	Vermont	71.14	6	3
5	Colorado	70.17	2	23
6	Virginia	69.37	7	5
7	New Hampshire	68.28	5	13
8	Minnesota	66.28	8	14
9	Washington	64.86	9	11
10	New Jersey	64.6	10	10
11	Utah	64.58	11	8
12	New York	57.44	18	16
13	Illinois	56.89	17	19
14	Delaware	56.08	24	6
15	Oregon	55.77	12	39
16	Montana	55.39	13	32
17	Hawaii	54.19	16	36
18	North Dakota	53.29	22	20
19	Wisconsin	53.28	25	12
20	Kansas	52.83	15	44
21	Nebraska	52.53	19	30
22	Maine	52.45	20	29
23	Rhode Island	52.16	21	27
24	Iowa	50.92	27	18
25	Alaska	50.78	14	48
26	California	50.28	36	4
27	Wyoming	48.56	23	43
28	Michigan	48.5	26	33
29	Florida	48.42	37	7
30	Pennsylvania	47.71	29	25
31	North Carolina	46.53	33	21
32	Missouri	46.18	31	28
33	Georgia	45.46	35	22
34	South Dakota	45.4	28	41
35	Ohio	45.17	34	24
36	Arizona	43.43	32	38
37	Idaho	42.97	30	46
38	Indiana	40.74	40	17
39	Texas	39.11	43	15
40	South Carolina	36.52	39	45
41	New Mexico	36.11	38	49
42	Oklahoma	35.58	41	35
43	Tennessee	35.52	42	31

TABLE 7.1. (*continued*)

Overall rank	State	Total score	Educational attainment rank	Quality of education rank
44	Nevada	32.84	44	37
45	Kentucky	31.8	46	26
46	Alabama	31.33	45	40
47	Arkansas	27.18	47	34
48	Louisiana	22.96	48	47
49	West Virginia	21.71	50	42
50	Mississippi	21.06	49	50

Source: Adam McCann, "2018's Most & Least Educated States in America," *WalletHub*, January 23, 2018, https://wallethub.com/edu/most-educated-states/31075/. McCann's article also describes WalletHub's methodology.

compiled two comprehensive and exhaustive indexes of educational attainment and quality of education. The educational attainment scores were based on the share of adults with at least a high school diploma, some college, a bachelor's degree from college, or a graduate or professional degree. The quality of education score built on a measure of the quality of a state's schools, the graduation rate from high school and college, grade school test scores, scores on advanced placement exams, and gaps in educational attainment by race and gender. The result was an overall index of "the most educated states," ranging from the top states (Massachusetts, followed by Maryland, Connecticut, Vermont, and Colorado) to the bottom states (Alabama, Arkansas, Louisiana, and West Virginia, with Mississippi at the bottom). Massachusetts scored nearly four times higher than Mississippi (see table 7.1). Moreover, each state's ranking was very closely connected with its income. The richer the state, the higher the educational performance.[33]

Just as there are differences in educational performance and household income, there are disparities, both among and within states, in how much state and local governments spend on education. The per-pupil spending gap between relatively rich and relatively poor school districts is enormous. In some states (including Delaware, Colorado, Utah, Iowa, and Washington), spending is about the same for both rich and poor districts. In other states (including Vermont, Missouri, Illinois, and

Virginia), the gap is very large. In Pennsylvania, the state with the biggest disparity in spending between rich and poor school districts, the richer districts spent one-third more on each student in 2012 than poorer districts did. Since inequalities in spending help drive inequalities in educational outcomes, these gaps are enormously important.[34]

Although Americans often criticize education policy overall, they treasure their local schools and their ability to shape education to fit their goals and aspirations. A 2014 survey, for example, showed 47 percent of Americans giving their local public schools a grade of A or B. However, just 20 percent of those surveyed gave the nation's public schools overall one of these top two grades.[35] "Americans dislike one-size-fits-all solutions when it comes to how their children are educated," one analyst explained. They much prefer to set education policy locally, using local standards, because "Americans have a libertarian streak in our DNA."[36]

What Americans spend on education, however, and the education their children receive vary enormously from school district to school district and from state to state. Local control of education means inequality in spending, and inequality in spending leads to inequality in educational outcomes.

The same pattern holds true in corrections. Consider the rate at which states imprison convicted criminals, which ranged from 137 per 100,000 citizens in Maine in 2016 to 760 per 100,000 in Louisiana. Among the fifteen most-leading states, the rate was half the rate of the fifteen least-leading states (see table 7.2). The most-leading states are much less likely to punish convicted criminals with longer prison sentences.

TABLE 7.2. State Imprisonment Rate, 2016

	Imprisonment rate per 100,000 citizens	Percentage change, 1996 to 2016
Fifteen most-leading states	255	16
Fifteen least-leading states	503	26

Source: US Bureau of Justice Statistics, "Imprisonment Rate of Sentenced Prisoners under the Jurisdiction of State or Federal Correctional Authorities per 100,000 US Residents," December 31, 2016. Generated using the Corrections Statistical Analysis Tool at www.bjs.gov.

Great Disunity

With Lyndon B. Johnson's promise of a Great Society and the reinforc-
ing decisions of presidents, both Republican and Democrat, afterward,
there had been a sense that the great disunity that had long afflicted the
nation was waning. The federal government had gained predominance
in policymaking, and state and local governments seemed to have been
transformed into administrative agents of this national policy. The
common threads seemed increasingly interwoven to produce greater
unity of policy with greater uniformity in policy outcomes. Analysts,
meanwhile, applauded the states as "laboratories of democracy," as "chem-
ists" like an up-and-coming Arkansas governor named Bill Clinton devised new formulas for state-driven success.[37] Indeed, the "laboratories"
label, popularized by US Supreme Court justice Louis D. Brandeis in 1932,
came to characterize an era of enthusiastic embrace of a progressive
federalism.

As the states took on greater responsibility for these programs,
however, the results were neither greater unity of policy nor greater
uniformity of outcomes. Today there are big and often growing differences between the states. Moreover, as our examination of health care,
environmental policy, education, and infrastructure has made clear, a
common theme is not so much that the best are getting even better,
but that the worst are getting worse, and faster. Not only is the gap
among the states growing, but conditions in some states are also
deteriorating.

These differences have typically flowed from very different political choices made by the states and their elected officials. Although
surely legitimate, these choices have incurred substantial costs, a logical by-product of the delegation of federal responsibility to the states.
There was a strong sense at the height of the Great Society in the
1960s and in the early days of the New Federalism in the 1970s that
the nation had committed itself to shrinking the gaping inequalities
in American society. There was a time when that commitment seemed
to be producing results, through government programs designed to
narrow the gaps.

But in the generation that followed, the result has been more in-equality, not the shrinking gaps that the golden age had promised. Where will this trend lead us? And how much inequality is the country prepared to accept as the price of allowing states so much freedom to chart their own course?

8

Engines of Inequality

Of all the inequalities that have rippled across the states, none is more fundamental or serious than inequality in income. It is fundamental because income inequality limits the ability of many states to provide the same level of services as other states. It is serious because income inequality fuels many of the deepest and most pernicious pathologies of American life, including the problem of trust in government.

Income Inequality

Consider the portrait painted by the US Census Bureau's American Community Survey. In the fifteen most-leading states, both the degree of poverty and the poverty rate are substantially lower. So too are the unemployment rate and the share of families receiving food stamps. Income inequality (as measured by the Gini coefficient, with lower numbers representing lower levels of inequality) is lower than in the fifteen least-leading states. The share of families without health insurance is far higher in the least-leading states, and the number of individuals with at least a bachelor's degree is far higher in the most-leading states (see table 8.1). The story is consistent: the most-leading states tend to provide their citizens with better outcomes, in a host of areas that fundamentally matter to their daily lives.

What accounts for these differences? The most important driver is, quite simply, income. The most-leading states, as a group, are richer than

TABLE 8.1. Poverty, Income, Employment, Health, and Education Outcomes by State, 2016

	Poverty rate (three-year average, 2014–2016)	Median household income	Gini coefficient	Percentage of families below the poverty line	Percentage of families receiving food stamps	Unemployment rate	Percentage with no health insurance	Percentage with a bachelor's degree (population age twenty-five and older)
Fifteen most-leading states	10.2	$67,020	46.3	7.9	11.1	6.0	8.3	21.4
Fifteen least-leading states	16.4	$50,831	47.0	13.0	14.6	7.8	14.0	15.8

Source: US Census Bureau, American Community Survey 2016, https://www.census.gov/acs/www/data/data-tables-and-tools/data-profiles/2016/.

the least-leading states. The most-leading states lead because they can afford to provide their citizens with better services and with the better quality of life that produces better outcomes on health, education, infrastructure, the environment, and many other functions that matter to citizens. The least-leading states lag because, very often, they are reluctant to ask their citizens to dig even deeper to pay higher taxes—taxes that many citizens simply could not afford to pay without further undermining the quality of their lives.

Consider the case of Lowndes County in Alabama, where citizens have long struggled with disease that flows directly from the county's inadequate sewage system.[1] The county, partway between Montgomery and Selma, is among the nation's poorest. It has a poverty rate of 27 percent—far higher than Alabama's rate of 19 percent, which is itself one of the highest in the country. The county's residents are mostly black, mostly poor, and mostly in areas without municipal sewage service. They must rely instead on septic systems, but these systems work poorly. In fact, one reporter found that "many people who live in Lowndes County have open pits of human waste in their yards or raw sewage backing up into their homes after heavy rains."[2]

In 2017 Baylor University researchers reported that they had found hookworm in more than one-third of the county's residents. The researchers were stunned. They had believed that Franklin D. Roosevelt's New Deal had effectively eliminated the disease, which causes a wide array of debilitating symptoms, including anemia, nausea, vomiting, and diarrhea.[3] Philip Alston, investigating the issue for the United Nations, said, "I think it's very uncommon in the First World. This is not a sight that one normally sees."[4] Other poor counties, researchers discovered, were struggling with the issue as well. As Catherine Flowers, an advocate for cleaning up the Lowndes County sewage system, concluded, "This is a problem around the country that shouldn't exist."[5]

If an inadequate sewage system shouldn't exist but does, the question is *why*? Flowers said that the explanation was simple: "The problem with Lowndes County is that Lowndes County has no money." Residents don't have the money to improve their sewage systems. The county is poor, and Alabama, a poor state itself, can't afford to help. The county tried to force residents to pay for improving their own systems by threatening to put thirty-seven residents in jail. But when it became clear that these residents just didn't have the money to pay for better sewage treatment, the county retreated. Moreover, it did little good for residents to complain to local officials. As Flowers explained, "If you complain to the health department, you're mandated to fix it yourself. So people don't complain, because at the end of the day, they're going to be held responsible," and if they fail to keep their systems up to local requirements, they are "maybe even subject to arrest." "People are literally being poisoned," Sen. Cory Booker (D-NJ) said to reporters after visiting the county. "These are our children and elderly folks living in a toxic environment."[6]

On another front, the spread of tropical diseases in poor American towns, from dengue fever to Chagas disease, has become part of a "plague of poverty," a 2012 *New York Times* op-ed argued. Citizens there become infected with tropical diseases that "we ordinarily think of as confined to developing countries." Moreover, these diseases "can even increase the levels of poverty in these areas by slowing the growth and intellectual development of children and impeding productivity in the work force."[7] Among the American states, poverty and performance are inextricably linked, and inequalities in income lead to inequalities in policy outcomes.

Figure 8.1 strongly makes this point. It charts the rank of each state's level of poverty (from 1, the lowest, to 50, the highest) against the rank of key policy outcomes (with 1 the highest and 50 the lowest). In a country as diverse as the United States, there is wide variation in the distribution of the states. But several important themes emerge. In general, the states that rank lowest in poverty tend to produce the best policy outcomes. All of the states with the strongest policy results cluster toward the bottom left hand of the chart (in bold face). That contrasts sharply with the states that rank lowest in policy outcomes, which cluster toward the top right hand of the chart, among the states with the highest levels of poverty (in italics). The states with the lowest levels of poverty have more money to spend on policy, and that greater wealth tends to produce stronger outcomes. More money, not surprisingly, means better results.

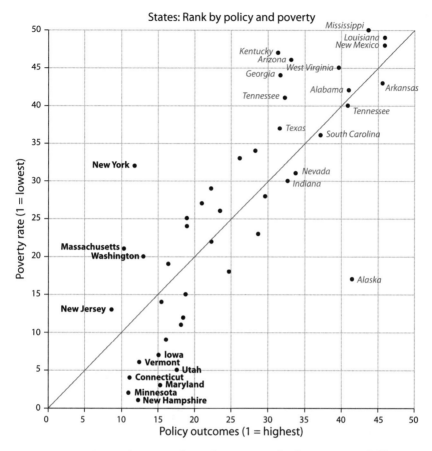

FIGURE 8.1. Among the states, policy and poverty are related. *Source:* Compiled by the author from the sources cited in table 5.1. "Least-leading states" are italicized. "Most-leading" states are not.

The ten least-leading states provide the clearest examples of how poverty affects policy outcomes. These are the states straining most under their citizens' burdens, and they are the states where high poverty—and the resulting struggle to raise tax revenue—makes the biggest difference in the services that citizens receive. This is the crucial backstory for the case of sewage treatment in Lowndes County in Alabama, and in many other policy areas and other similar counties.

Two sets of states cluster together in between. There are three states that punch far above their weight, given their levels of poverty: policy outcomes in California, North Carolina, and Florida are significantly higher than their level of poverty would suggest. On the other hand, there are three states that punch far below their weight: Missouri, Hawaii, and Wyoming have policy outcomes that are lower than one might expect, given their levels of poverty.

Policy outcomes in Louisiana, for example, regularly rank near the bottom of the scale. It is no higher than forty-first among the fifty states in most policy measures. In fact, it ranks forty-ninth or fiftieth in health, crime and corrections, and outcomes for children. There is a simple explanation: it also ranks forty-ninth in poverty among the states. Regardless of which policies state officials might *want* to pursue, they simply do not have the resources to do so. At the other end of the spectrum are states like New Hampshire, Minnesota, Maryland, and Connecticut, which regularly rank at the top on policy outcomes. They also have the lowest rates of poverty among the states, and with relatively more money, they can provide substantially better policy outcomes to their citizens. It is often the case that what separates the most-leading and least-leading states is their capacity to tax themselves and provide benefits to citizens.

Often—but not always. New York, for example, regularly ranks relatively high in policy outcomes (number two in education, number four in the environment, number five in crime and corrections) even though it ranks below average—number thirty-two—in poverty. Some of this disparity is explained by the state's high income inequality; relatively well-to-do portions of the state can provide good policy outcomes from relatively high incomes. And part of it is that New York has aggressive redistributive policies. On the other side of the policy spectrum, Alaska ranks number seventeen in poverty, significantly above the national average, but it regularly ranks toward the bottom in policy outcomes, including number thirty-eight in education, number forty-two in infrastructure, number forty-six in children's' policies, and number forty-seven in environment and crime and corrections. Some states simply choose to tax their citizens less and spend more on services that benefit them. These big variations—and fundamental differences in their causes—lead to very big questions about the impact of federalism on American life.

Why Does Inequality Matter?

Some scholars have long debated whether federalism is an institution with any real meaning—or whether, given the rise of the federal government, we are seeing the "end of federalism."[8] But that's not the right question. As long as the American constitutional republic exists, there will be federalism, so it doesn't really need to be saved. The fundamental question then becomes one about the mechanisms shifting the balance of power in the system: there have been shifts in federal and state predominance as the system has shifted back and forth between laws and boundaries, on the one hand, and bargaining and balance, on the other. The First Generation of Federalism saw the predominance of boundaries set in law, especially in resort to the Tenth Amendment. The Second Generation featured a sharper battle over state power, especially in the "separate but equal" doctrine that sought to advance the predominance of the states, even though the forces supporting federal power had won the Civil War. The Third Generation saw a swing back to law and boundaries, with the Supreme Court's ruling in *Brown* and the rise of the civil rights movement. The Fourth Generation brought renewed state preeminence, especially in Medicaid and the Affordable Care Act, based on big differences in state politics and state policy preferences.

Madison's federalism has never been a stable structure. He deliberately designed it to bend to local norms and politics without breaking. But with the dramatic rise in inequality during the Fourth Generation—rising inequality in the country overall, and more inequality among the states—the pressures on Madison's great invention have rarely been greater. The Civil War, of course, almost proved catastrophic for the republic. But that was an issue focused principally on slavery. In the Fourth Generation, by contrast, virtually every policy issue has been affected by growing inequality among the states, and that is sowing the seeds for much bigger problems through far sharper conflicts.

So the question is not so much whether we have seen "the end of federalism." More fundamentally, we need to ask where to set the balance between federal and state power, what the consequences of that balance are, and how those consequences—growing inequality—have strained the American polity. To an unprecedented degree, the government that Americans get increasingly depends on where they live.

The founders' decision to hard-bake great variation into the Constitution and give the states great autonomy over the course of their policy decisions lay at the core of the republic. It is at the core of the "laboratories of democracy" argument, the notion that competition among the states leads to policy innovation and better results, and it is the foundation for limited government. Pietro Nivola, for example, argues that federalism in all of its diversity has been the best way to improve the federal government:

> The sensible way to disencumber the federal government and sharpen its focus is to take federalism seriously—which is to say, desist from fussing with the management of local public schools, municipal staffing practices, sanitation standards, routine criminal justice, family end-of-life disputes, and countless other chores customarily in the ambit of state and local governance.[9]

This great variation, federalism's friends have long argued, is the foundation of liberty in the nation.

The political theorist Martin Diamond made a powerful case for the virtue of variation in American life through variation in American federalism. He argued that the genius of federalism lies in its decentralization and its function for citizens as "the school of their citizenship, a preserver of their liberties, a vehicle for flexible response to their problems—petty to others, perhaps, but profound to them—and the source of the distinctive energies of American life."[10] In the rich tradition of the American constitutional republic, variation is the fullest expression of liberty. Efforts to pursue uniformity always mean strong action by a powerful federal government, and that in turn is seen as a rejection of the very principles of liberty on which the founders built the country.

But the pursuit of liberty through the very different actions of very different states has far-reaching implications, including great variation in the government that different citizens receive. The fundamental story of federalism in the twenty-first century is the story of inequality: in resources to support government services, and in results and policy outcomes. This inequality brings variations in important areas like education, health care, infrastructure, and the environment. For citizens like those in Lowndes County, Alabama, it has meant exposure to diseases that most Americans assume exist nowhere outside of developing countries. Some variation in services is inevitable—perhaps even desirable—as the natural product of local choice and the exercise of liberty. But behind the liberty that Madison fought so hard to win and sustain in the American constitution, there has always been a dark side—levels of inequality that challenge basic values about what the majority of Americans find acceptable.

If Americans wanted to shrink this inequality, they could surely do so at the national level, with both tax and spending programs that would level the differences. We have some federal programs that do this, of course. Leveling the differences was the goal of many New Deal programs, especially Social Security, and the focus of Great Society programs. There is Medicaid (1965) and the related Children's Health Insurance Program (CHIP, 1997), which fund health care for the poor. There is the Supplemental Nutrition Assistance Program (SNAP, or food stamps, permanently created in 1964). There is the Supplemental Security Income Program (SSI, 1972), which provides cash payments to the blind and disabled. There is the Earned Income Tax Credit (EITC, 1975), which provides tax credits—mostly tax refunds—to individuals whose income is under the federal income limit. We have housing assistance programs, which in 1974 transformed the public housing program of the 1930s into a voucher program. And Temporary Assistance for Needy Families (TANF), updated in 1996, provides a safety net for poor families.

These programs are vast and expensive, although estimates of their total costs, across all levels of government, vary widely. One estimate from the Cato Institute, using a very sweeping definition of "welfare" and estimating state and local government contributions to the programs, puts the amount at $1 trillion a year.[11] Estimates vary widely, depending on whether one wants to make the case that we are already spending a lot or that we need to spend more. Furthermore, simply putting the "welfare" label on programs can stir political opposition. As *New York Times* columnist R. M. Schneiderman explained in 2008, "'welfare' remains a catch-all pejorative, a word that continues to connote indolence and idle," and it is a label that often has racial overtones. If the American dream has always been premised on individual responsibility and hard work leading to a better life, government-funded benefits without work requirements have always seemed to undermine that dream.[12]

There is no escaping the basic point: in spite of how substantial inequality in the United States is, we could reduce it if we wanted to. And yet, rather than shrinking, it is growing. Most-leading states have set an aggressive course toward expanding the role of government by working to increase government services and widen government protections. Some least-leading states have not been able to keep up simply because they cannot afford the same level of services, while other least-leading states have sought to peel back government's role in their pursuit of lower taxes and more individual freedom. And even if we want to reduce inequality, the evidence shows we are not succeeding.

Trust and the American States

This inequality breeds another problem: distrust in government. Although scholars fiercely debate the proposition, there is substantial evidence that the higher the level of inequality, the lower the level of trust in government—and the lower the level of trust in government, the less confidence citizens have in government and in the decisions it makes.[13] Distrust tends to lower political participation, including voting, and to increase political polarization. It decreases compliance with functions like tax collection, since so much of the tax system relies on citizens' voluntary agreement to do what the law requires; less trust can lead people to decide that they don't want to pay. Distrust increases the incentives for corruption, since trust lowers barriers to accepting the norms about how things ought to work. It is expensive, since more distrust leads to more regulation and litigation. It can slow innovation, because individuals become more cautious about taking risks. And it weakens the legitimacy of political institutions.[14]

There are two basic facts about trust in American government that have endured over a very long time. The first is that trust in government has been declining since the 1950s. The second is that the smaller the government and the closer they are to it, the more Americans trust their government. In general, trust is higher in local governments than in state governments, and it is much higher for both state and local governments than for the federal government.

In 2016, for example, 71 percent of Americans said that they had a "great deal" or a "fair amount" of trust in local governments to handle their problems—an increase from the 63 percent who said this in 1972. For state governments, the figure was 62 percent, a very slight decline from 63 percent in 1972. At the federal level, however, distrust has soared. In 2016, the share of Americans with a "great deal" or a "fair amount" of trust in the federal government was 49 percent, a precipitous drop from the 75 percent level in 1972.[15]

Moreover, among state governments, trust is higher in smaller governments than in larger ones. When surveyed about whether they had trust in their state government, 64 percent of the residents of the ten smallest states expressed confidence. Among the ten largest states, the number was thirteen points lower, 51 percent. There were only scant differences in trust depending on which party held the governorship or whether the state had a divided or unified government (see table 8.2).[16] In general, the farther people get from government, and the larger the government they deal with, the more they distrust it.

For those making the case for relying more on state and local governments, there is good news here, since trust is stronger the closer the government is to the people. That is a plus for federalism, with its heavy

TABLE 8.2. Citizens' Confidence in State Government, 2015

	Percentage confident
Largest ten states	51
Second-largest ten states	54
Ten middle states	56
Second-smallest ten states	59
Smallest ten states	64

Source: Jeffrey M. Jones, "Illinois Residents Least Confident in Their State Government," *Gallup Politics*, February 17, 2016, https://news.gallup.com/poll/189281/illinois-residents-least-confident-state-government.aspx.

reliance on state and local governments. But a deeper and more important story is also apparent here: one of the biggest drivers of distrust in government, in the United States and around the world, is inequality. Trust is greatest, on the other hand, where income is more equally distributed.[17] In the United States, distrust is rising. So is overall inequality. Inequality among the states is increasing. And as we will see in the pages that follow, the increase in inequality among the states is a product of both different public policies in state capitals (themselves the product of state action) and wide differences in state financial capacity (over which they have less control). Put together, these forces have become one of the most important but most understated forces shaping American public policy in the twenty-first century.

Reversing the rising trends of inequality and distrust in government is a heavy load to saddle on American federalism. Its necessity is also a profound irony, since Madison and the founders had designed federalism to increase trust in government and to promote liberty. For the nation's first two centuries, federalism created a tug-of-war between central control and state discretion. But then, toward the end of the twentieth century, that tug seemed to change. The golden age of federalism emerged, with a striking if fragile national commitment to the pursuit of equality. Then, with rising opposition to "big government," growing state concern about the cost of programs like Medicaid, rising political polarization, and its assault on programs like Obamacare, that golden age evaporated almost as quickly as it emerged. The story of federalism today is a story of rising inequality, with a new reality coming into focus: the quality of government services—and the quality of life—increasingly depend on where Americans live.

If trust in the nation's politics depends on some measure of equality, and if inequality is rising, the threats to the American experiment are real and profound. Is Madison's grand bargain breaking down, with potentially disastrous implications for the stability of the American polity? Can American federalism be reborn, by energetic and entrepreneurial steps in the states? Is it likely that some states are more likely to lead the way to a new future?

9

Can Some States Lead?

The core of Justice Brandeis's "laboratories of democracy" argument was that the states were experimental creatures. Some states, he believed, would discover what worked best, and that would set a path that other states would follow. In some measure, by this notion, federalism would inevitably generate inequality—but it would also fuel an engine of innovation, and that innovation could be put to use reducing inequality.

The "laboratories" argument thus frames the fundamental dilemma about how best to shrink inequality among the states. If some states lead, will other states follow? And if other states do not follow, does this make a case for shifting the balance of power toward the federal government, threatening Madison's grand experiment?

This, of course, is the debate that Riker—dismissive of federalism as a crutch supporting states that sought to infringe on the rights of their minorities—and Derthick—confident in the ultimate imagination of the states and their resolute stand against federal power—would find familiar. As with so many other big policy debates of the twenty-first century, the front lines of this one are found in California.

"I Don't Trust Air I Can't See"

The comedian Bob Hope was long America's king of the one-liners, and his fans continued to recite their favorites even after his death in 2003. In one performance in Montana, he reeled off one of his most famous quips about his hometown of Los Angeles. "You folks live in a magnificent part of the country," he told his Montana audience. "Yeah, the fresh air's great, even though I don't trust air I can't see."[1] With that line, Hope helped make cars, smog, and Los Angeles synonymous.

California grew so rapidly after World War II, in large part because of the spread of cars and highways, that Californians popularized "smog"—a mixture of smoke and fog that was the inescapable partner of the state's expansion.[2] Cars were central to Californians' identity and helped the state grow by generating far-flung suburbs connected by freeways (highways that were cost-free, in stark contrast to toll roads back east). But the network of freeways combined with California's peculiar topography (sprawling urban areas between the ocean and hills) to make the state one of the best spots in the country to generate smog—and Bob Hope's jokes about it.

Of course, the smog was no laughing matter. It sickened some individuals and shortened the lives of others. The more the cars and freeways spread, the more smog became a problem that demanded attention. Factories were a problem too. In one especially nasty crisis in 1943, Los Angelenos fought off nausea, burning lungs, and irritated eyes in what they called a "gas attack" that reduced visibility to just three blocks in the city; locals blamed a plant producing butadiene, used in synthetic rubber. Los Angelenos often could not see their famous HOLLYWOOD sign or the hills that gave the city much of its character.

Soon after, the state decided that it was time to act. In 1947, California created a regional air pollution control district, the nation's first unit of government focused on dealing with pollution. They were not alone in this pioneering effort. Oregon created the first statewide air pollution control agency in 1951, and California followed soon thereafter, with its regional district becoming a statewide authority.[3]

This was the birth of modern environmental policy, built on the Brandeis argument that individual states should be encouraged to "try novel social and economic experiments without risk to the rest of the country." He concluded, "If we would guide by the light of reason, we must let our minds be bold."[4] In the first years after World War II, as the country was trying to build an economy that could put millions of returning veterans to work, few things could be bolder—or riskier—than to regulate the pollution produced by cars and the factories that employed so many citizens. There was the constant, nagging fear, then as now, that tighter environmental standards might produce cleaner air at the cost of fewer jobs. But officials in California, followed by Oregon and other states, decided to let their minds be bold. Other states stood back, waiting to see whether that risk would pay off.

Among the state-based laboratories, California evolved into an especially aggressive workshop. It set the nation's first standards for tailpipe emissions of carbon monoxide, nitrous oxide, and diesel-based particulates. It led the way on requiring the use of catalytic converters, which transformed toxic pollutants into less dangerous emissions. In mandating that cars include on-board diagnostic computers, California was responsible for the CHECK ENGINE light that sometimes plagues motorists. It required automakers to produce a growing supply of zero-emission vehicles and demanded better fuel economy for the entire fleet of car manufacturers. It set the nation's first greenhouse gas emission standards for cars and then upped the ante with tougher "advanced clean car standards."[5]

Not only did these new regulations establish California as a bold environmental laboratory, but in a state that had been the emerging hotbed of the automobile—and become the country's single largest car market—they effectively set national standards. It was unthinkable for car manufacturers to produce different cars for the California market, and so California's pollution standards became market-shapers.

California transformed the idea of state-based laboratories. With one lab bigger than all the others, experiments there frequently became de facto policy everywhere. The future that arrived first in the Golden State quickly moved to the rest of the country. We often think of public policy in America as a process built in Washington that filters down to the states. But in a remarkable number of cases, water has flowed uphill. National policy has moved up from the states to the nation—particularly from California.

As climate change has become a larger, inescapable policy challenge, particularly in states like California where climate issues have surfaced with great ferocity, the movement of policy from the states to the nation has taken on ever more importance. The core problem of climate change is the emission of greenhouse gases—methane, nitrous oxide, and especially carbon dioxide. These gases trap heat in the atmosphere and then, in turn, increase pollution and contribute to weather extremes, from heavy rains to droughts. Transportation—cars, trucks, and buses—is the largest single source of greenhouse gases, accounting for about one-fourth of all such emissions.[6] By a significant margin, the United States accounts for the largest amount of per capita greenhouse gas emissions, although China is responsible for substantially more greenhouse gas emissions overall; analysts expect those emissions to continue to grow significantly over time, even though emissions in the United States have leveled off and the level in the European Union nations has diminished.[7] For more than a generation, to meet the core challenge of finding new ways to improve the air without weakening economic growth, California has become the nation's leading lab. And the most important piece of its laboratory apparatus has been the policy waiver.

Waivers for Flexibility

The significance of California's leadership in climate policy—a process we can call "Californiazation"—lies not only in its role as the nation's foremost policy laboratory but also in the translation of its state initiatives into national policy. California has used a complex process called "waivers," in which the federal government effectively creates federally sanctioned laboratories by granting some states the explicit authority to set their own standards and to assess the results. The labs, in turn, establish the foundation for the transformation of national policy.

From Oregon's first statewide air pollution standards in 1951 until the passage of the federal Clean Air Act of 1963, the door was wide open for state action. California passed its first statewide air pollution law in 1956, but only after New Jersey and Massachusetts had beaten it out of the gate two years earlier. Hawaii and Florida followed soon afterward, in 1957. All in all, nine states passed air standards laws before the 1963 act. With that legislation, the federal government began ramping up national standards; focusing on auto exhaust, it provided state and local governments with grants to create pollution control programs. The forty-one other states gradually established their own programs, until Ohio and South Dakota became the last states to establish air pollution control standards, in 1970. Before the creation of the US Environmental Protection Agency in 1970, the United States had a national network of air pollution regulations. The network, however, was a loose confederation more than an iron dome of protection. Some states had surged into the lead, others lagged behind, and the federal government sought to carve out a stable middle ground.

The story here is very much a part of the Fourth Generation of Federalism. In many areas of American public policy, a handful of states have led the way. National policy often emerges as state officials experiment, federal officials take the temperature on the results of state action, and then the federal government nudges forward the most promising state practices, often by providing grants that lure other states into the arena. Much more often than not, innovation in American federalism has typically followed the process of Californiazation: a vanguard of states—often California itself—take the lead; federal policymakers embrace an emerging national consensus before all states have joined; and then the rest of the state governments—sometimes reluctantly, often unhappily—are swept in at the end of the process.

In air pollution, California has regularly led the country in developing new standards, including the nation's first tailpipe emissions standards and its promotion of catalytic converters, in-car computers, and zero-emission vehicles.[8] For more than fifty years, the first big jumps forward in managing automobile air pollution have been made in California.

This Californiazation strategy, however, raises a big problem: many private companies hate huge variations in their marketplaces, and they dislike having to create different goods with different properties to sell in different places. It is one thing for a state to blaze a trail through a relatively uncharted forest. But once the federal government begins to act, national standards begin to emerge. Despite the Tenth Amendment, which reserves powers to the states, the presumption is that national policy will trump state law. That's partly political reality, since interest groups often find it much easier to fight a battle once in Washington than to have to stage repeated campaigns in fifty state capitals, and partly fundamental pragmatism. States may be laboratories, but there is often substantial variation in their results, and few manufacturers want to create different products, print different labels, run different payment systems, and manage other variances from state to state. Thus, there is a strong force in American government to push policies up to the federal government and then out to all the states.

This is where the waiver process comes in. In a wide range of federal programs that states administer, the states have wanted to experiment beyond the boundaries of what the federal government required. Sometimes, as in California, the state wanted to create regulations that went much further than federal standards. In other cases, including welfare and Medicaid, states sometimes believed that they could produce better results for less money if the feds gave them additional flexibility. In general, the federal government does not permit states to experiment with *lower* standards, but it has been increasingly flexible in allowing states to experiment if they pledge to do at least as well as federal standards require.

In environmental policy, the EPA granted California an unusually broad collection of waivers. The agency approved waivers for on-board diagnostics, portable diesel equipment, large engines, commercial harbor craft, off-road recreational vehicles, refrigeration units on-board vehicles, urban buses, cargo handling equipment in rail yards, idling in heavy-duty trucks, zero-emission vehicles (including battery-powered cars), heavy-duty tractor-trailers, light- and medium-duty trucks, personal watercraft, motorcycles, on-board vapor recovery during fueling, methanol-fueled vehicles, exhaust emission standards, and warranties.[9] The list of California's waivers runs to almost seventy pages.

The waiver process has produced a stunning transformation in how federal policy is made. It is no exaggeration to say that most federal clean-air standards could have a "made in California" label. The process has given Sacramento enormous power in driving national policy change from a substantial but relatively narrow base. The state's scale is small enough to galvanize action, but large enough to create markets too large to be ignored.

But while liberals have warmly embraced the Californiazation of air pollution policy, the state's policy entrepreneurship has enraged conservatives, who often find it difficult to hold the line in Washington against an expanding federal role being shaped in Sacramento and other state capitals. In 2018, EPA Administrator Scott Pruitt argued, "Cooperative federalism doesn't mean that one state can dictate standards for the rest of the country." Finding the balance between national air pollution standards and compliance costs, he argued, ought to be a decision made in DC.[10]

Automobile manufacturers found themselves torn. On the one hand, they resisted the rapid march of new—and expensive—technology. On the other hand, they wanted to seize the technological lead.[11] The fundamental question was not only how best to set that balance, but also who ought to make the call—the federal government or the states.

California undoubtedly had made great progress in reducing air pollution, especially compared with where it would have been without its waiver-driven policies. Despite its aggressive attack on pollution, however, it has remained the most polluted state in the country, at least in terms of ozone, which is the principal pollutant produced by gas-burning cars. In fact, in the American Lung Association's "State of the Air" report card for 2015 to 2017, California cities occupied seven of the ten most polluted spots: Los Angeles–Long Beach, Visalia, and Bakersfield ranked one, two, and three. Phoenix-Mesa, Arizona; Houston–The Woodlands, Texas; and New York–Newark, New Jersey, were the only non-California cities in the top ten.[12] The state's population has continued to grow, the highways are even more clogged with cars, and the state's warm temperatures and mountains still combine to make it hard for pollution to escape. "It is getting better here, but it's still the worst," explained Steve LaDochy, an air pollution expert at California State University–Los Angeles.[13] That is why California ranks in the middle of the over-achieving states: its policy outcomes exceed what one might expect given its level of income inequality, but its overall results lag behind the nation's most-leading states because its scale is so large.

Of course, California's performance is far better than would have been the case without its aggressive intervention, a strategy that helped deflate some of Bob Hope's favorite lines. He loved to quip, "The smog was so bad that I opened my mouth to yawn and chipped a tooth!" If the state had waited to follow national patterns, the results might have been much poorer. California's pollution—and the health impacts on its citizens—would have been far worse if the state had not chosen to lead the way on national environmental policy. Its strategy was built on its clever use of waivers to federal legislative requirements.[14]

The Trump administration has pushed back hard on California's environmental policy waivers, precisely because they have been so successful—not only in framing the state's policy but, far more important, because the state's waivers have fundamentally reshaped national policy, without changes in federal law or regulation. In fighting back against broader, more expensive regulations, top administration officials see California's waivers as a critical part of their strategy: if they are to reshape national policy, they have to prevent California from getting there first. The administration's challenges to California's waivers have triggered protracted legal battles. It turns out that the Californiazation of policy, once established, is not easily pushed aside.

Waiving at Federalism

At the core of the Californiazation of federalism is the federal government's policy of granting waivers to allow state governments to experiment—a process that has led to fundamental transformation not just of environmental policy but of welfare and health policy as well. The waiver movement got a rapid start in the 1980s with efforts in the states to find new welfare strategies: to end what some saw as a "cycle of dependence," increase work incentives, reduce states' costs, and balance the interests of Republicans (in cutting the programs) and Democrats (in protecting beneficiaries). The strategy rapidly grew in importance in the Reagan and Bush administrations as they tried to loosen federal strings on state innovation.

The welfare reform movement of the 1990s, for example, had its foundations in these waivers. Wisconsin Governor Tommy Thompson conceived of a strategy to get people off welfare and into work by building a network of supporting programs, including job training and child care. His "Wisconsin Works" caught national attention with its dramatic 36 percent reduction in the welfare caseload, which beat by far the efforts of other states. Wisconsin officials estimated that two-thirds of those on welfare spent at least eight years in the program—and that most of those on welfare could work. Wisconsin Works focused on training, not employment. Officials believed that the existing program led to dependency and rewarded mothers who had additional children. "W2," as it was known, required parents to work but focused on encouraging self-sufficiency.[15]

Conservatives hailed Thompson as "the real star of welfare reform" and his W2 as a "Wisconsin miracle," but they complained that Democrats, especially in the Clinton administration, had made waivers too hard to get. Democrats feared that programs like W2 were part of a Republican strategy to roll back welfare programs under the guise of increasing efficiency, and they were reluctant to license such efforts.[16] In time, however, Democrats recognized W2's success, and it became the model for national welfare reform. "Wisconsin took the idea (of welfare to work) to extremes not seen anywhere else in the country," said the welfare policy expert Lawrence Mead. "Wisconsin Works, the eventual system that it implemented, is the most radical reform in the country . . . and is a triumph of government."[17]

It wasn't a flawless effort, Mead explained in his powerful book on W2, "but it still struck the most telling blow against family poverty that government has managed in forty years of struggle."[18] And it was a blow remarkable in its political genesis. For the previous generation, most big policy innovations, especially those focused on the needs of the poor, had come from Democrats, often with Republicans fighting back before reluctantly conceding the battle. That was the case with Johnson's Model Cities, Medicare, Medicaid, civil rights, voting rights, and housing rights. In W2, however, Republicans led the way, despite the Clinton

administration's initial efforts. But in time, Wisconsin's efforts became a
true national model, one that grew into a large package of intricately
interwoven waivers designed by state policymakers, all on the foundation of the aggressive expansion of waivers that began under Republican
presidents in the 1980s. W2 showed that the Californiazation strategy
was not restricted to Democrats or to the West Coast.

On the heels of welfare reform came even more experiments with
Medicaid. The program raised all the ideological issues that had surfaced
with welfare—coupled with the program's budget pressures, which fueled the states' efforts to slow its soaring costs. Frank Thompson found
that the federal government had approved just fifty waivers in the program's first thirty years. But with the Clinton administration the pace
changed dramatically: by 2006, the federal government had approved 150
Medicaid waivers, with forty-four states and the District of Columbia operating under some form of waiver. The waivers continued to grow, in
part because first the Clinton administration and then the Bush administration eased the waiver approval process. From there, the waiver strategy rolled over into the Bush administration's landmark "No Child Left
Behind" educational policy, in which states sought waivers from its requirements for tough testing.[19] Waivers also proved an important foundation for administering the Affordable Care Act during the Obama
administration—and for unwinding it during the Trump years.[20]

The waiver strategy marks a major break from the traditional strategies of federalism. For most of American history, big changes in national
policy typically flowed from federal decisions in Washington designed
to create uniform standards across the country. Policies tended to be top-
down. But as the federal government's policy ambitions grew, so too did
the weight of the federal bureaucracy's actions on state governments.
That, in turn, increasingly worried state officials, both on the left (in
California on environmental policy) and on the right (in Wisconsin on
welfare). By the 1950s, the Tenth Amendment might have seemed truly
redundant, but its basic principle remained quietly in play: there were, in
fact, boundaries between federal and state authorities, and the federal
government could not simply cross those lines when new problems or
initiatives surfaced. In each case, if there was to be a stronger federal

role, the proponents of that step needed to think creatively about how to use—or circumvent—the features of federalism to advance their goals. The federal government might make policy—from ending slavery to the Fourteenth Amendment to stimulus spending to civil rights to health care—but the states often ended up with important administrative responsibilities that gave them the last word on how that policy would actually affect citizens. The boundaries of federalism have sometimes seemed an artificial barrier around which policymakers have to steer, but federalism remains remarkably strong despite the many years that have passed since the apparently least essential of the first ten amendments to the Constitution came into being.

Waivers, moreover, have allowed Congress to create ambitious programs while delegating some of the biggest problems to the states. States that can make a convincing case that they can produce better results earn waivers that give them the ability to run federal programs in their own way.[21] That change has marked a major shift in federalism: from federal design to state-based initiatives, from uniform policy to state-driven variation, and from congressional control to federal administrators' discretion. It marks an era, at the federal level, of executive-centered federalism that has profoundly transformed the way policy is made at the top and the way states connect with the federal government. The nation has moved from the federal government trying to incentivize state governments to implement federal policies to the federal government giving the states the freedom to exempt themselves from federal politics. In fact, many federal elected officials have made significant efforts to explore giving many of the most difficult administrative questions to the states instead of resolving the problems themselves.

Perhaps most important, waivers have become especially attractive because they provide a road for policy innovation in an era of gridlock. The more federal policymakers find themselves tied up in can't-pass-can't-win struggles over legislation, the more attractive it is to them to delegate to the states the ability to propose waivers and to give federal administrators the responsibility for approving or denying them. And the more frustrated with the federal impasse governors with ambitious ideas become—to expand, reform, or shrink designed-in-Washington programs—the more waivers have become a way to do what otherwise cannot be done. Governors have licensed a wide range of experiments, from Wisconsin's W2 to efforts in Massachusetts to provide universal health care. The Clinton administration, no fan in its early years of W2, became more enthusiastic about waivers to encourage states to experiment with health reform after its own health care plan collapsed. Moreover, waivers were integral to the Obama administration's strategy for rolling out health reform.

The waiver approach has become remarkably bipartisan, and it has won substantial political support from many experts in the field, for programs ranging from health care to environmental policy.[22] In an era of partisan polarization in Washington, the waiver process provides a way for states to carve out new strategies while allowing reluctant members of Congress to sidestep issues in which they would prefer not to be engaged. In an era of hyperpolarization, therefore, the waiver process provides a surprisingly versatile tool that allows state officials to do more of what they want while allowing federal officials to avoid the issues they do not want to deal with.[23]

Waivers thus not only are the tools for the states' laboratories of democracy but they have also created those laboratories, without which many of the policy advances of the last generation—in welfare, health, the environment, education, and other areas—simply would not have been possible. Indeed, as the states have won tremendous authority over the shape of national policy, they have become the purest manifestation in modern federalism of what Madison imagined.

Much of federal policy in the 1950s and the 1960s was designed to eliminate state variation. The waivers, in contrast, were designed not only to allow but also to create and feed state variations. It would have been impossible to pass many federal programs, from the environment to health, without giving the states a substantial role. Indeed, members of Congress have often pushed their coalitions as far as gridlock will allow and then simply passed off remaining decisions—often the critical administrative ones—to the states. Waivers have thus become the truly essential component of policy innovation in the era of political polarization—and the way in which Madison's factions, however mischievous, continue to thrive. The centralization in the Third Generation of Federalism has become the experimentation of the Fourth Generation, in ways that feed the continuing evolutionary cycles of federalism in the United States. Indeed, the major national policy initiatives in federalism since the 1980s are, for the most part, children of waivers launched by the states. Without the waivers, it is doubtful that the Californiazation of policy—imaginative and innovative state experiments, licensed by federal agencies under grants of authority from Congress—would ever have happened.

Ronald Reagan worried in 1982 that growing gridlock would paralyze federal policy. In making his case for helping Americans weighed down by rising interest rates and unemployment, he asked,

> Do we tell these Americans to give up hope, that their ship of state lies dead in the water because those entrusted with manning that ship can't agree on which sail to raise? We're within sight of the safe port of economic recovery. Do we make port or go aground on the shoals of selfishness, partisanship, and just plain bullheadedness?[24]

Waivers provided a way to steer around the shoals on which legislative proposals increasingly foundered. Both Republicans and Democrats came to embrace this strategy. Without waivers, there would have been no welfare reform. There would have been no Obamacare, on the one hand, or Trump administrative tactics to unwind it, on the other.

The waiver strategy has strong support. It has enabled presidents of both parties to advance their initiatives without the inconvenience of congressional gridlock. It has enabled some presidents to reverse the policies of their predecessors in far more streamlined fashion than would have otherwise been possible. It has allowed the states far more flexibility than previous programs allowed. And the waiver strategy multiplied the genuine experimental quality of state laboratories. It is little wonder that the movement has attracted such strong and bipartisan support.

But as the legal scholar Edward H. Stiglitz points out, the waiver movement has big downsides. Waivers, he argues, tend to worsen inequality.[25]

They create competition among the states, and state discretion over benefit levels tends to drive overall benefits down.[26] When the economy takes a turn for the worse, the states rarely have the resources to reinforce their safety nets, precisely at the time when program recipients need them most. This "undermines the core purpose of safety nets," Stiglitz notes, "and threatens increases in inequality."[27] At the least, by their very nature, waivers increase the differences among the states. More generally, Stiglitz worries, they tend to make the poor worse off.

Moreover, waivers introduce an enormous information difference between the states proposing them and the federal officials approving them. State officials tend to be especially good at framing their applications in broad and glowing terms, emphasizing the necessity of tailor-made tactics that fit the special needs of their state and their bold, experimental plans that make the ideas especially attractive. "A permissive posture on waivers," Stiglitz worries, "is likely to exacerbate the tendency of states to falsely represent their motivations for pursuing a waiver, which may in truth have ideological, partisan, or electoral roots."[28] Federal officials almost never have enough information to know how much of the case to believe—and that is before strong pressures to grant a waiver foreclose an extra close look at a state's application. The waiver sets up a classic case of information asymmetry, one of economists' classic worries in explaining why market failures occur—although in this case the problem would be a failure of federalism. Once granted, waivers are hard for the federal government to claw back. It would take powerful countervailing evidence to lead federal officials to withdraw their permission. Rarely do the states evaluate their waivers systematically enough to make that possible—even if federal officials were inclined to do so, which is rarely the case.

Finding the Balance

Having started down this road in the 1980s, federal and state governments cannot retreat from the embrace of waivers now. There is simply too much paralysis in the system to believe that policymakers could go back to pre-waiver days, and too much uncertainty about what works best to foreclose the chance for experimentation. States, not surprisingly, tend to declare victory before the results are in, and other states are often tempted to follow their ideas without knowing how well they actually work. Indiana's Healthy Indiana Plan 2.0, for example, promised to reduce costs and improve care by charging premiums to poor beneficiaries. But state officials discovered, not surprisingly, that it was much harder to implement the experiment than they had anticipated. Working out the kinks took longer than expected, and getting good evidence on results took even more time. But along the way Arizona, Ohio, and Kentucky proposed going down Indiana's road before the evidence was in.[29]

That, of course, is an old story. Much policy is driven by how well new ideas fit established ideologies, and by how well the promise of a proposal matches the goals that policymakers seek. The great attraction of waivers is that they can grow quickly on new ideas and established ideologies. But it's also deceptively easy for ideas to percolate and spread before evidence emerges about whether they work. W2, one of the most-studied policy innovations in history, was a program developed by a Republican governor dealing with a Democratic federal administration, and that partisan balance injected a note of skepticism and caution that slowed the pace of innovation in other states. However, the stronger the ideological or partisan push behind a proposal, the more pressure there is to move before the facts are in. When the Trump administration announced its effort to unwind Obamacare, there were Republican governors who looked to waivers to do just that, often with extremely clever and innovative plans, like Indiana's HIP 2.0, but without much evidence that they would work. The more partisan and ideological interests align, the easier it is for waivers to outstrip evidence.

The overall result is a deeply rooted risk that waivers will encourage more innovation in policy at the cost of greater inequality among the states. The *Wall Street Journal's* investigation of some states' efforts to roll back the Affordable Care Act found that "health-care coverage is increasingly determined by where you live."[30] The conservative waiver proposals, in fact, often provided a test of just how far a federal administration was prepared to roll back existing policy, just as liberal waiver proposals tested the boundaries for advancing policy.[31]

The Political Stakes in Californiazation

Inequality is being fueled not only by policy entrepreneurship in the states but also by the rising party polarization among the states.

In the states, there is no stronger bedrock of grassroots political power than the composition of state legislatures. From 1967 to 2017, the number of states with split party control dropped from eleven to three. Legislatures controlled by Republicans increased from eighteen to thirty-two, while legislatures controlled by the Democrats dropped from twenty to fourteen.[32] Each party got much better at redistricting, but there was no escaping the fundamental conclusion: party splits became deeper and sharper.

And what difference has this growing polarization made for the fundamental challenge of inequality? Especially in challenging Republicans, Democrats often portray themselves as the champions of programs to reduce income inequality. The Gini coefficients for income inequality in the American states, however, show a very different story (the higher the Gini coefficient, the greater the income inequality). It is no surprise, given the forces described in previous chapters, that income inequality in *every* state increased from 1969 to 2014. But in states where the Democrats controlled the state legislature in 2015, income inequality increased almost 30 percent more than the national average. In contrast, for state legislatures controlled by Republicans, the increase in income inequality was about 10 percent less than the national average (see table 9.1). Democrats champion strategies for reducing inequality, but states where the Democrats control the legislature have had bigger increases in inequality.

Researchers have found broader patterns afoot here. The economist James Galbraith found that "fourteen states with the largest increases in inequality after 1990 without exception voted for Hillary Clinton." On the other hand, "the seven states with the smallest increase in inequality, and ten of the lowest twelve, all voted for Donald Trump." Indeed, he concluded, "the correspondence of inequality-change to the election outcome is almost uncanny."[33]

What could explain this phenomenon? States with large enclaves of workers in areas like finance, government, technology, and insurance,

TABLE 9.1. Party Control of State Legislatures, 2015

Legislative control	Number of states	Gini: Change from 1969 to 2014	Gini: Compared with average
Democratic	11	0.1263	128.8%
Republican	30	0.0891	90.8
Split	8	0.0863	88.0
Average of all states	49	0.0981	

Source: National Conference of State Legislatures; James Galbraith, University of Texas Inequality Project, LBJ School of Public Affairs, http://utip.gov.utexas.edu.

Note: The legislature in Nebraska is nonpartisan.

along with large numbers of low-income individuals and immigrants, tend to vote Democratic. As incomes among the former group rise and incomes among the latter barely budge, it is little surprise that income inequality in these states has grown. States with large numbers of middle-class workers, especially those who once worked in factories, tend to be "rural, conservative, and white."[34] For middle-class voters, incomes stagnated during the Fourth Generation, after accounting for inflation—and that is after more middle-class families had acquired two wage-earners. Indeed, it was Trump's message that the economy was not treating those who worked hard fairly that helped win him the presidency.

And there's one further paradox lurking here. The more Democrats in these states promoted strategies aimed at redistributing income to the poor, the more likely they were to make the poor into middle-class voters and turn them into Republicans. On the other hand, the more Republicans championed programs to help the rich, the more they might have manufactured Democrats.

The portrait here of the Fourth Generation of Federalism is inescapable. An important cause—and effect—of the nation's political polarization is its increasing inequality. The widening political divide *within* the states produced growing economic and social divides *among* them. No gulf is more important than differences in income, and income inequality has certainly increased in the United States. But income inequality among the states shows very different patterns, and the gap between states led by different parties has created a wider gulf.

That in turn has created substantial barriers to the belief that entrepreneurial states can lead the other states out of the worsening trap of inequality. Some states have indeed set off on fresh, new, energetic courses. But there is growing reluctance in Washington to allow these states to set national policy indirectly, and there is growing pushback in many states to having changes—big, often expensive, and expansive changes—forced on them by other states. The result is an increasingly two-track system, with states heading down diverging roads. And within even the most aggressive states, the strategy has not reduced income inequality. From 1969 to 2014, income inequality increased more in California than in any other state save Connecticut (which only barely surpassed it). The waiver process has begun to break down as an engine of policy innovation, at least by the standards of California's environmental policies and Wisconsin's welfare reform. Through it all, inequality has remained stubborn and persistent.

The Californiazation of federalism, especially since the 1980s, was an important milestone with truly significant implications. At a time when crafting policy ideas in Washington increasingly proved difficult—even impossible—it was tempting to count on the states to lead the way. But relying on state leadership had large, significant, and often hidden implications. Turning to the states emphasized *pluribus* over *unum*, accelerating the disunity of the states of America. And sometimes divisions among the states popped up in unlikely places—like the surprisingly fierce struggle over the legalization of marijuana, which prompted a fresh battle over where to draw the lines between federal and state power.

Weed as a Force for Change

New Year's Day 2018 brought big bottlenecks to Californians, and this time it wasn't highway congestion. Happy shoppers stood in long lines—up to forty minutes in some places—to buy marijuana for recreational purposes. Anyone over the age of twenty-one could purchase pot for personal use and grow up to half a dozen plants at home. Comedians joked that people who used to meet secretly in back alleys to buy their weed now stood in public lines. Sometimes it was a family affair. Ellen Peter, a sixty-one-year old mom, brought her twenty-three-year-old son Bryce to a Santa Ana dispensary, glad not to have to sneak around to snag her supply. In Berkeley, Mayor Jesse Arreguin came to a ribbon-cutting ceremony to launch pot sales in his city.[35]

Buyers had a huge array of choices. There were buds and cigarettes as well as cannabis-infused popcorn, sushi, drinks, and candy, with "budtenders" giving advice about how consumers could best get their high. For those who did not want to make the trip to the pot store, home delivery services sprang up, promising to get weed to the front door as fast as a pizza. State investors sunk their cash into marijuana start-up companies, such as one run by gourmet chefs who promised to make marijuana consumption into a fine dining experience. The state's chefs eyed Oregon's Laurie Wolf, who had become nationally famous—in some circles—for her creativity in cooking (legally) with marijuana, even though legalization had taken only halting steps to date.[36]

Californians were determined to take a backseat to no one else, and analysts projected that the market would grow to $7 billion annually within two years. "This is the most populous state. We've popularized yoga. We've popularized sushi," explained Daniel Yi, a spokesman for a West Hollywood shop called MedMen. "I think this is going to move the needle like nothing else when it comes to the national conversation."[37]

The debate over recreational pot had grown out of efforts to legalize marijuana for medical purposes, to ease the pain of the chronically ill. Many patients with AIDS and cancer found that conventional treatments simply were ineffective, and the medical marijuana movement promised them relief. In 1996, California became the first state to approve the medical use of marijuana, and by the time California legalized recreational use of pot in 2018, twenty-nine other states and the District of Columbia had legalized the use of marijuana in some form, and eight states and the District had voted to allow recreational use. Citizens who did not live in one of these states could only vicariously take part in the conversation. For those states, federal law still held—and federal law still classified marijuana as a prohibited "Schedule 1" drug, along with heroin, cocaine, ecstasy, and LSD, because of a "high potential for abuse."

During the Obama administration, as states first began to legalize weed for recreational use, federal officials faced a dilemma: enforce federal laws and fight the rising tide of state legalization votes, or allow state votes to change policy despite federal law. They took the latter approach. Obama's deputy attorney general, James Cole, announced that the federal government would concentrate enforcement on keeping marijuana out of the hands of minors and reducing gang activity in distributing and selling the drug. Marijuana was still illegal under federal law, he reminded federal prosecutors, but he slyly suggested that they should exercise their prosecutorial discretion "on a case-by-case basis." Obama himself had said that the administration had "bigger fish to fry" than going after recreational drug users who were complying with state law.[38]

But by the time California legalized marijuana, a new administration was in place. For new US Attorney General Jeff Sessions, the big California celebrations were simply too much. He rejected the Cole memo and told federal prosecutors, "Given the Department's well-established general principles, previous nationwide guidance specific to marijuana enforcement is unnecessary and is rescinded, effective immediately."[39] The Obama-era guidance, Sessions said, "undermines the rule of law." But Sessions was careful not to order US attorneys to arrest pot buyers who were following their state's laws. Rather, he said, his policy "simply directs all US Attorneys to use previously established prosecutorial principles that provide them all the necessary tools to disrupt criminal organizations, tackle the growing drug crisis, and thwart violent crime across our country."[40]

But what had really changed? The Obama administration had suggested that US attorneys use their prosecutorial discretion by focusing on problems other than state-sanctioned marijuana use. The Trump administration suggested that US attorneys use their prosecutorial discretion to weaken criminal organizations and reduce violence. Colorado US Attorney Bob Troyer immediately said that was just what he was going to do—and that his office would not do anything differently. His plan, he announced, was "identifying and prosecuting those who create the greatest safety threats to our communities around the state."[41] For Troyer, that plan did not include going after those involved in Colorado's legal recreational pot industry. Meanwhile, Sessions encountered pushback even from senators of his own party. Sen. Lisa Murkowski (R-AK) described the new guidance as "disruptive to state regulatory regimes and regrettable."[42] Sen. Cory Gardner (R-CO) tweeted that "the Justice Department has trampled on the will of the voters in CO and other states."[43] Gardner pointed to a 2016 interview with then-candidate Trump. A reporter asked whether Trump's attorney general would "try to shut down marijuana legalization" if he were elected. Trump replied, "I think it should be up to the states, absolutely."[44]

Sessions had other ideas—but his gambit crumbled on the states' defiance. His announcement had little effect except to drive down the stock prices of some marijuana-related companies. The value of Canopy Growth Corporation stock, a Canadian company that had blossomed into one of the largest pot production companies, fell 19 percent. Even Scotts Miracle-Gro—a company that was best known for helping suburbanites make their lawns green but that was also building a big business in the fertilizer and lighting equipment used in cannabis production—saw its stock price fall 5.2 percent, then struggle to recover.

The battle over recreational pot grew directly out of the fundamental—and eternal—debate over who should make the most basic decisions in American government. Should such decisions be made by the states, in the spirit of experimentation and in pursuit of small government? Local opinions about what to do about pot varied widely across the country, and perhaps this was just one more example of where local views ought to rule. Or should the federal government set national policy, in the interest of preventing wide and often-confusing variations? Some employers prohibited the use of illegal drugs and subjected their workers to drug tests. Could an employee go on vacation to a state where the recreational use of marijuana was legal, enjoy the local delicacies, and return home to a state where it was illegal and be punished for testing positive for drug use? And did state decisions to legalize pot make the debate even more confusing in light of the federal prohibition of recreational use? What was the best way to deal with such variations in policy and practice around the country?

The conflict between federal and state-level policy was particularly tricky for individuals caught in the middle—such as veterans receiving care in facilities operated by the US Department of Veterans Affairs (VA). As a federal agency, the VA was governed by federal law even if the facility was in a state that legalized medical marijuana—and even if a vet could legally obtain pot from a state-licensed dispensary down the street. As pressure for allowing the medical use of marijuana for vets continued to build, the VA created a tiny crack in the door. VA medical providers could not recommend medical marijuana to patients, but the VA gave approval for physicians to talk with vets about how medical marijuana might affect their symptoms and interact with their other medications. Even though they could not make referrals to non-VA providers who could legally dispense marijuana, the VA allowed its health care providers to hint at its use. With this guidance, vets didn't risk losing their benefits, VA health care professionals didn't violate federal law, and the vets received some direction to the alternative treatments they sought.[45]

The explosive growth of the marijuana industry led to other legal issues—like the practical problem of what to do with all the cash coming into the booming industry. Here again, the conflict between federal prohibition and state legalization created a tough puzzle. Big banks wanted no part of this business, because federal regulators tended to look at large cash deposits from marijuana sales as money laundering subject to investigation. So even in states where pot was legal for recreational or medical uses, most entrepreneurs could not use banks to manage their cash or to process credit card transactions. This left these businesses no alternative but to deal in cash—billions of dollars of cash—and become tempting targets for thieves.

To help the budding businesses deal with the problem, a handful of small financial institutions began flaunting the federal prohibition. Partner Colorado, a Denver credit union, provided checking accounts for merchants in the weed business. It matched every deposit and withdrawal with precise details of the transaction to demonstrate that they were legal by state standards, in the hope that federal regulators would decide that an investigation was not worth the trouble. In other towns, armored car businesses sprang up and security companies offered to sell safes that could be bolted to the floor to prevent thieves from carting them away.

State Attorneys General in Partisan Conflict

The tension around marijuana legalization is hardly the first time that state and federal policies have come into conflict. Similar patterns of state nullification stretch back to the constitutional debates in Philadelphia. State assertions of their power to nullify federal policy on slavery nearly pulled the country apart in the nineteenth century, and the battle continued until nearly the end of the 1900s. The questions are always the same: How much uniformity do we want? How much variation can we take? And what happens when state initiatives stretch national policy toward two starkly opposing polls? The battle over pot raised, yet again, the puzzle over just how united the United States of America ought to be and where the decisions ought to be made.

Such battles have opened a new frontier for intergovernmental contests, and many are being decided in the courts. State attorneys general once worked more or less collaboratively on the legal issues they faced. But in the 2010s, the separate Republican and Democratic attorneys general associations began moving aggressively down different paths. To push back on what they saw as federal overreach, state attorneys general devised a combination of new strategies, joined along partisan lines and pushing in very different directions—but all under the flag of fighting for federalism.

During the Obama years, columnist Fred Barnes applauded Republican attorneys general as "the resistance" and as "a scourge of President Obama."[46] Barnes quoted Texas Attorney General Greg Abbott (who would later be governor) as saying, "What I really do for fun is I go into the office [and] sue the Obama administration." Many Republican attorneys general accused the Obama administration of "overreach." Dan Branch, a powerful Texas state legislator who unsuccessfully vied to replace Abbott as attorney general, promised that he would be even tougher. "The state AG's role is to use all the tools in the toolbox to push back. The independent authority of the AG's office is the platform to do it," he said. Abbott himself filed more than thirty lawsuits against the Obama administration, including seventeen against the EPA. He led the legal campaign by Republican attorneys general against Obamacare that resulted in the Supreme Court's decision on Medicaid.[47] The movement was so powerful, columnist George Will wrote, that "state attorneys general are revitalizing federalism."[48] They surely did not win all their battles, but they did slow many of the Obama initiatives.

The highest-profile victory of the Republican attorneys general was in their challenge to Obamacare, but they also won a major victory against the Obama administration's signature environmental policy initiative. The EPA issued a rule limiting the emission of pollution from oil- and coal-fired power plants, which substantially expanded federal regulation. A team of Republican attorneys general challenged the decision and argued that the EPA had to consider the costs of compliance in setting the standard. The new EPA rules, the Republicans argued, imposed unreasonable costs on power plants and intruded on private-sector operations; in 2015, the US Supreme Court agreed. In *Michigan v. EPA*, Justice Antonin Scalia, in writing for the majority, concluded that federal regulators had to weigh the costs of rules before imposing new standards. The law, Scalia pointed out, gave the EPA authority to regulate pollutants if "regulation is appropriate and necessary." The phrase, Scalia concluded, required the EPA to consider cost and, since the agency argued that it had not considered cost in imposing the rules, the 5–4 majority struck down the rule.[49]

Challenges to federal action by state attorneys general were not limited to Republicans. Democratic attorneys general joined together to fight Donald Trump's immigration policies, forcing the administration to repeatedly redraft its guidelines, and also collaborated to block the sale of 3-D printed guns. They fought in the courts against the Trump administration's effort to restrain the expansion of recreational marijuana. When President Trump announced a national emergency on the southern border, sixteen Democratic attorneys general—including California's—filed suit to stop it.

The state attorneys general once had a national association that worked collaboratively on issues of shared interest. But that association split into one for Democratic attorneys general and another for Republicans. The efforts carved out very different policy positions, but what they shared was a bottom-up effort by state officials to block federal action—and to split state action along partisan lines.[50]

In 2018, the noted attorney Elbert Lin concluded, "There is no question that the states have been suing the federal government (and the executive in particular) more often in recent years." Lin argued that there was real value in state litigation against federal action, but he worried "that state attorneys general are taking federalism's name in vain in support of the rise of state-led litigation against the federal government."[51]

State attorneys general, once mainly supporting players in state politics, had become truly major players not only in their capitals but also in national politics. On one level, that is perhaps surprising, because it transforms the law, often seen as a matter of rationality and balance, into a political battle. Of course, federalism, from its very first days, has always been harshly political, and partisans on all sides have always seized on any instrument at hand to advance the points of view. As conflicts grew during the Fourth Generation of Federalism and sometimes festered, it was therefore scarcely surprising that legal battles became more important and that state attorneys general took on a far greater role. As their role grew, so too did the partisan divisions between Republican and Democratic AGs, and with that polarization only grew.[52]

There is rich irony in the rising role of state attorneys general. In the First Generation of Federalism, the rule of law was created to draw clear boundaries between federal and state power, with the states standing (more or less) shoulder to shoulder to prevent an encroaching federal role. In this Fourth Generation, the states split along partisan lines, arguing when politically expedient against the policies of the opposing power in the White House—and often against each other. That trend has become even more important as the states have taken on a growing share of the burden for managing regulatory policy in the United States. In part, that is the story of Flint, where the decision of state environmental policy officials led to the contamination of the city's water.

But it is a much broader story as well. The states have responsibility for managing a wide array of environmental policy regulations promulgated by the federal government, ranging from air standards to the use of pesticides. State inspectors in Michigan checking a local grocery store found *Listeria* in hummus, a contamination that can lead to death in people with compromised immune systems and miscarriages in pregnant women, and their discovery led to a massive recall. Tennessee inspectors found *E. coli* in ground beef, which led to a recall of more than 100,000 pounds of the product. Both the federal and state governments have enacted labor laws that cover everything from the minimum wage to child labor. The most stringent laws apply in each state—and state officials play a leading role in enforcing them. The federal government defines weights and measures—what officially is known as a "pound," a "gallon," or an "inch"—but state inspectors are in charge of ensuring that the goods that Americans buy, whether filling up at a gas station or food shopping at a grocery store, deliver honest value. This intermingling of policymaking and policy administration, in fact, has become one of the great sleeper stories of federalism in the early years of the twenty-first century—the growth of a vast, though mainly invisible interdependence between the federal and state governments, often with big differences in how the states play their roles. This growing interdependence has not only shaped the overall level of equality in the system but also affects the health and safety of Americans everywhere—their trust in the products sold across the nation depends heavily on how individual state inspectors examine products in individual stores.

The result has been greater variability, more conflict, greater complexity, and even more ferocious battles over fundamental American values. The rise of state-based initiatives, to be sure, has fueled more state policy experimentation. Many of the greatest advances in environmental policy would not have occurred but for actions taken by the states. But many of the deepest and most polarizing struggles in American politics have developed along the fault lines of federalism, which have only been deepened and widened by the states. The states may have created the country in the first place and then, with Madison's pen, crafted its greatest constitutional inventions—the separation of powers and federalism—but they are now tugging on the threads that keep the country together. Congress has indeed become the broken branch, but it is also true that federalism—Madison's truly essential invention—has become a driver of deeper conflict and more inequality. The Fourth Generation of Federalism is a tale of states divided, with profound implications for the future of American democracy. The biggest puzzle is whether a new generation of federalism could remedy the problems that federalism has brought on itself.

10

Madison's Invention
Comes Undone

From its very first days, American federalism has been a profoundly messy affair. The colonies found unity in their eagerness to beat the British and in their great ideals, but they had far less consensus on how to deal with each other once they had won independence. They worried about how much centralization to bake into the Constitution (in the interest of framing a truly national policy) and how much decentralization (in the interest of securing the support of the states). They sought an answer just strong enough to pull the states together without generating so many problems that the tensions would drive them apart.

It was an exquisitely difficult challenge, to which Madison responded with his brilliant tactical answer: federalism. He and the other founders surely hoped that they were creating exciting new institutions and a new model for government that would endure through a long and prosperous history. However, their first priority was getting the nation onto its feet and ensuring that it didn't stumble.

Madison understood better than anyone just how fragile a system the founders had designed. In *Federalist 10*, he pointed to the mischiefs that factions, within and among the states, could cause. And even though he was a slave-owner himself, he knew that slavery was the flash point that could blow apart the new country's hard-won unity. He and the other founders have drawn fierce criticism over the years for choosing expediency over principle and allowing slavery to continue. We will never know if the situation in the country's first years left them any practical choice; allowing slavery to continue may have been the inescapable, awful cost of creating the new country. But there was a deep, foreboding sense in the hearts of many of the founders that sooner or later they would have to deal with the unspeakable legacy of the nation's founding—and they soon did, when it pushed the country into civil war.

After the Civil War's many bloody battles, the nation might have been forgiven for thinking that the biggest challenges to a United States that was truly united had been resolved. Yet that was anything but the case, because of two inescapable features of federalism.

First, federalism is not just a governing institution. It is a political cauldron into which Americans have always poured their toughest domestic problems—problems that federal officials want to address but cannot agree on how to go about it, or problems that federal officials want to duck and pass along to the states. The very flexibility of federalism has spawned a complex range of bargains and outcomes that, in turn, have allowed this enormously varied nation to bend and twist without ever breaking.

Second, federalism has long had both political and administrative components. On the political side, there has been the constant search for balance between the power of the federal government and the power of the states, as well as the periodic instinct to draw lines and clarify responsibilities. On the administrative side, state and local governments have been used as agents of federal policy, fueled by federal grants that have drawn them into partnerships without forcing them to surrender all control.

Federalism thus has always been about both very high strategy and very practical tactics—about seeking clear boundaries while creating programs that blur them. It has given Americans the confidence to press ahead through a host of problems without having to clearly confront them. It is this combination—and sometimes collision—of principle and pragmatism that lies at the core of the American state. That is why federalism was Madison's most essential invention. If, at any point, Americans had been required to draw a clear boundary between federal and state power, if they had been forced to choose clearly between federal and state administrative instruments, the tensions underlying the great American republic might well have fractured the uneasy compromises that have kept the disparate nation together, if sometimes only just barely.

It kept the nation together, that is, until the early twenty-first century, when Madison's great invention came undone. Federalism, instead of bridging the gaps in the polarization and inequality of the new century, fed and accelerated them. Instead of focusing on a relatively narrow range of contentious issues in domestic policy, federalism found itself drawn into virtually every one of them, and none proved more important than health policy. The states became both political decision-makers and administrative agents for Medicaid, a program vitally important to a growing number of Americans. As more Americans lived longer, more found themselves supported by Medicaid in nursing home care. And as the Medicaid-eligible population needed ever more expensive care, state budgets became dominated by a federal program that they once had had a chance to pass back to the feds. Then, when the Obama administration sought to expand health insurance to all Americans and the Republicans pushed back against the expansion of government, the states found themselves on the front lines of both the politics and the administration of the reform.

With the states playing a larger role in shaping national policy on this intensely polarizing issue, it was scarcely surprising that the gaps between the states grew. Once again, federalism was the obvious cauldron to throw these tough issues into—and not just these, but other divisive questions around the environment and transportation and education and corrections. But handling all these divisive questions at once was more than the federalism cauldron could hold, and the issues boiled over. The result was not only great differences among the states but also differences that increased over time, with the best states getting better and the worst states lagging farther behind. Madison's most essential invention had begun feeding America's worst pathology: inequality.

This has all happened largely out of public view because it has been the domain of practical rather than principled conflict, of gradual changes on the margins rather than epic battles. More and more frequently, every new domestic policy battle has been fought around the question of how much to nudge the boundaries of federalism one way or the other. The political scientist Aaron Wildavsky explains that Americans have a "romance with federalism," which has been more focused on providing the setting for an "armed truce between rival versions of the good life."[1] But this is not a World War I trench-style conflict that, in spite of big clashes and enormous casualties, does nothing to change the overall balance. Rather, this armed truce has subtly, in often unnoticed ways, shifted the notion of what the "good life" is, and who ought to decide it. The outcome has been greater inequality. The romance with federalism—the reverence for the founders and for American self-government—has made it easier to ignore the deep-seated conflicts lurking under the surface, but these conflicts have profoundly shaped the nation and its pursuit of the public interest. The rising tide of inequality and polarization has come to threaten the very republic that Madison and his colleagues worked so hard to build.

That threat leads to the fundamental question: Can we reset the balance to reduce inequality without eroding liberty in a way that Americans would find unacceptable? Decisions in the states might help drive this rising inequality, but Americans would never countenance undermining the states that, even divided, form America. Can we frame a Fifth Generation of Federalism?

The Fifth Generation of Federalism

The history of American federalism is a tale of rising tensions that sparked new versions of federalism, or generations, each characterized by new policies, politics, pressures, and players. The First Generation, based on the effort to define a separate sphere of state power through the Tenth Amendment, eroded after the Civil War. Political bargains rather than constitutional law drove federalism in the Second Generation. Some of those bargains were uneasy deals that advanced state power, especially through practices under the "separate but equal" banner; some of them helped fuel the rise of federal power, especially through the federal grant program during the Great Depression. In each case, it was the shifting balance, constantly recalibrated through political bargains, that defined federalism.

With the Supreme Court's ruling in *Brown*, the Third Generation arose, reasserting the rule of law to support the principle of equality. The Third Generation saw a dramatic increase in federal power, first through the rule of law and then through new federal grant programs designed to reinforce *Brown*'s momentum toward equality. It didn't take long, however, for aggressive state bargaining to reassert itself. The resulting Fourth Generation grew from a host of federal programs—most especially those administering health policy. But just as the Third Generation quickly evolved into the Fourth, it did not take long for the Fourth Generation to be destabilized by the rise of inequality and polarization. Federalism, the institution designed to bring balance to the country, had become a force fueling increasingly fierce warfare.

With this quickening pace of change and instability, the forces of history suggest the need for federalism's Fifth Generation. What will it look like? Will it be a new generation focused on greater devolution of power to the states? That could make for a more law-based collection of guarantees, like the First Generation and its foundation in the Tenth Amendment, or it could be a more state-based system, like the Second Generation and its adherence to the "separate but equal" doctrine. Or will it be a generation based on more centralization of power in the federal government, like the Third Generation and its pursuit of civil rights through the courts and through the vast sweep of the Great Society?

Over the course of the intellectual history of federalism, the nation has tended to go down one of two roads in answering these basic questions. William Riker captured one, Martha Derthick the other. But with the challenges that have arisen during the Fourth Generation, neither road will solve the core problems of inequality and polarization. The answer, as we shall see, depends on finding a new path.

Riker saw federalism as an accommodation to slavery and not, therefore, as an institution worth saving. Following Riker, one answer would be to push the states aside and build the Fifth Generation purely around federal primacy. But Americans have so much invested in their states that this step would be structurally difficult and politically unworkable. Moreover, the federal government has so much invested in state implementation of national policy that stepping away from federalism would require an increase in the federal bureaucracy so vast that any such plan would die before its ink could dry. Riker's course seems unworkable.

Derthick insisted that the states could provide the essential protection of American liberty, though that protection would prove increasingly feeble if federalism fueled further division. Derthick often pointed to *Federalist 51*, where Madison argued the virtues of a "compound republic" with "two distinct governments," federal and state. "The different governments will control each other, at the same time that each will be controlled by itself," he argued. With the rise of federal power in the twentieth century, along with the increasingly intertwined federal and state governments, Derthick worried that Madison's "double security" was eroding. She proposed sorting out functions between the federal government and the states to keep Madison's dream alive. So the nation could seek a new balance between federal and state power by drawing sharper lines between their functions, much as the founders anticipated with the Tenth Amendment.

We seem unlikely to take Derthick's course, however, since the 1960s federal policy has moved in precisely the opposite direction. Instead of clearly delineating which government should perform which function, the federal and state governments have become ever more interconnected. As the federal government's ambitions have grown, so too has the puzzle about how to develop the administrative mechanisms to make it happen. There has been no eagerness to grow the federal bureaucracy, nor even to define sharply what federal policy ought to be. It has become increasingly attractive, therefore, to blend federal and state responsibility, both to enlist the states as administrative agents and to disperse to them the political consequences of the big decisions in play. Quite simply, it has become impossible within American federalism to determine precisely just who really does what, let alone define who *should* do what. With the lines of responsibility so blurred, even policy experts sometimes get swallowed up in the system's complexity. In a 2009 CNN interview, the famed economist Arthur Laffer said, "If you like the Post Office and the Department of Motor Vehicles and you think they're run well, just wait till you see Medicare, Medicaid and health care done by the government."[2] But of course, Medicare, Medicaid, and health care *are* done by the government, and much of the work is done through complex partnerships between the levels of government. Medicaid in particular has become so complicated that even many state decision-makers are only vaguely aware of the details of its operations.

We are far past the point where sorting out functions and clarifying intergovernmental roles are possible. That reality has strangled Derthick's plan for rescuing the compound republic. On the other hand, the interweaving of federal and state government responsibility has made it impossible to accept Riker's argument that federalism has become obsolete.

Federalism has thus become ever more politically strained and administratively disorderly. Accountability—who is responsible for what—has become increasingly impossible to identify, let alone disentangle. The interconnections have become so deep that there is no going back, but they are so complex that the system is increasingly hard to manage. And despite the strong role of federal programs, state variations have grown to the point that the government citizens get depends increasingly on where they live. It might be tempting to try to solve this problem by making the intergovernmental boundaries neater, but as Wildavsky pointed out, the system is "disorderly, no doubt, but still without a viable alternative—neatness has never been a prime American virtue."[3]

Federalism's Struggle with Inequality

The political scientist Theodore Lowi concluded that looking at a nation's system of government is something like looking in a mirror. "Every regime ultimately creates a politics consonant with itself," he wrote.[4] If we have drifted into a world where accountability is elusive and federalism nurtures inequality, it must be, in some measure, because that is what we the people have decided we want—or that we have proven incapable of producing anything else. Despite the worries of many analysts in the 1960s that federalism was sick and dying, and even though it is drifting in a direction that Madison and the founders worried about but thought they had found a way to forestall, it remains alive and well. Indeed, American federalism not only survives but thrives, because it helps Americans get the government they want without forcing them to confront questions they would just as soon not answer.

In talking about French democracy, that country's famous post–World War II prime minister Charles de Gaulle famously complained, "No one can bring together a country that has 265 kinds of cheese." Only "the threat of danger," he argued, would bring unity.[5] The United States is not divided by cheese, but its fifty states can produce deep divisions, as Lowi pointed out. "In France there is no Republic of Brie or a Republic of Camembert or a Republic of Roquefort," he wrote, "but in the United States there is a Republic of Alabama, a Republic of New York, a Republic of California." The result is a strategy for allowing the interest of each section to flourish without imposing local regimes on everyone nationwide.[6] That strategy, however, is producing a republic that badly needs rescuing.

In the story of American federalism, patterns of federal and state dominance are regularly shifting, with continuous tension between the push toward equality and the pull of inequality. In the pursuit of equality, there has been the Fourteenth Amendment, the Progressive era, and the programs from the golden age of equality in the twentieth century—the New Deal, interstate highways, civil rights, the Great Society, and Medicaid. Most of these initiatives originated with and, at least in the early stages, were dominated by the federal government.

For the forces driving inequality, there has been slavery, the "separate but equal" doctrine, the rise of urbanization and the cities' struggle to provide basic services for many of their residents, and especially the constellation of issues encountered in those areas where inequality has risen since the end of the twentieth century (see figure 10.1).

The underlying story is this: American political institutions have fed both equality and inequality since the nation's founding. But most of the forces driving equality forward grew from Washington. Most of the forces dragging equality down grew from the states.

This fundamental divide is scarcely surprising. Reducing equality requires a nation to speak with one voice and act with resolute strength, and a harmonious and unified policy voice is unlikely to emerge from the often dissonant chords of the fifty states. Reducing equality must reckon with this special challenge in the United States, a country whose states long preceded the creation of the national government;

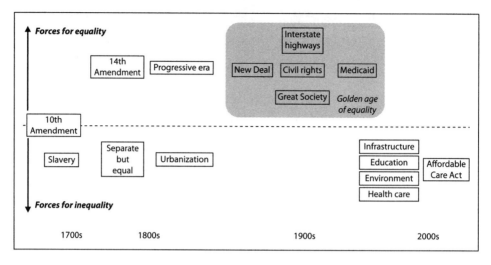

FIGURE 10.1. The flow of federalism.

whose states fought and won a revolution to champion that national government; but whose national government from the very beginning was constrained by the insistence of the states on an amendment asserting their primacy in anything they chose not to give to the national government.

Federalism, American-style, is thus not only a strategy of government but also, and more important, a study in Americans' historical unwillingness to surrender their authority and vision to a national government, even though that government has unquestionably grown in political power, financial leverage, and legal influence. When many of the world's most advanced nations created a vast array of social welfare programs after World War II, the United States took only partial steps in that direction, with the states sharing responsibility with the federal government for the expansion of government.[7] That strategy insulated the federal government from the charge that it was advancing socialism, but it also inevitably created a system far more complex in politics, policy, and management than any of the other Western democratic systems that traveled down the same road. That, in turn, built the foundation for the rising inequality of American life.

Since the 1970s, rising inequality has steadily if quietly increased the pressures on American federalism. The pressures have indeed been almost inaudible because the roots of inequality in federalism are difficult to see. But as we have explored in this book, those roots are more and more deeply entrenched. The consequences, both for trust in government and for the broader welfare of citizens, are large and significant. We must ask: Where is this movement heading? And could the implications of decentralization and inequality rise to the point of recentralizing decisions in Washington?

The Pressures on Federalism

These questions are vitally important because of a fundamental dilemma: state governments' responsibility for programs designed to reduce inequality is growing, but their capacity and will to advance these programs is shrinking. These trade-offs are important beyond issues around the conduct of federalism. How they are resolved could also dramatically shift the ideological balance of power between left-leaning big-government forces and right-leaning small-government cohorts. Four pressures are shaping the emerging debate.

America's Population Is Increasingly Concentrated

In 2018, the University of Virginia's Weldon Cooper Center took a careful look at the population projections for each state. Their finding was startling: by 2040, half of the nation's population will live in just eight states: California, Texas, Florida, New York, Pennsylvania, Georgia, Illinois, and North Carolina. Sixteen states will account for 70 percent of the population: in addition to the eight largest states, these eight additional population centers will include Ohio, Virginia, Michigan, New Jersey, Washington, Arizona, Massachusetts, and Colorado.[8] The country will be dominated by the West Coast (California and Washington), the East Coast, and three midcountry powerhouses (Texas, Arizona, and Colorado).

These trends will have dramatic repercussions. As the political analyst Norman Ornstein points out, half of the population will control 84 percent of the US Senate's 100 seats, and just 30 percent of the population—in the thirty-four remaining states—will control 68 percent of the Senate seats. In these thirty-four states, the population will be more rural, older, whiter, and more male.[9] Moreover, these states are likely to be more polarized than they already are, as part of the movement that the journalist Bill Bishop calls "the big sort": a tendency for like-minded people to cluster together. In this case, that tendency is likely to lead to even deeper divisions in the country.[10]

The implications for federalism and inequality are enormous. The states are likely to become even more deeply divided, and there will be large majorities in the Senate aligned with the interests of smaller states. One of the most important reasons why the founders invented their version of federalism, of course, was to preserve political balance in constructing the new Congress. With a large and growing gulf between the larger and smaller states, Madison's delicate congressional balance could well be lost, and that could make it even harder to craft legislation that a majority can embrace. The fastest-growing states, facing even more difficulty getting national support to help them meet the challenges of rapid growth, are more likely to be on their own. Their rapid expansion will generate more tax revenue, but it will be difficult for them to invest fast enough in the government programs that a rapidly growing population will require. On the other hand, the slowest-growing states will face the challenge of supporting basic services with a tax base that lags behind other states—or may even be shrinking. That could well increase inequality even further; newer schools in fast-growing regions, for example, will benefit from an expanding tax base, while existing schools in shrinking communities struggle to catch up. The same problem seems certain to be replicated with the nation's infrastructure and environmental policies—in fact, in any area in which citizens are concerned.

These forces may not only deepen the inequality among the states but also reinforce political tensions in ways that will be difficult to overcome. One strategy to counter them would be old-fashioned log-rolling: small states supporting programs that benefit large states in exchange for help on their own needs. That could work for distributive policies that sprinkle money around broadly, like the model of the interstate highway system. But that strategy would require enough tax money, and there is little support now for funding even a trickle of new investment. All of the projections for the coming generation suggest that the budget will be even tighter, especially with the rising costs of entitlements and a tax base struggling to keep up.[11] Redistribution of money from older, whiter, smaller states to younger, more diverse, larger states could prove a very tall order indeed. The result is likely to be even sharper tensions among the states.

America's Aging Population Will Squeeze the Federal Budget

The aging of the nation's population is a familiar story. By 2060, almost 95 million Americans—nearly one in four—will be over the age of sixty-five. The number of people over the age of eighty-five is projected to triple—and those over the age of one hundred will grow more than six-fold.[12] The aging population is quickly driving up federal spending for older Americans as well. The two biggest federal programs for the elderly—Social Security and Medicare—accounted for 7.8 percent of GDP in 2018. The Congressional Budget Office projects that this figure will grow to 11 percent by 2048 (assuming no reductions in benefits), principally because of the aging population. If the federal budget as a share of the economy stays constant, that would mean that these two programs alone would grow from 38 percent to 53 percent of the entire federal budget.[13] By concentrating the expenditures of the federal government on national defense and programs for the elderly, that shift would inevitably crowd out programs to even out the differences between society's rich and poor, leaving more of the burden to the states, which will have an increasingly difficult time in meeting it.

Budget Pressures on the States Widen the Inequality Gap

The pressures of an aging population will squeeze state budgets as well, leaving them with few prospects for filling in the gap that the federal government cannot. In its long-range projections of state government finances, the US Government Accountability Office (GAO) has concluded that, without a major shift in state budgets, state governments will run in the red until at least the year 2064—and possibly beyond, depending on the long-term trends in demographics, the economy, and state policy choices. The upshot is that not only will state governments have no extra money to deal with income inequality, but the pressures of an aging population—especially spending for Medicaid and pensions for retired government employees—will continue to put enormous pressure on state budgets. The states, quite simply, will not be able to make good on the promises already made for pensions, deal with the rising costs of Medicaid, balance their budgets as required by their constitutions, *and* address the many challenges that flow from the increasing gap between the rich and the poor. In fact, the gap between states with well-run and worse-off pensions systems is large and growing, and that is certain to increase the pressures on many states' budgets as well as increase the gap between them.[14]

One strategy to address income inequality would be to focus on programs for kids. The percentage of children living in poverty (18 percent) is twice the level for seniors (9 percent). Nevertheless, the Urban Institute projected in 2018 that federal spending on programs designed for children is likely to drop by one-fourth by 2028, from 9 percent to 6.9 percent of the federal budget. Meanwhile, spending for seniors will increase, from 45 to 50 percent of the budget.[15] With federal spending for redistributive programs shrinking and irresistible pressures to spend on seniors growing, the burden of redistributive programs—addressing the needs of the poor—is shifting to the states. And with state budgets in near-paralysis for the coming generations, there is little prospect that they will be able to shrink the gap.

Polarization Is Locking Inequality into Place

State legislatures are polarized—and are becoming more so. The political scientists Boris Shor and Nolan McCarty have found that polarization is very high in most states, concluding: "About half the states are even more polarized than Congress—which is saying a lot." Moreover, polarization has increased over time, and some states—California, Colorado, and Nebraska—are polarizing especially quickly.[16] Much of this polarization is the direct product of gerrymandering, as those in power have become ever more clever in drawing state legislative boundaries that benefit their party. And this skill has carried over to district-drawing for the US House of Representatives, which is done by state legislatures and which has increased polarization in Congress as well. It's a case of water flowing uphill—growing polarization in the states has fed greater polarization in Washington. But even more fundamentally, polarization is increasing because of an increasing tendency of citizens to sort themselves into like-minded communities, as Bishop found. That, in turn, has reinforced the instinct of state policymakers, armed with ever more sophisticated computer models, to reinforce existing enclaves and make existing legislative boundaries, for both state legislators and members of Congress, into ever-safer seats.

The National Conference of State Legislatures found that some strategies can help states deal with the effects of polarization, including constitutional provisions, such as requiring a single subject for bills, limited sessions, and balanced-budget requirements; a nonpartisan staff for key legislative organizations; and "a determination to get things done," coupled with strong leadership by governors and key legislators. "We're not DC" can sometimes prove an effective rallying call.[17]

Another idea has been to force a less partisan strategy for drawing legislative boundaries that is focused less on gerrymandering lines to create safe legislative seats and that relies more on nonpartisan commissions. The more Americans decide they want to live among other Americans with whom they agree, however, the harder it is to draw legislative boundaries to address the underlying polarization. Indeed, this cuts to the heart of a problem that has plagued federalism since its very start. Most of the boundaries of the original thirteen states came from colonial days and were the product of natural barriers, especially rivers, and charters issued by the British king. When Delaware, Maryland, and Pennsylvania squabbled over confusing boundaries as laid out in their charters, two surveyors, Charles Mason and Jeremiah Dixon, laid out the famous Mason-Dixon Line. The Potomac River set the boundary between

Virginia and Maryland, so that when it came to carving out land for the new capital city, both states gave up a bit (though in the end Maryland gave up what would constitute the District of Columbia). The border between Texas and New Mexico emerged from the Compromise of 1850, and most of the West was carved up by straight lines on the map. None of these boundaries did a very good job at the time of responding to the big policy issues at play, and the story since has been one of big policy problems gradually emerging that almost never fit well with the jurisdictions trying to solve them. State identity lacks real state leverage over many policy issues.

The more social forces drive the unquestionably increasing polarization of the states and this polarization infects polarization in Washington, the harder it is to uproot. A sustained attack on inequality requires extraordinary consensus, but growing polarization makes that consensus almost impossible.

Is Centralized Power the Answer?

In the history of American federalism, the strongest policies to deal with inequality, both legal and administrative, have come from the federal government. The administrative steps to carry out these federal policies have tended to flow to the states, because Americans have always resisted creating a federal government large and powerful enough to push forward these policies on its own. But as more responsibility has come to rest with the states, the seeds of inequality have flourished anew. Now, with polarization increasingly woven into this cycle, it has become harder for the federal government to act, since the graying of the population is squeezing the budget and polarized policymaking is making consensus elusive. As a result, the key decisions not only about carrying out policy but also about what policy ought to be are flowing to the states. And as has been the case since the beginning of the republic, putting such responsibility on the states only increases inequality.

The interplay of these four forces—the increasing geographic concentration of the population, the aging of the population, the budget pressures on the federal government and especially on the states, and the growing polarization of the states—has locked inequality into place and made it harder to close the gap. The government a citizen gets depends on the state where the citizen lives. Getting a different government most often means moving to a different state—and those at the bottom of the inequality scale have the fewest options for finding new jobs or homes.

Add to these forces the nationalization of politics and political conflict. The political scientist Daniel Hopkins argues that politics has become increasingly driven by the big issues framed and debated in Washington.[18] State politics is a reflection of national clashes, often with a different cast of characters but rarely with fresh ideas about how to resolve them. As Lee Drutman concludes, "America has local political institutions but nationalized politics. This is a problem."[19] The United States, he argues, is more and more united—in shared conflicts. Reformers once called for parties that stood for clear ideas that gave voters equally clear choices. In the polarized world of the twenty-first century, they have gotten their wish. The result, however, has been sharper divisions, driven from the top.

There is a deep debate about whether the American polity—indeed, the broader American social fabric—has unraveled. Hopkins points to the squeezing out of local shops by homogenized superstores like Walmart and Home Depot. "Just as an Egg McMuffin is the same in every McDonald's, America's two major political parties are increasingly perceived to offer the same choices throughout the country," he argues.[20] The noted journalist James Fallows, on the other hand, believes that there might be sharp partisan divisions at the national level, but local communities have a surprising amount of social glue. He flew around the country with his wife, Deb, visiting a wide range of communities. There are, he concluded after his 54,000-mile adventure, "eleven signs a city will succeed," including a local belief that "divisive national politics seem a distant concern," "they have a downtown," and "they have craft breweries."[21] All eleven of Fallows's findings point to the vibrant civic life of strong communities that live happily quite apart from the battles of national polarization. Tocqueville never sampled an Egg McMuffin, but he surely would have recognized the fundamental debate about America's national character.

American politics is thus enmeshed in a deep debate: about whether strong national forces are homogenizing the country and driving the pressures of polarization into the states; or whether local communities are developing their own distinctive character below the national political hurricane, though at the risk of further driving the nation apart. This debate frames Madison's dilemma even more sharply. Madison was not only a leader of great vision but also an architect of balance. His instinct was not to push on one polar side or the other but rather to create institutions that could produce a fine, changing balance among competing forces. That was his strategy for organizing the power of the federal government, with countervailing branches holding each in check. It was also his plan for dealing with the even more difficult problem of gluing the thirteen colonies into a single nation.

None of the colonies was about to surrender its autonomy to the others—or to a national government that could overrule what were often widely different values. As the conservative political economist William Niskanen put it in his reflection on Madison's argument for the American compound republic,

> The most promising means to sustain the constitution of a compound republic is to make the federal government the guarantor of individual rights against an abuse of power by the states and to make the state governments the guarantor of those rights against an abuse of power by the federal government.[22]

That is the core of America's treacherous balancing act, and it has great merit. But it also brings with it two great challenges. One is deciding just where the boundaries between federal and state power lie. What this book makes clear is that those boundaries have never been stable and that, in fact, the process of setting them has always been full of conflict. The other challenge is managing whatever boundaries do get defined. It is one thing to argue for where a fence ought to go. It is quite another to lay it out, build it, and maintain it. The underlying story of American federalism is that its administrative dimensions have tended to bring its principles to life and define what those principles actually mean.

It is one thing to point to the virtues of America's compound republic. But it is quite another to define and maintain it. And since this compound republic is in deep trouble, rescuing the republic requires both political and administrative dimensions. Franklin was right about the difficulty of keeping the republic that the founders had created.

There are many ways to celebrate the genius of Madison's compound republic—and to advance its virtues into the turmoil of the twenty-first century. His formulation broke the deadlock that had immobilized the new country during the era of the Articles of Confederation. The strategy for balancing federal and state powers made it possible for the states to ratify the Constitution. The compound republic has provided vast elasticity in the generations since, allowing the country to stretch almost to the breaking point during the Civil War, to produce an administrative solution for responding to the Great Depression, to survive the traumatic civil rights revolution, and to evolve from horses and buggies to interstate highways to private companies selling tourist seats on rockets into space.

It is important to recognize just how durable the founders' inventions have been. The country has had just one republic in the time that the French have had five, the British have joined and then renounced union with Europe, and the Germans have moved from the Weimar Republic through Nazi rule and the division of the country after World War II, to a reunited Germany after the fall of the Berlin Wall. The guiding hand of the US Constitution has truly been one of the most remarkable inventions of the human era. It has demonstrated vast capacity to endure, to promote basic values, and to bend without breaking under the pressure of enormous challenges.

The foundation of this compound republic has been Madison's genius for creating self-correcting forces to deal with the inescapable frictions of federalism. Some of these self-correcting forces are hard-wired into the basic document, including the relatively limited specification of federal domestic responsibilities. If federal power threatened individual liberty, the states had the power to push back, through the Tenth Amendment and all of its elements. If the states threatened minority rights, the federal government had its own armaments, especially since the ratification of the Fourteenth Amendment. The system would adjust over time to an equilibrium of constitutional and political balance. That was the theory.

Over time, however, the balance in the system has unquestionably moved toward federal dominance in policymaking but growing state dominance in policy administration. That shift, in turn, has challenged the pursuit of equality, all in the shadow of the Tenth Amendment. In a 1976 decision, *National League of Cities v. Usery*, the US Supreme Court held that the "traditional governmental functions" of state and local governments were exempt from federal regulations.[23] That ruling was in keeping with the long efforts, dating back to the nation's founding, to draw clear boundaries between the federal government's power and the autonomy of state and local governments; in *Usery*, the Court sided with those seeking a clear line. A decade later, however, in *Garcia v. San Antonio Metropolitan Transit Authority*, the Court backed away from that position.[24] The San Antonio Metropolitan Transit Authority relied on *Usery* and refused to pay its employees overtime pay, as federal regulations required of most employers. Joe Garcia, along with other Transit Authority employees, countered that this was unfair and inconsistent with the law, and they took the Authority to court. The lower court invoked *Usery* and sided with the Transit Authority, concluding that mass transit was not a "traditional government function." But the US Supreme Court held in Garcia's favor, concluding that there really was no such thing as a "traditional" (as opposed to a "nontraditional") government function. What governments do is what they do, after all. In a 5–4 vote, the Court ruled in favor of Garcia and concluded that laws passed by Congress could extend to state and local governments as well.

In a series of decisions that followed, the Court upheld the growing reach of congressional legislation and federal regulations into state and local governments. Scholars continued to debate whether the Tenth Amendment had crawled into a corner to die or whether it retained rhetorical power, in the abstract, to push back against federal power. But the basic principle of federal primacy seemed more firmly established than ever. The Tenth Amendment reserved to the states the powers that the Constitution did not otherwise give the federal government, but federal policymakers read the Constitution as giving them the power that the Congress decided was theirs. As a result, the federal government's role became ever more solidified.

But two factors pushed back against this point of law. One was that the states took on a larger role as administrative agents of federal policy. To a large degree, federal policy became whatever state governments made it. The other factor was that some states took advantage of their role to push back not only against the federal government but also against other states that sought to expand government's role. That, in turn, broke down what had seemed to be a growing consensus about equality in the American system. In practice, it also increased inequality in the system.

These counterpressures have broken down the self-correcting forces in the system. The federal government has continued to set bold and ambitious national standards, but it has increasingly left the administration of details to the states. In the 1960s, despite widespread struggles over civil rights and violence in the cities, a national consensus about equality showed signs of emerging. But as has always been the case throughout America's history, no policy—or progress—is ever stable because the federal government is unable on its own to make it stick, and also because the underlying policy implementation rests so heavily on the wide differences in capacity, energy, enthusiasm, and support among the states. That was the deal that Madison made to get the young nation to its feet. But inequality has flourished in its wake.

Americans simultaneously harbor demands for redistribution of income in the pursuit of equality but withdraw authority from those who have to make good on promises to do so. Wildavsky noted in 1984: "Federalism is barely possible without a semblance of a center. Centralization without a center is a contradiction in terms."[25] There is nothing fundamentally new in that anomaly. It has been the story of the compound republic from the very beginning. But Wildavsky noticed that the frictions between Americans' aspirations and the government they would tolerate and build were growing. At the same time, and more subtly, these frictions have widened the gap and weakened the institutions that, in the past, had always addressed the big differences that are inevitable in a country as vast and diverse as the not-so-United States of America.

Inequality grew, and so too did distrust in government. The result was the emergence of a quiet yet increasingly dire crisis for American democracy, rooted in the very innovation that had originally created it and then sustained it.

Madison's essential invention to create the American republic thus has sailed into a deepening dilemma: growing inequality and polarization, which threaten the republic; and diminishing chances that the periodic, self-correcting swings in federalism will provide an answer. Americans have long tolerated differences—and inequalities—as the cost of state autonomy and individual liberty. Those costs have now become crippling, and Madison's great invention has come undone. Federalism no longer functions as originally envisioned, whether as a relief valve for the mischiefs of faction or as a mechanism to experiment with policy before building a national consensus to shrink the nation's sprawling differences. The founders knew very well that if they pressed any harder on the early tensions at the nation's core, they risked splitting the country before it could get started. They also knew very well the big risks they were taking with the inventions they made. Federalism has proved remarkably pliable and resilient, through tremendous pressures, over the nation's remarkable life. But in the twenty-first century, it's impossible to escape the stark conclusion that federalism just doesn't work well any longer.

The puzzle is whether Hamilton's great alternative offers a solution. We will turn to that in the book's conclusion.

11

Hamilton's Solution to Madison's Dilemma

Madison and the other founders had little choice but to begin with the states as the building blocks for the new nation. They had, after all, just won a surprising victory against the world's most powerful army. Unity for that effort had not come easily, and there was no chance of keeping the new country together in the postwar years without giving the states a prominent role. Allowing the states to spin back into separate orbits—or, worse, to break into factions—would have spelled a quick death to the newly united states. The invention of federalism provided the essential ingredient to create the nation: it brought enough unity to give the country identity while it created a relief valve to prevent the "mischiefs of faction" from producing ruin.

But over the course of the nation's history, disunity was never far away. Federalism worked well enough to prevent centrifugal forces from spinning the country apart, but never well enough to solve the problems of inequality in any stable or permanent way. Those forces grew into the twenty-first century with fierce cross-pressures that seriously challenged Madison's great invention.

Madison's Dilemma

Madison wanted, of course, to build a government for the ages, but supreme tactician that he was, he worried first about creating a constitution that could win approval from the disparate states. Hamilton, of course, was just as determined to win ratification of the Constitution. He had fought alongside Washington during the war for independence, and he joined the close partnership with Madison and Jay to write *The Federalist Papers*. But as the new nation's foremost strategist, he focused singularly on the policy problems that it needed to solve, not the political boundaries within which it needed to solve them. His concern was building what the nation needed not only to survive but also to thrive in the long run. The states, for Hamilton, were instruments of (and sometimes impediments to) this broader national vision.

So, as the Fourth Generation of Federalism has created deep fissures, the competing insights of these two founders frame the fundamental choice: whether to redefine the role of the states in order to reduce inequality and polarization, in keeping with Madison's vision, or craft an alternative way of solving the nation's problems using the states as key players but not ultimate deciders, in keeping with Hamilton' view.

Madison's insight into balancing political power remains as keen as it ever was, but his boundary-based strategy has become far less effective. The boundaries of the American republic were never a good match for the problems it was trying to solve. Tiny Rhode Island and Delaware have always had challenges that spilled over to adjacent states. The big ports were often far from farms and plantations, so it was hard to build the infrastructure needed to connect them across state boundaries. Great cities like Philadelphia and Boston (and later New York, Chicago, Los Angeles, and Phoenix) stirred up great envy from other urban areas, and rural areas have never trusted any of the cities. But as the country waded deeper into the Fourth Generation of Federalism, its problems became broader and ever more wrapped up in the increasingly intractable problems of inequality. States were the wrong scale at which to attack these problems, and the challenges of inequality often swept over their borders. Not only could the states not adequately attack the issues of inequality, but their decisions also tended to aggravate inequality and widen the gap.

Madison and Hamilton agreed that a too-weak federal government would inevitably cause problems. In *Federalist 19*, Madison considered Germany, whose subnational governments were so strong that the country was left with "a feeble and precarious Union" and ran the risk of functioning as a "disjointed machine" on the verge of "falling entirely to pieces." Hamilton always campaigned for a larger, more robust national government than others—most notably Thomas Jefferson, with his agrarian roots—were ever prepared to accept. In his monumental 1790 analysis, *Report Relative to a Provision for the Support of Public Credit*, Hamilton argued the need for the federal government to drive the national economy, starting with a system of borrowing to support important national priorities. Since Madison's and Hamilton's competing ideas for the federal government staked out the opposing poles of the national debate, Hamilton's vision is a good place to start looking for clues as we consider how to deal with the costs of Madison's great invention.

Hamilton's Strategy

Hamilton was perhaps the strongest champion among the nation's founders of a powerful, robust central government. That position, of course, got him into endless trouble (as did his considerable passion for ideas, his pride, and his considerable number of female friends, even after his marriage to Eliza). Hamilton, the historian Richard Brookhiser concludes, had "an all-pervading ardor."[1] But he had no ardor for weak government in general, and for the Articles of Confederation in particular. When he criticized it in *Federalist 22* for "the intrinsic feebleness of its structure," he was just getting warmed up. The Articles, he said, was "one of the most execrable forms of government that human infatuation ever contrived." For Hamilton, liberty rested "on the solid basis of THE CONSENT OF THE PEOPLE. The streams of national power ought to flow immediately from that pure, original fountain of all legitimate authority." And the solutions for what the people needed ought to flow, he argued, from the engine of government best positioned to deal with their most fundamental needs: the federal government. As his biographer Ron Chernow observed, "Hamilton engineered the transition to a postwar political culture that valued sound and efficient government as the most reliable custodian of liberty."[2]

On that, Hamilton was in sync with his mentor, George Washington, who laid out four basic principles the new nation needed if it was to be great: a strong federal government to bring the states together, repayment of the substantial debt accumulated to fight the war, a new army and navy to preserve liberty, and true harmony among the country's new citizens.[3] Hamilton had little respect for the role of the states as the country's building blocks. He once called for breaking up the larger states into smaller ones, a plan that Chernow calls "a crackpot scheme," as indeed it was.[4] Hamilton believed that fragmentation of power would forever deny America its chance at greatness, that putting too much power into the hands of the states would lead to dangerous disintegration, and that only a strong and vibrant federal government would ensure the place in the world order that the country deserved—and had earned.

Hamilton's argument was not a brief for tyranny or an unaccountable government. He fervently believed in a democratic government strictly under the control of the people. But he did not believe that the states could ever shape the country its destiny warranted.

Indeed, his philosophy led to his singular contribution to American federalism. Madison might have constructed the instrument of balance, but Hamilton recognized the powerful forces that would define where the balance would fall. Hamilton believed that the heavy weight of the state debt incurred from fighting the Revolutionary War would handicap the new nation, perhaps fatally, and that it would prevent strong commerce among the states. The only solution, he believed, was having the federal government assume that debt, and indeed, the federal government's eventual assumption of that debt would prove essential in keeping Madison's invention afloat.

Among the founders, it was Hamilton who most clearly saw the inevitable role that the federal government would need to play. And it was Hamilton who most clearly would have seen the necessity today of recentralizing power in the federal government. If he were to survey the prospect of a country sliding into increasing inequality and polarization, he surely would have been deeply worried. It is a problem he would have recognized as rooted in the power of the states, and it certainly is one that he would have insisted that the nation address and that the federal government take the reins in solving. He was no spendthrift. As secretary of the treasury, he felt the enormous weight of stabilizing the new country's finances and being careful about overstretching them, so he surely would not have favored throwing money at the problem of inequality in an effort to solve it. But neither would he have counseled patience with the states as they wrestled with it.

The cycles of federalism are increasing in speed through new generations, the federal and state roles are becoming increasingly intertwined, and the political and administrative dimensions are ever more inseparable. That has set the system up for a new Fifth Generation of Federalism, one that requires a rebalancing of the system, a more Hamiltonian solution to Madison's dilemma. That challenge frames three big questions.

First, in which areas of policy should the federal government invest its most intense energy—and cash—to redress the problems of inequality? The crucial frontiers for the twenty-first century are certain to be health care and climate policies. As Americans live longer and advanced health care offers more options, costs will surely rise. Because the American health care system involves a complex partnership between government and private insurers, paying these costs will bring tougher policy choices about just who ought to pay for what. And because government's responsibility is divided awkwardly between the federal government and the states, the debate over how to allocate government's responsibility in health care is even more difficult. The same sets of issues apply to climate policy, where government and the private sector share uneasily the question of who ought to be most responsible for what—and how much responsibility the federal government ought to share with the states—on issues ranging from reducing air pollution to ensuring water quality to incentivizing renewable energy. Shared governmental responsibility in these areas has not only led to big differences

among the states but also to growing differences over time. Huge variations will never produce stable politics or effective policy.

Second, what control should the federal government have over the
grant money that it chooses to spend, through the states, on these issues?
Americans have never been satisfied with allowing the federal government to dictate policy decisions in the states. Indeed, the great invention
of federal grants, in both land and money, allowed the federal government
to shape state and local policies without dictating their actions. Through
incentives, the federal government sculpted the contours of policy without having to wield a mallet and chisel. The federal grant program has
proven to be a remarkably resilient and effective instrument, but it is also
a very expensive one. It requires supplying enough inducements to encourage the states to do what they otherwise would not have done. The
harder the job is to do, the larger the inducements need to be. Given the
tight budgets that all American governments face in the coming decades,
that strategy might well cost more than the country decides it can afford.
Moreover, the grant strategies of the Fourth Generation have only led
to widening gaps, so reversing that trend would require a heavier hand
in federal grants than federalism has seen.

Third, how should the federal government regulate the vastly complex
relationships between itself and the states—and among the states? The
scarcer money becomes, the more tempting it is to replace cash with
rules. The history of the regulatory regime since the 1960s, however, is
that more rules only produce more gaming among the players and less
accountability for results. Where national standards are important—on
issues ranging from water quality to public health—state-based experimentation can lead the way. It is one thing, however, to learn which experiments work best. It is quite another to replicate the results outside
any single state's lab. It is likewise tempting to litigate these battles in the
courts, and federal courts have become increasingly flexible in granting
hearings to individuals arguing mistreatment at the hands of the states.

Meanwhile, the courts have ordered state and local jails to provide
methadone to prisoners struggling with addiction, more sleep for prisoners facing noisy cells, and gender confirmation surgery. As the courts

have expanded their reach, however, they have also become forums for increasing political polarization in the country. Forums at one level provide remedies for problems that develop at other levels, but the greater the breakdown of Madison's other great invention, the Congress, the more likely it becomes that interests will push their way onto court dockets. As long as the separation-of-powers system remains viable and polarization encourages venue-shopping to resolve public policy problems, this trend is likely to continue. Conservatives and liberals once differed in their willingness to use federal power to push back on state policies they opposed. That has radically changed, with conservatives and liberals joined in their eagerness to use federal power to push back on state decisions—and differing only in *which* state actions they seek to block. Moreover, the US Supreme Court has become increasingly willing to allow partisans in state legislatures to use their power to draw legislative districts in distinctly partisan ways. That has fueled the eagerness of partisans to push policy agendas in the states, from immigration to abortion, in an effort to change national policy from the state capitals. All of these efforts have only fueled polarization, precisely as Madison feared but, ironically, through the very institution of federalism he had hoped would prevent it.

Madison's invention depended on the states, which have always operated within their own boundaries, but those boundaries no longer match society's problems. Moreover, the frictions caused by attacking problems within those boundaries have only created a new and increasingly dangerous collection of pathologies.

That points to the need for shifting the balance in federalism toward Hamilton's vision of America. Hamilton's great insight was that the country might have been formed from the states, but that the federal government, not the states, needed to be the prime actor if the country was to advance. Hamilton's grand strategy depended on a federal approach to problem-solving. Madison's pragmatic tactics, on the other hand, depended on a state-based, boundary-constrained approach. The growing tensions within Madison's approach, especially in the Fourth Generation of Federalism, build the case for rebalancing the system.

A Hamiltonian solution to Madison's modern dilemmas would have three dimensions.

First, it would transform the role of federal grants by focusing intergovernmental aid primarily on inequality-busting initiatives. Over the course of the nation's history, the repeated pattern is that the prime driver of redistributive policies has been the federal government. That has been true for regulatory action, for civil rights, and for grant programs, especially in health care. The more the states have driven policy decisions, the more disparities between them have developed, ranging from acceptance of slavery before the Civil War to reluctant implementation of the Affordable Care Act in the 2010s. Stronger national action to reduce inequality, both within and between the states, would require a larger federal role in shaping the Fifth Generation of Federalism.

A larger federal role raises a host of political problems, of course. The increase in inequality between the states flows from the states' policymaking role, which provides for local discretion as a pushback against federal power. But a strong federal policymaking role would not necessarily enfeeble the states. It could flow from a fundamental shift in federal strategy as the federal government focuses its regulatory authority, as well as its grant money, on programs with a redistributive twist, and then relies on state and local governments as administrative agents. States could tailor their actions to fit federal policy to state and local conditions, while the federal cash could ensure that their efforts are concentrated on redistribution: across incomes (with a focus on the poor), across generations (with a focus especially on the very young and the very old, who most need assistance), and across boundaries (so that lines once drawn for different reasons do not frustrate the focus on attacking inequality).

Federal aid, of course, has increasingly focused on redistributive programs, through grants for payments to individuals. That has grown from 34 percent of all grants in 1940 and 36 percent in 1980 to 74 percent in 2020.[5] But much of this growth has come through Medicaid, and disparities among the states in how they administer Medicaid have been a major driver of inequality. The states can surely maintain their central role as administrators of intergovernmental programs, in keeping with the historic sentiment of the Tenth Amendment, but if we care about reducing inequality, we cannot allow a broad state role in shaping these programs to drive a greater wedge between the rich and the poor. It would take a herculean shift in policy strategy to do so, but the federal government could retake the reins of Medicaid in particular and revert to the role it took when the program was originally created in the 1960s.

Second, a stronger federal role in shaping intergovernmental policy does not necessarily mean abandoning the states' role as laboratories of democracy. There would still be plenty of state experimentation, but less commitment to using the lessons that individual states learn to redefine national policy. The federal government—and the states—could make a stronger commitment not only to experimenting with policy alternatives but also to transforming federalism into a system that genuinely learns the lessons with true national import. Built into the idea of the states as "laboratories of democracy" has always been the notion that the national government could determine what works best through the states' entrepreneurship. A more explicit strategy of learning from state experiments, such as welfare reform in Wisconsin and environmental policy in California, could provide a more effective strategy for national progress.

Third, in many debates about federalism, local governments are often the forgotten player, not only by the federal government but also by their state governments. The irony is that any quest to improve trust in government could start by acknowledging that trust in local governments ranks highest in the United States. Local governments have some of the most advanced and energetic governance systems in the country. Former Indianapolis mayor Stephen Goldsmith and urban analyst Neil Kleiman, in fact, have pointed to innovations at the local level as a foundation for a completely new governmental operating system built on data and transparency to advance resilient and more equitable communities.[6] As former Baltimore mayor and Maryland governor Martin O'Malley explained,

> Mayors and county executives deliver very visible services, and they've embraced this revolution in openness, transparency, performance management, the use of the data, and the use of the map. That gives their citizens a view of service delivery in the life of their city in real-time. That's never happened before, and that's happening now.[7]

The Fifth Generation of Federalism not only requires rebalancing federalism toward the Hamiltonian vision but also focusing that vision on improving government's results in ways that reduce inequalities among its citizens. And that, in turn, means giving the nation's local governments a more prominent place in our federal system—a place in the debate over intergovernmental power that they have never enjoyed.

In the long sweep of American history, however, the even deeper truth is that an attack on inequality requires redistributive politics, and redistributive politics requires a far stronger federal role. Indeed, the federal government is the only level with sufficient leverage and resources to get results. State and local governments can deal with issues like infrastructure, but there's no hope that the states, left to their own policies and politics, could narrow the widening gaps between them. That would require the federal government.

In fact, the great public policy challenges of the twenty-first century are health and climate. Both of them raise questions that require redistributive answers, and the redistributive answers inevitably require a robust federal role, in leadership, policy, and funding—a Hamiltonian role, in fact. And therein lies the fundamental challenge of American democracy—and American federalism. Because of the deep fissures in Madison's other invention, the separation of powers, it's increasingly hard for government to act, but where it can mobilize itself to action, it tends to come through distributive policies. What the country most needs is an attack as well on the problems of inequality through redistributive policies. These are problems in which the federal government increasingly shows an instinct to pass problems along to the states—or duck them completely.

This basic test either shows the path forward—the steps that America needs to take if it is to solve the great challenges of the century—or the detour into conflict—the steps that will lead to a gradual weakening of American democracy, or worse. Just as was the case at the very beginning of the nation, it's possible to achieve success on even the most difficult journey—but also just as at the nation's founding, the steps lead through federalism.

Join, or Die?

In the long and often difficult history of the American republic, there has always been an enthusiastic embrace of liberty. That has been the cornerstone for leaders of every partisan stripe. The question has always been how best to preserve that liberty, how to ensure enough unity in the country to fulfill its aspirations, and how to protect its citizens. On these central questions, the United States has never developed a firm answer—or at least, not an answer that was able to stick for long. The great virtue of the invention of American federalism has been its very elasticity, its capacity to stretch and bend to accommodate shifting ideas about what the country ought to be without shredding the fibers that hold it together. From Madison to Hamilton, Derthick to Riker, the pursuit of liberty has been at the core. The debate has always been about how to proceed.

That was Franklin's great point in America's first great political cartoon, in which he raised the question: join, or die? In the twenty-first century, has Madison's solution, based on the search for balance, finally come undone, with a federalism that no longer works—and could Hamilton's vision of a stronger federal government be the way forward? The pursuit of liberty remains paramount. But so too does the quest to reduce inequality and to ensure that the quality of government that citizens receive does not depend on the state in which they live. Indeed, this question brings forward, for the twenty-first century, the original sin of America's eighteenth-century decisions about slavery: if all men (and women) are created equal, to what lengths is American government prepared to go to fulfill this promise?

For the Madisonian vision to survive, let alone thrive, it will need to find a way to advance the Hamiltonian dictum that saw a "sound and efficient government as the most reliable custodian of liberty," as historian Ron Chernow put it.[8] Even then, the puzzle will be whether the delicate intergovernmental balance can adjust quickly enough to the fast-moving pressures of twenty-first-century challenges, to a country that is aging rapidly and concentrating geographically, and to a political process that is increasingly polarized and distrusted.

The nation's founders would recognize the puzzles, even if they would be unhappy at their twenty-first-century incarnations. After all, they had fought many of the same battles, during the years of the Articles of Confederation and in the debates over the Constitution. But even Madison recognized that one of the country's biggest challenges was preventing majorities from tyrannizing minorities—and preventing minorities from steering the country off track. Madison and his followers were forever nervous about Hamilton's ideas about a strong federal government, but in the end Hamilton won many of those debates. The best way to preserve Madison's compound republic will likely be to embrace Hamilton's concept of a stronger, sounder, and more efficient federal government— the one player in American government with the resources and capacity to deal with the bottom-up issues of inequality and polarization threatening the nation's political stability—as the best custodian of liberty and the keeper of the founders' vision. That, in turn, will prove the best way to bring the divided states of America together, in a way that all the founders hoped.

What the founders would not recognize is the large and growing gap between fierce national politics and the operating realities of federalism. And at the core of the problem is the rise of light-fare television. In a 2019 paper, a team of Italian researchers argued that those who watched a lot of light-fare reality TV shows came to expect light-fare entertainment from the political campaigns they watched. That, in turn, set the stage for a generation of populist leaders who gave them reality-TV politics.[9] In Italy, for example, the more light-fare television voters watched, the more they became attuned to short sentences, simple messages, and less sophisticated ideas.

The same phenomenon has spilled over into American politics and has fundamentally transformed our political campaigns. To break through the vast congestion of the Internet and the noise of political campaigns, candidates began sliding in the 2010s to ever-simpler slogans (Democrats and Republicans alike, from "Medicare for All" to "Make America Great Again") and away from complicated ideas (like climate change) that require a lot of words to explore. And that, in turn, has radically transformed national politics dealing with states and cities. Until the early years of the twenty-first century, no self-respecting candidate could aim for the presidency without at least a couple of local policy arrows in their quiver. Even in the 2016 presidential campaign, the pledge to invest in infrastructure seemed a sure bet to pass a divided Congress. But that goal evaporated in the blizzard of reality-TV national politics. The label "infrastructure" just did not sell. That surely wasn't solely because it was expensive, because Congress and the Trump administration joined to produce the largest peacetime budget deficits in history. The complexities of infrastructure investment just didn't have a sound-bite appeal. The snappy slogans of reality-TV national politics simply do not fit the operating realities of state and local governments, where officials must focus on making government work, from putting out forest fires on California hillsides to ensuring safe drinking water in Newark's homes. Local realities do not fit national reality-TV politics.

This large and growing gap has strained the tendons of federalism. Federal policy, even policies like welfare and health care that rely on state and local governments for implementation, is increasingly disconnected from state and local realities. It's surely not for lack of policy ambition. Democratic political strategist Stan Greenberg argued, "People are desperate for government to show it can do big things."[10] Moreover, what they seem to want from the federal government is what mayors and governors, Republican and Democratic, do every day: deliver results that matter to citizens. But what they do in local communities doesn't translate well to national reality-TV slogans—and reality-TV politics doesn't work well on the ground. It has become harder for tangible local issues to break through on the national stage or for performers on the national stage to play their roles in ways that make sense in the nation's states and towns.

The result has been the development of two tiers of American politics—the snappy reality-TV national campaigns and the driving realities of state and local policies. Those tiers have fed very different kinds of debate about public policy in America, and those debates have, in turn, driven federalism from the national stage.

The founders, of course, were no strangers to short, snappy slogans or the popular media. Patrick Henry's "Give me liberty or give me death!"

has endured for centuries. Benjamin Franklin, among his many professions, was a magazine publisher, and his "Join, or die" cartoon is emblazoned on twenty-first-century T-shirts. James Madison and Alexander Hamilton were all-star bloggers, and their contributions to *The Federalist Papers* were essential to the ratification of the Constitution. But even though they sometimes found themselves on different sides of the issues, they could not have imagined a debate where national politics and federalism moved in opposite directions. They would surely have recognized and appreciated the rise of television and social media—one could imagine Franklin hosting his own cable talk show, and his aphorisms would have made for delicious tweets. They would have been horrified to discover that these media were helping undermine one of the inventions about which they were proudest.

Federalism remains the keystone of governance in America, just as it was for the founders, but it no longer has a place of prominence in national politics. That scarcely prevents state and local governments from continuing to play a pivotal role in national policies. From immigration to health care, state and local governments are where policy problems and proposals meet reality. However, state and local governments increasingly are where federal policymakers dump big issues that they cannot or choose not to resolve. The decline of federalism is thus tightly bound to the rise of reality-TV politics: it's attractive for federal officials to solve problems by wrapping them in slogans, and to duck the details by passing them along to the states. With the states, in turn, sliding in different directions, the result has been the rise of an especially insidious engine of inequality, with federal officials avoiding the implications of their decisions and state and local governments driving those decisions in ways that widen the gaps between them.

These forces have combined in ways that, left to their own devices, are likely to continue driving ever-deeper wedges between the nation's communities. The rise of reality-TV politics and the decline of federalism have combined to increase inequality in the nation. Moreover, there is a perverse irony in how the very institution that the founders created to accommodate differences in the early nation has become a force to widen them.

Federalism might have been the most essential invention to build and maintain the American republic. But it has become not so much the glue that keeps the country together but an engine driving it apart. The result is a divided states of America. The situation is serious, perhaps even bleak. However, it need not be fatal to the nation's grand democratic vision. But fixing federalism will require true vision and resolve, along with a fundamentally Hamiltonian solution to Madison's great dilemma.

NOTES

Chapter 1. Madison's Balancing Act

1. Joseph J. Ellis, *Founding Brothers: The Revolutionary Generation* (New York: Alfred A. Knopf, 2001), 53, 113.

2. Notes of Dr. James McHenry, a Maryland delegate, published in *The Records of the Federal Convention of 1787*, vol. 3, ed. Max Farrand (1911; reprint, 1934); see Bartleby.com, no. 1593, https://www.bartleby.com/73/1593.html.

3. Thomas E. Mann and Norman J. Ornstein, *The Broken Branch: How Congress Is Failing America and How to Get It Back on Track* (Oxford: Oxford University Press, 2006); Mann and Ornstein, *It's Even Worse than It Looks: How the American Constitutional System Collided with the New Politics of Extremism* (New York: Basic Books, 2012).

4. John D. Donahue, *Disunited States: What's at Stake as Washington Fades and the States Take the Lead* (New York: Basic Books, 1997), 5.

5. "Americans Say They Like Diverse Communities; Election, Census Trends Suggest Otherwise," Pew Research Center, December 2, 2008, http://www.pewsocialtrends.org/2008/12/02/americans-say-they-like-diverse-communities-election-census-trends-suggest-otherwise/; "The Partisan Divide on Political Values Grows Even Wider," Pew Research Center, October 5, 2017, http://www.people-press.org/2017/10/05/the-partisan-divide-on-political-values-grows-even-wider/. See also Cass R. Sunstein and Reid Hastie, *Wiser: Getting Beyond Groupthink to Make Groups Smarter* (Cambridge, MA: Harvard Business Review Press, 2015).

6. Charles Wise and Rosemary O'Leary, "Is Federalism Dead or Alive in the Supreme Court? Implications for Public Administrators," *Public Administration Review* 52:6 (November/December 1992), 559–72; David Corbin and Matt Parks, "Who Killed Federalism?" *The Federalist*, May 26, 2014, https://thefederalist.com/2014/05/26/who-killed-federalism/.

7. James Madison, letter to Lafayette, November 25, 1820, National Archives/Founders Online, https://founders.archives.gov/?q=%22dreadful%20fruitfulness%22&s=1111311111&sa=&r=1&sr=.

8. James Madison to Mr. Coles, October 3, 1834, James Madison Collection, Rare Books and Special Collections, Princeton University. More broadly, see Paris Amanda Spies-Gans, "James Madison," Princeton & Slavery Project, https://slavery.princeton.edu/stories/james-madison#ref-18.

9. "Declaring Independence: Drafting the Documents," Jefferson's "original Rough draught" of the Declaration of Independence (punctuation in the original), reconstructed by Julian Boyd, from *The Papers of Thomas Jefferson*, vol. 1, 1760–1776, ed. Julian P. Boyd (Princeton, NJ: Princeton University Press, 1950), 243–47, available at Library of Congress, https://www.loc.gov/exhibits/declara/ruffdrft.html.

10. Thomas Jefferson, "With the Declaration of Independence," January 6, 1821, in Jefferson, *Autobiography*, Yale Lillian Goldman Law Library, Avalon Project, http://avalon.law.yale.edu/19th _century/jeffauto.asp.

11. The authorship of *Federalist 54* has been attributed to Madison, although Alexander Hamilton may have written it.

12. Thurgood Marshall, "Remarks at the Annual Seminar of the San Francisco Patent and Trademark Law Association," May 6, 1987, Maui, Hawaii, Thurgood Marshall (website), http://thurgoodmarshall.com/the-bicentennial-speech/.

13. William H. Riker, *Federalism: Origin, Operation, Significance* (Boston: Little, Brown, 1964), 13, 140, 142, 143, 155.

14. William H. Riker, "Federalism," in *Handbook of Political Science*, vol. 5, ed. Fred I. Greenstein and Nelson W. Polsby (Reading, MA: Addison-Wesley, 1975), 159. See also Riker, *Federalism*.

15. Martha Derthick, "Whither Federalism?," no. 2 in "The Future of the Public Sector" series, Urban Institute, June 1, 1996, http://webarchive.urban.org/publications/306767.html. See also Martha Derthick, *Keeping the Compound Republic: Essays on American Federalism* (Washington, DC: Brookings Institution Press, 2001).

16. Derthick, "Whither Federalism?"

17. US Census Bureau, "Historical Income Tables: Income Equality, Table H-2: Share of Aggregate Income Received by Each Fifth and Top 5 Percent of Households," https://www.census .gov/data/tables/time-series/demo/income-poverty/historical-income-inequality.html.

18. Data from James Galbraith, University of Texas Inequality Project, LBJ School of Public Affairs, http://utip.gov.utexas.edu.

19. Gloria G. Guzman, "Household Income 2017," US Census Bureau, September 2018, https:// www.census.gov/content/dam/Census/library/publications/2018/acs/acsbr17-01.pdf.

20. Organisation for Economic Cooperation and Development (OECD), "Inequality," http:// www.oecd.org/social/inequality.htm.

21. Fabrice Murtin and Marco Mira d'Ercole, "Household Wealth Inequality across OECD Countries: New OECD Evidence," *OECD Statistics Brief* 21 (June 2015), 5, 7, http://www.oecd .org/sdd/household-wealth-inequality-across-OECD-countries-OECDSB21.pdf.

22. Thomas E. Mann and Norman J. Ornstein, "Republicans Created Dysfunction. Now They're Paying for It," *Washington Post*, March 8, 2016, https://www.washingtonpost.com/news /in-theory/wp/2016/03/08/republicans-created-dysfunction-now-theyre-paying-for-it/?utm _term=.38c36714b59b.

23. Deil S. Wright, *Understanding Intergovernmental Relations: Public Policy and Participants' Perspectives in Local, State, and National Governments* (North Scituate, MA: Duxbury Press, 1978).

24. Ron Chernow, *Alexander Hamilton* (New York: Penguin Press, 2004), 221.

25. Chernow, *Alexander Hamilton*, 290.

26. Michael Lind, "The Legacy of Alexander Hamilton," in *Hamilton's Republic: Readings in the American Nationalist Tradition*, ed. Michael Lind (New York: Free Press, 1997), 4–5.

27. James Barron, "Did 'Hamilton' Get the Story Wrong? One Playwright Thinks So," *New York Times*, January 13, 2019, https://www.nytimes.com/2019/01/13/nyregion/hamilton-lin -manuel-miranda-the-haunting.html.

28. Jacob E. Cooke, *Alexander Hamilton* (New York: Macmillan, 1982), 94.

Chapter 2. E Pluribus Unum

1. Samuel Johnson, *A Dictionary of the English Language* (1755), digital edition, https://johnsonsdictionaryonline.com/magazine/.

2. "The Great Seal of the United States," US Department of State, Bureau of Public Affairs, July 2003, https://2009-2017.state.gov/documents/organization/135450.pdf.

3. Jimmy Stamp, "American Myths: Benjamin Franklin's Turkey and the Presidential Seal," *Smithsonian.com*, January 25, 2013, https://www.smithsonianmag.com/arts-culture/american-myths-benjamin-franklins-turkey-and-the-presidential-seal-6623414/; Benjamin Franklin, "To Sarah Bache (unpublished)" (letter to his daughter), January 26, 1784, Papers of Benjamin Franklin, digital edition by Packard Humanities Institute, http://franklinpapers.org/framedVolumes.jsp.

4. Benjamin Franklin, *Pennsylvania Gazette*, May 9, 1754.

5. "On Independence," AmericanRevolution.org, 1776, http://www.americanrevolution.org/war_songs/warsongs38.php.

6. On the authenticity of this quote, see *Ben Franklin Laughing: Anecdotes from Original Sources by and about Benjamin Franklin*, ed. Paul M. Zall (Berkeley: University of California Press, 1981), 154; see Bartleby.com, no. 395, http://www.bartleby.com/73/395.html.

7. Hans Beck and Peter Funke, eds., *Federalism in Greek Antiquity* (Cambridge: Cambridge University Press, 2015), frontmatter.

8. Article 2, Articles of Confederation; see "A Century of Lawmaking for a New Nation: US Congressional Documents and Debates, 1774–1875," Library of Congress, https://memory.loc.gov/cgi-bin/ampage?collId=llsl&fileName=001/llsl001.db&recNum=127.

9. "The Articles of Confederation and Perpetual Union," 1777, USHistory.org, http://www.ushistory.org/documents/confederation.htm.

10. US Continental Congress, "By the US in Congress Assembled," November 1, 1783, Library of Congress, https://www.loc.gov/resource/bdsdcc.08901/.

11. W. Brooke Graves, *American Intergovernmental Relations: Their Origins, Historical Development, and Current Status* (New York: Charles Scribner's Sons, 1964), 61, 64.

12. James Madison, "Vices of the Political System of the United States, April 1787," National Archives/Founders Online, https://founders.archives.gov/documents/Madison/01-09-02-0187.

13. Andrew Glass, "Patrick Henry Dies, June 6, 1799," *Politico*, June 6, 2012, https://www.politico.com/story/2012/06/this-day-in-politics-077065.

14. Patrick Henry, "Virginia Ratifying Convention," in Herbert J. Storing, ed., *The Complete Anti-Federalist* (Chicago: University of Chicago Press, 1981), 211.

15. "Amending America: Proposed Amendments to the United States Constitution, 1787 to 2014," National Archives/Open Government at the National Archives, https://www.archives.gov/open/dataset-amendments.html.

16. James Madison, *Federalist 10*. For this paper and others in the collection, see Congress.gov Resources, "The Federalist Papers," https://www.congress.gov/resources/display/content/The+Federalist+Papers.

17. James Madison, letter to Thomas Jefferson, October 24, 1787, National Archives/Founders Online, https://founders.archives.gov/documents/Madison/01-10-02-0151.

18. Cato, "To the Citizens of the State of New York" (1788), in *The Anti-Federalist Papers and the Constitutional Convention Debates*, ed. Ralph Ketcham (New York: Signet Classics, 2003), 344.

19. Patrick Henry, "Speech," June 5, 1788, in Ketcham, *The Anti-Federalist Papers*, 200.

Chapter 3. The Search for Unity

1. "The Federal Farmer," no. 4, October 12, 1787, in *The Complete Bill of Rights: The Drafts, Debates, Sources, and Origins*, ed. Neil H. Cogan (New York: Oxford University Press, 1997), 699.

2. George Mason, speech delivered June 14, 1788, in Cogan, *The Complete Bill of Rights*, 692.

3. Speeches by Patrick Henry and by James Madison, delivered June 24, 1788, in Cogan, *The Complete Bill of Rights*, 697–98.

4. Cited in Abraham Baldwin, letter to Joel Barlow, June 14, 1789, in Cogan, *The Complete Bill of Rights*, 703.

5. James Madison, letter to Richard Peters, August 19, 1789, in *The Founders' Constitution*, vol. 1, chap. 14, document 53, from *The Papers of James Madison*, ed. William T. Hutchinson et al. (Chicago: University of Chicago Press, 1962–1977), http://press-pubs.uchicago.edu/founders/documents/v1ch14s53.html.

6. Thomas Jefferson, letter to James Madison, December 20, 1787, in Cogan, *The Complete Bill of Rights*, 702.

7. James Madison, letter to George Washington, December 5, 1789, in Cogan, *The Complete Bill of Rights*, 704.

8. *McCulloch v. Maryland*, 17 U.S. (4 Wheat.) 316 (1819). The text of the decision is available at the Legal Information Institute, Cornell Law School, https://www.law.cornell.edu/supremecourt/text/17/316.

9. For discussions, see Gordon Wood, *The Creation of the American Republic, 1776–1787* (Chapel Hill: University of North Carolina Press, 1969); Stanley Elkins and Eric McKitrick, *The Age of Federalism: The Early American Republic, 1788–1800* (New York: Oxford University Press, 1993).

10. Graves, *American Intergovernmental Relations*, 486.

11. Article IV, Constitution of the Confederate States, March 11, 1861, Yale Lillian Goldman Law Library, Avalon Project, http://avalon.law.yale.edu/19th_century/csa_csa.asp.

12. Confederate States of America, "Declaration of the Immediate Causes Which Induce and Justify the Secession of South Carolina from the Federal Union," December 24, 1860, Yale Lillian Goldman Law Library, Avalon Project, http://avalon.law.yale.edu/19th_century/csa_scarsec.asp.

13. "Civil War at 150: Still Relevant, Still Divisive," Pew Research Center, April 8, 2011, http://www.people-press.org/2011/04/08/civil-war-at-150-still-relevant-still-divisive/.

14. Quoted by the Editorial Board, "America Started over Once. Can We Do It Again?," *New York Times*, July 3, 2018, https://www.nytimes.com/2018/07/03/opinion/trump-supreme-court-nominee.html.

15. *Slaughterhouse Cases*, 83 U.S. 36 (1872).

16. *Plessy v. Ferguson*, 163 U.S. 537 (1896).

17. "Martin Luther King Jr., National Historic Park Georgia: Jim Crow Laws," National Park Service, last updated April 17, 2018, https://www.nps.gov/malu/learn/education/jim_crow_laws .htm.

18. "Freedom Riders," *American Experience*, PBS, 2011, http://www.pbs.org/wgbh /americanexperience/features/freedom-riders-jim-crow-laws/.

Chapter 4. Washington Rising

1. US Bureau of the Census, "Population and Housing Unit Counts, Table 4: Population, 1790–1990," https://www.census.gov/population/censusdata/table-4.pdf.

2. Upton Sinclair, *The Jungle* (New York: Doubleday, 1906); Jane Addams, *Twenty Years at Hull-House* (New York: Macmillan, 1912).

3. "Muckraker: 2 Meanings," *New York Times*, April 10, 1985, http://www.nytimes.com/1985 /04/10/us/muchraker-2-meanings.html.

4. For an analysis, see John Kenneth Galbraith, *The Great Crash, 1929* (Boston: Houghton Mifflin, 1955).

5. Louise V. Armstrong, *We Too Are the People* (Boston: Little, Brown, 1938), 10.

6. "Government Spending Chart," compiled by Christopher Chantrill, USGovernmentSpending.com, https://www.usgovernmentspending.com/spending_chart_1820_1930USt _19s2lio11tcn_FofFosFol.

7. Graves, *American Intergovernmental Relations*, 806.

8. William Y. Elliott, *The Need for Constitutional Reform* (New York: McGraw-Hill, 1935).

9. John Joseph Wallis and Wallace E. Oates, "The Impact of the New Deal on American Federalism," in *The Defining Moment: The Great Depression and the American Economy in the Twentieth Century*, ed. Michael D. Bordo, Claudia Goldin, and Eugene N. White (Chicago: University of Chicago Press, 1998), 156.

10. Michael Schuyler, "A Short History of Government Taxing and Spending in the United States," Tax Foundation, February 19, 2014, https://taxfoundation.org/short-history-government -taxing-and-spending-united-states/.

11. J. S. Maloy, *The Colonial American Origins of Modern Democratic Thought* (New York: Cambridge University Press, 2008).

12. *City of Clinton v. Cedar Rapids and Missouri River Railroad*, 24 Iowa 455, 475 (1868). For an analysis, see Jay P. Syverson, "The Inconsistent State of Municipal Home Rule in Iowa," *Drake Law Review* 57 (2008), 263–317; Jesse J. Richardson Jr., Meghan Zimmerman Gough, and Robert Puentes, "Is Home Rule the Answer? Clarifying the Influence of Dillon's Rule on Growth Management," Brookings Institution Center of Urban and Metropolitan Policy discussion paper, January 2003, https://www.brookings.edu/wp-content/uploads/2016/06 /dillonsrule.pdf.

13. Derthick, *Keeping the Compound Republic*, 17.

14. John Joseph Wallis, "The Birth of the Old Federalism: Financing the New Deal, 1932–1940," *Journal of Economic History* 44:1 (March 1984), 139–59.

15. *United States v. Darby*, 312 U.S. 100, 124 (1941).

16. *Brown v. Board of Education of Topeka*, 347 U.S. 483 (1954).

17. Kate Ellis and Catherine Winter, "An Imperfect Revolution: Voices from the Desegregation Era," *American RadioWorks*, American Public Media, 2018, http://americanradioworks.publicradio.org/features/deseg/e1.html.

18. *Brown v. Board of Education of Topeka*, 347 U.S. 483 (1954).

19. National Commission on Civil Disorders, "The Kerner Report" (1968), http://www.eisenhowerfoundation.org/docs/kerner.pdf.

20. Robert A. Caro, *Master of the Senate* (New York: Alfred A. Knopf, 2002).

21. Tim Alan Garrison, "Government & Politics: US Supreme Court Cases: *Worcester v. Georgia* (1832)," *New Georgia Encyclopedia*, April 27, 2004, updated February 20, 2018, https://www.georgiaencyclopedia.org/articles/government-politics/worcester-v-georgia-1832.

22. "Highway History: Interstate Frequently Asked Questions," Federal Highway Administration, updated December 18, 2018, https://www.fhwa.dot.gov/interstate/faq.cfm#question3.

23. Charlie Savage, "As Trump Vows Building Splurge, Famed Traffic Choke Point Offers Warning," *New York Times*, February 6, 2017, https://www.nytimes.com/2017/02/06/us/politics/a-pennsylvania-highway-town-at-the-junction-of-politics-and-policy.html.

24. Federal Highway Administration, "Highway History."

25. Eric Pianin, "A Mover on the Hill: Shuster Follows His Own Road Map," *Washington Post*, September 16, 1997, A4, https://www.washingtonpost.com/wp-srv/politics/special/highway/stories/hwy091697.htm; Associated Press, "House Panel to Resume Ethics Probe of Shuster," *Washington Post*, December 5, 1998, A4, https://www.washingtonpost.com/wp-srv/politics/special/highway/stories/shuster120598.htm.

26. Theodore J. Lowi, "Four Systems of Policy, Politics, and Choice," *Public Administration Review* 32:4 (July/August 1972), 298–301.

27. James Wilson, speech delivered October 6, 1787, in *The Anti-Federalist Papers and the Constitutional Convention Debates*, ed. Ralph Ketcham (New York: Signet Classics, 2003), 185.

28. *Budget of the United States Government, Fiscal Year 2019: Historical Tables*, US Office of Management and Budget, https://www.whitehouse.gov/omb/historical-tables/.

29. "Federal Aid to State and Local Governments," Center on Budget and Policy Priorities, April 19, 2018, https://www.cbpp.org/research/state-budget-and-tax/federal-aid-to-state-and-local-governments.

Chapter 5. America's Struggle with Inequality

1. Alexis de Tocqueville, *Democracy in America* (New York: Penguin Books, 2003), 784–85.

2. "OECD Income Distribution Database (IDD): Gini, Poverty, Income, Methods, and Concepts," OECD, updated April 10, 2019, http://www.oecd.org/social/income-distribution-database.htm.

3. Central Intelligence Agency, "The World Factbook," https://www.cia.gov/library/publications/the-world-factbook/rankorder/2172rank.html.

4. Emmanuel Saez, "Table 1. Real Income Growth by Groups," in Saez, "Striking It Richer: The Evolution of Top Incomes in the United States," June 25, 2015, https://eml.berkeley.edu/~saez/saez-UStopincomes-2014.pdf.

5. Heather Knight, "Income Inequality on Par with Developing Nations," *SFGate*, June 25, 2014, http://www.sfgate.com/bayarea/article/Income-inequality-on-par-with-developing-nations -5486434.php; Natalie Holmes and Alan Berube, "City and Metropolitan Inequality on the Rise, Driven by Declining Incomes," Brookings Institution, January 14, 2016, https://www.brookings.edu /research/city-and-metropolitan-inequality-on-the-rise-driven-by-declining-incomes/.

6. Estelle Sommeiller, Mark Price, and Ellis Wazeter, "Income Inequality in the US by State, Metropolitan Area, and County," Economic Policy Institute, June 16, 2016, https://www.epi.org /publication/income-inequality-in-the-us/.

7. Barack Obama, "Remarks by the President on Economic Mobility," The White House, Office of the Press Secretary, December 4, 2013, https://obamawhitehouse.archives.gov/the-press -office/2013/12/04/remarks-president-economic-mobility.

8. Adam Smith, *The Theory of Moral Sentiments* (1759), chap. 3.

9. Dennis C. Rasmussen, "The Problem with Inequality, According to Adam Smith," *Atlantic*, June 9, 2016, https://www.theatlantic.com/business/archive/2016/06/the-problem-with -inequality-according-to-adam-smith/486071/. Compare Dennis C. Rasmussen, "Adam Smith on What Is Wrong with Economic Inequality," *American Political Science Review* 110:2 (May 2016), 342–52.

10. The data for these comparisons come from: on poverty, US Census Bureau, "Income and Poverty in the United States, 2016: Tables: Poverty: Percentage of People in Poverty by State Using 2- and 3-Year Averages: 2013–2014 and 2015–2016," report P60-259, September 2017, https://www .census.gov/data/tables/2017/demo/income-poverty/p60-259.html; on health, "America's Health Rankings: 2017 Annual Report: State Rankings," United Health Foundation, https://www .americashealthrankings.org/learn/reports/2017-annual-report/findings-state-rankings; on infrastructure, "Infrastructure Rankings," *U.S. News & World Report*, 2017, https://www.usnews .com/news/best-states/rankings/infrastructure; on the environment, Daniel Fiorino and Riordan Frost, "The State Air, Climate, and Energy (ACE) Index: A Tool for Research and Policy" (draft), 2018; on crime and corrections, "Crime Rankings," *U.S. News & World Report*, 2017, https://www.usnews.com/news/best-states/rankings/crime-and-corrections; on education, National Center for Higher Education Management Systems Information Center, citing US Census Bureau, "ACS [American Community Survey] Educational Attainment by Degree-Level and Age Group," 2015, http://www.higheredinfo.org/dbrowser/?level=nation&mode=data&state =0&submeasure=245; on children, Annie E. Casey Foundation, *2018 KIDS COUNT Data Book: 2018 State Trends in Child Well-being*, http://www.aecf.org/resources/2018-kids-count-data-book /, especially "Appendix A: Child Well-being Rankings," http://www.aecf.org/m/databook /2018KC_databook_rankings.pdf.

11. Compare Paul E. Peterson, *The Price of Federalism* (Washington: Brookings Institution Press, 1995).

Chapter 6. Health, Unequal

1. "President Truman's Proposed Health Care Program: November 19, 1945," Harry S. Truman Presidential Library and Museum, https://www.trumanlibrary.org/anniversaries /healthprogram.htm.

2. "Q&A with Robert Caro," C-SPAN, May 18, 2017, https://www.c-span.org/video/?428765-2/qa-robert-caro.

3. "Medicaid's Share of State Budgets," Medicaid and CHIP Payment and Access Commission, https://www.macpac.gov/subtopic/medicaids-share-of-state-budgets/.

4. National Association of State Budget Officers, *2018 State Expenditure Report: Fiscal Years 2016–2018*, https://www.nasbo.org/reports-data/state-expenditure-report.

5. "Medicaid in the United States," Kaiser Family Foundation, November 2018, http://files.kff.org/attachment/fact-sheet-medicaid-state-US.

6. Adam Clymer, "Governors Oppose Reagan on Medicaid," *New York Times*, February 24, 1981, A1, https://www.nytimes.com/1981/02/24/us/governor-s-oppose-reagan-on-medicaid.html.

7. "Transcript of President's State of the Union Message to Nation," *New York Times*, January 27, 1982, A16, https://www.nytimes.com/1982/01/27/us/transcript-of-president-s-state-of-the-union-message-to-nation.html.

8. "Poverty and Spending over the Years," Federal Safety Net, http://federalsafetynet.com/poverty-and-spending-over-the-years.html; "State and Local Expenditures on Welfare," Federal Safety Net, http://federalsafetynet.com/state-and-local-expenditures-on-welfare.html; "State and Local Budget Spending Details," compiled by Christopher Chantrill, USGovernmentSpending.com, https://www.usgovernmentspending.com/year_spending_2016USbt_18bs1n_0002101712404147202425018086_551_605_609_502_504_376_604_501_506#usgs302.

9. Bill Adair and Angie Drobnic Holan, "PolitiFact's Lie of the Year: 'A Government Takeover of Health Care,'" *PolitiFact*, December 16, 2010, http://www.politifact.com/truth-o-meter/article/2010/dec/16/lie-year-government-takeover-health-care/; Lori Robertson, "A Final Weekend of Whoppers?," FactCheck.org, March 19, 2010, https://www.factcheck.org/2010/03/a-final-weekend-of-whoppers/.

10. *National Federation of Independent Business v. Sebelius*, 567 U.S. 519 (2012).

11. Alana Semuels, "Indiana's Medicaid Experiment May Reveal Obamacare's Future," *Atlantic*, December 21, 2016, https://www.theatlantic.com/business/archive/2016/12/medicaid-and-mike-pence/511262/; Judith Solomon, "Indiana Medicaid Waiver Evaluation Shows Why Kentucky's Medicaid Proposal Shouldn't Be Approved," Center on Budget and Policy Priorities, August 1, 2016, https://www.cbpp.org/research/health/indiana-medicaid-waiver-evaluation-shows-why-kentuckys-medicaid-proposal-shouldnt-be.

12. Allie Bice, "Did Arizonans See 116% Increase in 'Obamacare' Premiums?," *azcentral.com*, November 27, 2017, https://www.azcentral.com/story/news/politics/fact-check/2017/11/27/did-arizonans-see-116-percent-increase-obamacare-premiums/842108001/.

13. Editorial board, "Wisconsin ObamaCare Howlers," *Wall Street Journal*, April 29, 2018, https://www.wsj.com/articles/wisconsin-obamacare-howlers-1535585135.

14. "Kaiser Health Tracking Poll," Kaiser Family Foundation, May 2011, https://kaiserfamilyfoundation.files.wordpress.com/2013/01/8190-f.pdf.

15. "Poll: Majorities Favor a Range of Options to Expand Public Coverage, Including Medicare-for-All," Kaiser Family Foundation, January 23, 2019, https://www.kff.org/health-reform/press-release/poll-majorities-favor-a-range-of-options-to-expand-public-coverage-including-medicare-for-all/.

16. Peterson-Kaiser, "Health System Tracker," May 22, 2017, https://www.healthsystemtracker .org/chart-collection/quality-u-s-healthcare-system-compare-countries/?_sft_category =quality-of-care#item-start.

17. Joachim O. Hero, Alan M. Zaslavsky, and Robert J. Blendon, "The United States Leads Other Nations in Differences by Income in Perceptions of Health and Health Care," *Health Affairs* 36:6 (2017), 1032–40.

18. United Health Foundation, "America's Health Rankings: 2017 Annual Report: State Rankings."

19. For life expectancy, cardiovascular deaths, and cancer deaths, see Institute for Health Metrics and Evaluation, 2014, http://www.healthdata.org/. For infant mortality and persons without health insurance, see Centers for Disease Control and Prevention, National Center for Health Statistics, "Life Expectancy," 2017, tables 12 and 114, https://www.cdc.gov/nchs/fastats/life -expectancy.htm. For drug overdose deaths, see Centers for Disease Control and Prevention, "Drug Overdose Deaths," December 2017, https://www.cdc.gov/drugoverdose/data/statedeaths .html. Health outcome data are occurrences per 100,000 people.

20. "State Health Facts: Health Insurance Coverage of the Total Population," Henry J. Kaiser Family Foundation, 2016, https://www.kff.org/other/state-indicator/total-population/ ?currentTimeframe=0&sortModel=%7B%22colId%22:%22Location%22,%22sort%22:%22asc% 22%7D.

21. Nancy E. Adler and David H. Rehkopf, "US Disparities in Health: Descriptions, Causes, and Mechanisms," *Annual Review of Public Health* 29 (April 2008), 235–52; National Institutes of Health, "Health Disparities," https://report.nih.gov/NIHfactsheets/ViewFactSheet.aspx?csid =124. More broadly, see Institute of Medicine, "Crossing the Quality Chasm: A New Health System for the 21st Century," March 2001, http://www.nationalacademies.org/hmd/~/media /Files/Report%20Files/2001/Crossing-the-Quality-Chasm/Quality%20Chasm%202001%20 %20report%20brief.pdf; Brian D. Smedley, Adrienne Y. Stith, and Alan R. Nelson, eds., *Unequal Treatment: Confronting Racial and Ethnic Disparities in Health Care* (Washington, DC: National Academies Press, 2003), https://www.nap.edu/read/12875/chapter/1.

22. OECD Health Statistics 2018, http://www.oecd.org/els/health-systems/health-data.htm.

23. "Paying Out-of-Pocket: The Healthcare Spending of 2 Million US Families," JPMorgan Chase & Co. Institute, September 2017, https://www.jpmorganchase.com/corporate/institute /report-affording-healthcare.htm.

24. Manatt, Phelps, and Phillips, LLP, "Medicaid's Impact on Health Care Access, Outcomes, and State Economies," in Robert Wood Johnson Foundation, *Briefing Series: Key Medicaid Issues for New State Lawmakers*, February 1, 2019, https://www.rwjf.org/en/library/research/2019/02 /medicaid-s-impact-on-health-care-access-outcomes-and-state-economies.html.

25. Sandra Hempel, *The Strange Case of the Broad Street Pump: John Snow and the Mystery of Cholera* (Berkeley: University of California Press, 2007).

26. Centers for Disease Control and Prevention, "Achievements in Public Health, 1900–1999: Control of Infectious Diseases," *Morbidity and Mortality Weekly Report* 48:29 (1999), 621–29, https://www.cdc.gov/mmwr/preview/mmwrhtml/mm4829a1.htm.

27. Micheal E. DeBakey, "The Role of Government in Health Care: A Societal Issue," *American Journal of Surgery* 191:2 (February 2006), 145–57.

28. Jocelyn Kiley, "Most Continue to Say Ensuring Health Care Coverage Is Government's Responsibility," Pew Research Center, June 23, 2017, http://www.pewresearch.org/fact-tank/2017/06/23/public-support-for-single-payer-health-coverage-grows-driven-by-democrats/.

29. DeBakey, "The Role of Government in Health Care," 154.

Chapter 7. E Pluribus Pluribus

1. *Bond v. United States*, 564 U.S. 211 (2011).

2. Patrick Gillespie, "Flint, Michigan: A Hollow Frame of a Once Affluent City," *CNN Money*, March 7, 2016, http://money.cnn.com/2016/03/06/news/economy/flint-economy-democratic-debate/index.html.

3. Merrit Kennedy, "Lead-Laced Water in Flint: A Step-by-Step Look at the Makings of a Crisis," *The Two-Way*, NPR, April 20, 2016, https://www.npr.org/sections/thetwo-way/2016/04/20/465545378/lead-laced-water-in-flint-a-step-by-step-look-at-the-makings-of-a-crisis.

4. City of Flint, "City of Flint Officially Begins Using Flint River as Temporary Primary Water Source" (press release), April 25, 2014, https://www.documentcloud.org/documents/2696071-Snyder-Emails.html#document/p16/a272881.

5. Lindsey Smith, "After Ignoring and Trying to Discredit People in Flint, the State Was Forced to Face the Problem," *Michigan Radio*, December 16, 2015, http://michiganradio.org/post/after-ignoring-and-trying-discredit-people-flint-state-was-forced-face-problem#stream/0.

6. Miguel A. Del Toral, Regulations Manager, Ground Water and Drinking Water Branch, memo to Thomas Poy, Chief, Ground Water and Drinking Water Branch, US Environmental Protection Agency (EPA), "High Lead Levels in Flint, Michigan—Interim Report," June 24, 2015, http://mediad.publicbroadcasting.net/p/michigan/files/201602/Miguels-Memo.pdf.

7. Lindsey Smith, "Leaked Internal Memo Shows Federal Regulator's Concerns about Lead in Flint's Water," *Michigan Radio*, July 13, 2015, http://michiganradio.org/post/leaked-internal-memo-shows-federal-regulator-s-concerns-about-lead-flint-s-water#stream/0.

8. Siddhartha Roy, "Our Sampling of 252 Homes Demonstrates a High Lead in Water Risk: Flint Should Be Failing to Meet the EPA Lead and Copper Rule," Flint Water Study Updates, September 8, 2015, http://flintwaterstudy.org/2015/09/our-sampling-of-252-homes-demonstrates-a-high-lead-in-water-risk-flint-should-be-failing-to-meet-the-epa-lead-and-copper-rule/.

9. Steve Carmody, "Team Testing Flint Water for Lead Sample by Sample," *Michigan Radio*, September 6, 2015, http://michiganradio.org/post/team-testing-flint-water-lead-sample-sample.

10. Kennedy, "Lead-Laced Water in Flint."

11. Robin Erb, "Doctor: Lead Seen in More Flint Kids since Water Switch," *Detroit Free Press*, September 24, 2015, https://www.freep.com/story/news/local/michigan/2015/09/24/water-lead-in-flint/72747696/.

12. Siddhartha Roy, "Public Health Advisory Regarding Lead in Flint Water from the Genesee County Board of Commissioners, Health Dept., and City of Flint," Flint Water Study Updates, September 29, 2015, http://flintwaterstudy.org/2015/09/public-health-advisory-regarding-lead-in-flint-water-from-the-genesee-county-board-of-commissioners/.

13. Dennis Muchmore, email to Rich Snyder and others, "Flint Water," September 25, 2015, https://www.documentcloud.org/documents/2696071-Snyder-Emails.html#document/p71/a5.

14. Flint Water Advisory Task Force, *Final Report*, March 21, 2016, https://www.michigan.gov/documents/snyder/FWATF_FINAL_REPORT_21March2016_517805_7.pdf.

15. EPA, Office of Inspector General, *Management Weaknesses Delayed Response to Flint Water Crisis*, Report 18-P-0221, July 19, 2018, https://www.epa.gov/sites/production/files/2018-07/documents/_epaoig_20180719-18-p-0221.pdf.

16. Samantha Raphelson, "Flint Residents Confront Long-Term Health Issues after Lead Exposure," *Here and Now*, NPR, October 31, 2017, https://www.npr.org/2017/10/31/561155244/flint-residents-confront-long-term-health-issues-after-lead-exposure.

17. Mona Hanna-Attisha, Jenny LaChance, Richard Casey Sadler, and Allison Champey Schnepp, "Elevated Blood Lead Levels in Children Associated with the Flint Drinking Water Crisis: A Spatial Analysis of Risk and Public Health Response," *American Journal of Public Health* 106:2 (2016), 283–90.

18. Kevin D. Williamson, "Political Poison," *National Review*, January 15, 2016, https://www.nationalreview.com/2016/01/flint-water-scandal-democratic-pattern/.

19. Abby Goodnough and Jennifer Steinhauer, "As Grilling over Flint Water Begins, Partisan Divisions Surface," *New York Times*, February 3, 2016, https://www.nytimes.com/2016/02/04/us/politics/as-grilling-over-flint-water-begins-partisan-worry-lingers-on-fringe.html.

20. Rachel Carson, *Silent Spring* (Boston: Houghton Mifflin, 1962).

21. Johnny Carson, *The Tonight Show*, https://www.youtube.com/watch?v=Kvoh-X2hTOs.

22. Lily Rothman, "Here's Why the Environmental Protection Agency Was Created," *Time*, March 22, 2017, http://time.com/4696104/environmental-protection-agency-1970-history/.

23. J. Alfredo Gómez, "Environmental Protection: Status of GAO Recommendations Made to EPA since Fiscal Year 2007," testimony before the House Committee on Energy and Commerce, Subcommittee on Oversight and Investigations, US Government Accountability Office, GAO-17-801T, September 6, 2017, https://www.gao.gov/assets/690/686946.pdf; GAO, "Environmental Protection: EPA-State Enforcement Partnership Has Improved, but EPA's Oversight Needs Further Enhancement," GAO-07-883, July 31, 2007, https://www.gao.gov/products/GAO-07-883; Avinash Kar, Shravya Reddy, Nikhil Vijaykar, and Ashley Eagle-Gibbs, *Effective Environmental Compliance and Governance: Perspectives from the Natural Resources Defense Council* (Washington, DC: National Resources Defense Council, December 2010), https://www.nrdc.org/sites/default/files/int_10051901a.pdf.

24. Frost and Fiorino, "The State Air, Climate, and Energy (ACE) Index"; Riordan Frost and Daniel Fiorino, email communication with the author, March 13, 2018.

25. Barry Rabe, "Race to the Top: The Expanding Role of US State Renewable Portfolio Standards," *Sustainable Development Law and Policy* 7:3 (Spring 2007), 10–16, 72.

26. Mary Graham, "Environmental Protection and the States: 'Race to the Bottom' or 'Race to the Bottom Line'?" Brookings Institution, December 1, 1998, https://www.brookings.edu/articles/environmental-protection-the-states-race-to-the-bottom-or-race-to-the-bottom-line/.

27. W. Brooke Graves, *American Intergovernmental Relations: Their Origins, Historical Development, and Current Status* (New York: Charles Scribner's Sons, 1964), 484–89.

28. Interstate Highway 80 has since replaced US Route 40 from Utah to San Francisco.

29. "Bridges & Structures: Deficient Bridges by Owner 2016," Federal Highway Administration, December 31, 2016, https://www.fhwa.dot.gov/bridge/nbi/no10/owner16.cfm.

30. Graves, *American Intergovernmental Relations*, 481.

31. Pearson, "Index—2014 vs. 2012," http://thelearningcurve.pearson.com/index/index-comparison/2014-lowest.

32. Melissa S. Kearney and Philip B. Levine, "Income Inequality, Social Mobility, and the Decision to Drop Out of High School," *Brookings Papers on Economic Activity*, March 3, 2015, https://www.brookings.edu/wp-content/uploads/2016/03/KearneyLevine_IncomeInequalityUpwardMobility_ConferenceDraft.pdf.

33. Adam McCann, "2018's Most and Least Educated States in America," WalletHub, January 23, 2018, https://wallethub.com/edu/most-educated-states/31075/.

34. US Department of Education, National Center for Education Statistics, "School District Current Expenditures per Pupil with and without Adjustments for Federal Revenues by Poverty and Race/Ethnicity Characteristics," table A-1, https://nces.ed.gov/edfin/Fy11_12_tables.asp.

35. Martin R. West, "Why Do Americans Rate Their Local Public Schools So Favorably?," Brookings Institution, October 23, 2014, https://www.brookings.edu/research/why-do-americans-rate-their-local-public-schools-so-favorably/; "*Education Next*: Program on Education Policy and Governance—Survey 2014," Education Next, http://educationnext.org/files/2014ednextpoll.pdf.

36. Nina Rees, president and chief executive officer of the National Alliance for Public Charter Schools, "An Education in Building Local Support," *U.S. News & World Report*, August 26, 2014, https://www.usnews.com/opinion/blogs/nina-rees/2014/08/26/common-core-and-charter-school-polls-show-americans-like-local-education.

37. David Osborne, *Laboratories of Democracy* (Boston: Harvard Business School Press, 1990).

Chapter 8. Engines of Inequality

1. See Daniel C. Vock, "'People Are Literally Being Poisoned': How Sewage Problems in Alabama Got So Bad—and Why Other States Should Worry," Governing (website), July 17, 2018, https://www.governing.com/topics/transportation-infrastructure/gov-alabama-hookworm-sewage.html.

2. Vock, "'People Are Literally Being Poisoned.'"

3. Megan L. McKenna, Shannon McAtee, Patricia E. Bryan, Rebecca Jeun, Tabitha Ward, Jacob Kraus, Maria E. Bottazzi, Peter J. Hotez, Catherine C. Flowers, and Rojelio Mejia, "Human Intestinal Parasite Burden and Poor Sanitation in Rural Alabama," *American Journal of Tropical Medicine and Hygiene* 97:5 (November 2017), 1623–28.

4. Ray Downs, "UN Official: Alabama's Poverty, Sewage Crisis 'Very Uncommon in First World,'" *UPI*, December 10, 2017, https://www.upi.com/Top_News/US/2017/12/10/UN-official-Alabamas-poverty-sewage-crisis-very-uncommon-in-First-World/1681512952225/.

5. Steve Dubb, "Medical Studies Expose America's Toxic Sludge Problem," *Nonprofit Quarterly*, July 18, 2018, https://nonprofitquarterly.org/medical-studies-expose-americas-toxic-sludge-problem/.

6. Vock, "'People Are Literally Being Poisoned.'"

7. Peter J. Hotez, "Tropical Diseases: The New Plague of Poverty," *New York Times*, August 18, 2012, https://www.nytimes.com/2012/08/19/opinion/sunday/tropical-diseases-the-new-plague-of-poverty.html.

8. See, for example, Martin Diamond, "The Ends of Federalism," *Publius* 3:2 (Autumn 1973); Derthick, *The Compound Republic*; Pietro Nivola, "Why Federalism Matters," Brookings Institution, October 1, 2005, https://www.brookings.edu/research/why-federalism-matters/; Daniel J. Elazar, *American Federalism: The View from the States* (New York: Crowell, 1972).

9. Pietro Nivola, "Why Federalism Matters," Brookings Institution, October 1, 2005, https://www.brookings.edu/research/why-federalism-matters/.

10. Diamond, "The Ends of Federalism," 152.

11. Michael D. Tanner, "The American Welfare State: How We Spend Nearly $1 Trillion a Year Fighting Poverty—And Fail," Cato Institute, April 11, 2012, https://www.cato.org/publications/policy-analysis/american-welfare-state-how-we-spend-nearly-$1-trillion-year-fighting-poverty-fail.

12. R. M. Schneiderman, "Why Do Americans Still Hate Welfare?" *New York Times*, December 10, 2008, https://economix.blogs.nytimes.com/2008/12/10/why-do-americans-still-hate-welfare/.

13. See, for example, Aina Gallego, "Inequality and the Erosion of Trust among the Poor: Experimental Evidence," *Socio-Economic Review* 14:3 (2016), 443–60; Guglielmo Barone and Sauro Mocetti, "Inequality and Trust: New Evidence from Panel Data," *Economic Inquiry* 54:2 (April 2016), 794–809; Robert D. Putnam, "E Pluribus Unum: Diversity and Community in the Twenty-First Century" (2006 Johan Skytte Prize Lecture), *Scandinavian Political Studies* 30:2 (2007), 137–74; Eric M. Uslaner and Mitchell Brown, "Inequality, Trust, and Civic Engagement," *American Politics Research* 33:6 (2005), 868–94; Eric M. Uslaner, *The Moral Foundations of Trust* (Cambridge: Cambridge University Press, 2002). For a contrary view, see Sander Steijn and Bram Lancee, "Does Income Inequality Negatively Affect General Trust?," GINI Discussion Paper 20, November 2011, http://www.gini-research.org/system/uploads/274/original/DP_20_-_Steijn_Lancee.pdf.

14. Donald F. Kettl, *Can Governments Earn Our Trust?* (Cambridge: Polity Press, 2017), chap. 1.

15. "Trust in Government," Gallup, https://news.gallup.com/poll/5392/trust-government.aspx; Justin McCarthy, "Americans Still More Trusting in Local over State Government," Gallup Politics, September 19, 2016, https://news.gallup.com/poll/195656/americans-trusting-local-state-government.aspx.

16. Jeffrey M. Jones, "Illinois Residents Least Confident in Their State Government," Gallup Politics, February 17, 2016, https://news.gallup.com/poll/189281/illinois-residents-least-confident-state-government.aspx.

17. See, for example, Uslaner and Brown, "Inequality, Trust, and Civic Engagement"; Jean M. Twenge, W. Keith Campbell, and Nathan T. Carter, "Declines in Trust in Others and Confidence in Institutions among American Adults and Late Adolescents, 1972–2012," *Psychological Science* 25:10 (October 2014), 1914–23; Eric D. Gould and Alexander Hijzen, "Growing Apart, Losing Trust? The Impact of Inequality on Social Capital," International Monetary Fund Working Paper WP/16/176, August 2016, https://www.imf.org/external/pubs/ft/wp/2016/wp16176.pdf; Edelman Trust Barometer, https://www.edelman.com/trust-barometer.

Chapter 9. Can Some States Lead?

1. "Master of One-Liner Who Entertained Troops from WWII to Gulf War Dies," *Billings Gazette*, July 28, 2003, http://billingsgazette.com/news/world/master-of-one-liner-who-entertained-troops-from-wwii-to/article_c5e98541-bd77-550d-b8fd-a5cb9a0be687.html.

2. "History," California Air Resources Board, https://ww2.arb.ca.gov/about/history; *National Geographic*, "Smog," https://www.nationalgeographic.org/encyclopedia/smog/.

3. Arthur C. Stern, "History of Air Pollution Legislation in the United States," *Journal of the Air Pollution Control Association* 32:1 (1982), 44–61, https://www.tandfonline.com/doi/pdf/10.1080/00022470.1982.10465369.

4. *New State Ice Co. v. Liebmann*, 285 U.S. 262 (1932).

5. California Air Resources Board, "History."

6. "Greenhouse Gas Emissions," EPA, https://www.epa.gov/ghgemissions/sources-greenhouse-gas-emissions.

7. "Climate Basics: Energy/Emissions Data: Global Emissions," Center for Climate and Energy Solutions, https://www.c2es.org/content/international-emissions/.

8. California Air Resources Board, "History."

9. "Vehicle Emissions California Waivers and Authorizations," EPA, https://www.epa.gov/state-and-local-transportation/vehicle-emissions-california-waivers-and-authorizations#authorization.

10. Eric Kulisch, "California Becomes an Emissions Battleground," *Automotive News*, April 9, 2018, http://www.autonews.com/article/20180409/OEM11/180409731/california-environment-waiver-emissions-epa.

11. Megan Geuss, "EPA Says Auto Emissions Standards Are Too High, Questions California's Waiver," *ArsTechnica*, April 2, 2018, https://arstechnica.com/cars/2018/04/epa-says-auto-emissions-standards-are-too-high-questions-californias-waiver/.

12. "State of the Air 2019," American Lung Association, https://www.lung.org/our-initiatives/healthy-air/sota/city-rankings/.

13. "California Named State with the Worst Air Quality (Again)," *ScienceDaily*, June 19, 2017, https://www.sciencedaily.com/releases/2017/06/170619092749.htm.

14. Richard M. Frank, "The Federal Clean Air Act: California's Waivers—A Half-Century of Cooperative Federalism in Air Quality Management," testimony before the California State Senate, Committee on Environmental Quality, February 22, 2017, https://senv.senate.ca.gov/sites/senv.senate.ca.gov/files/uc_davis_-_richard_frank_testimony_2-22-17.pdf.

15. Tommy G. Thompson, *W2: Wisconsin Works* (Madison: Wisconsin Division of Economic Support, 1996), http://content.wisconsinhistory.org/cdm/ref/collection/tp/id/49207.

16. Tommy Thompson and William J. Bennett, "The Good News about Welfare Reform: Wisconsin's Success Story," Heritage Lecture 593, Heritage Foundation, March 6, 1997, https://www.heritage.org/welfare/report/the-good-news-about-welfare-reform-wisconsins-success-story.

17. Lissa August, "Thompson Was a Leader in Welfare Reform," *Politifact*, June 1, 2007, https://www.politifact.com/truth-o-meter/statements/2007/jun/01/tommy-thompson/thompson-was-a-leader-in-welfare-reform/.

18. Lawrence M. Mead, *Government Matters: Welfare Reform in Wisconsin* (Princeton, NJ: Princeton University Press, 2005), ix.

19. Frank J. Thompson, "The Rise of Executive Federalism: Implications for the Picket Fence and IGM," *American Review of Public Administration* 43:1 (2013), 3–25; see also Frank J. Thompson, "State and Local Governance Fifteen Years Later: Enduring and New Challenges," *Public Administration Review* (special issue, December 2008), S8–19; Isabel V. Sawhill, Jennifer L. Noyes, and Pietro S. Nivola, "Waive of the Future? Federalism and the Next Phase of Welfare Reform," Brookings Institution, March 1, 2004, https://www.brookings.edu/research/waive-of-the-future-federalism-and-the-next-phase-of-welfare-reform/; Carol S. Weissert and William G. Weissert, "Medicaid Waivers and Negotiated Federalism in the US: Is There Relevance to Other Federal Systems?" *Journal of Health Service Research Policy* 22:4 (October 2017), 261–64.

20. Nicholas Bagley, "Federalism and the End of Obamacare," *Yale Law Journal* 127 (2017), http://www.yalelawjournal.org/forum/federalism-and-the-end-of-obamacare.

21. Thomas Gais and James Fossett, "Federalism and the Executive Branch," in *Institutions of American Democracy: The Executive Branch*, ed. Joel D. Aberbach and Mark A. Peterson (New York: Oxford University Press, 2005), 488–524.

22. See, for example, Samuel R. Bagenstos, "Federalism by Waiver after the Health Care Case," University of Michigan Public Law Research Paper 294, October 15, 2012, https://papers.ssrn.com/sol3/papers.cfm?abstract_id=2161599, reprinted in *The Health Care Case: The Supreme Court's Decision and Its Implications*, ed. Gillian Metzger, Trevor Morrison, and Nathaniel Persily (New York: Oxford University Press, 2013); Jonathan H. Adler, "Letting Fifty Flowers Bloom: Using Federalism to Spur Environmental Innovation," in *The Jurisdynamics of Environmental Protection: Change and the Pragmatic Voice in Environmental Law*, ed. Jim Chen (Washington, DC: Environmental Law Institute, 2003), 263.

23. See Jessica Bulman-Pozen, "Executive Federalism Comes to America," *Virginia Law Review* 102 (2016), 1030, http://www.virginialawreview.org/sites/virginialawreview.org/files/Bulman-Pozen_Online.pdf; Gillian E. Metzger, "Agencies, Polarization, and the States," *Columbia Law Review* 115:7 (2015), https://columbialawreview.org/content/agencies-polarization-and-the-states/.

24. Ronald Reagan, "Address to the Nation on Federal Tax and Budget Reconciliation Legislation," delivered August 16, 1982, The American Presidency Project, http://www.presidency.ucsb.edu/ws/index.php?pid=42860.

25. Edward H. Stiglitz, "Forces of Federalism, Safety Nets, and Waivers," *Theoretical Inquiries in Law* 18 (2017), 125–56. https://scholarship.law.cornell.edu/cgi/viewcontent.cgi?article=2610&context=facpub.

26. See, for example, Peterson, *The Price of Federalism*.

27. Stiglitz, "Forces of Federalism, Safety Nets, and Waivers," 129.

28. Stiglitz, "Forces of Federalism, Safety Nets, and Waivers," 129–30.

29. Judith Solomon and Jesse Cross-Call, "Evaluation Needed before Allowing Replication of Indiana's Medicaid Waiver," Center on Budget and Policy Priorities, April 14, 2016, https://www.cbpp.org/research/health/evaluation-needed-before-allowing-replication-of-indianas-medicaid-waiver.

30. Stephanie Armour, "Health-Care Coverage Is Increasingly Determined by Where You Live," *Wall Street Journal*, July 18, 2018, https://www.wsj.com/articles/health-care-coverage-is-increasingly-determined-by-where-you-live-1531933372.

31. Colleen M. Grogan, Phillip M. Singer, and David K. Jones, "Rhetoric and Reform in Waiver States," *Journal of Health Politics, Policy and Law* 42:2 (April 2017), 247–84.

32. Data are from the National Conference of State Legislatures.

33. James Galbraith, "Inequality and the 2016 Election Outcome: A Dirty Secret and Dilemma," *NewGeography*, July 5, 2017, http://www.newgeography.com/content/005678-inequality-and-2016-election-outcome-a-dirty-secret-and-a-dilemma.

34. Galbraith, "Inequality and the 2016 Election Outcome."

35. "The Latest: 40-Minute Wait for Newly Legal California Pot," *Associated Press*, January 1, 2018, https://www.apnews.com/9cc4624f16304bb8a9d0dbd6f4c04269.

36. Lizzie Widdicombe, "The Martha Stewart of Marijuana Edibles," *New Yorker*, April 24, 2017, https://www.newyorker.com/magazine/2017/04/24/the-martha-stewart-of-marijuana-edibles. See, for example, Laurie Wolf, *Cooking with Cannabis: Delicious Recipes for Edibles and Everyday Favorites* (Beverly, MA: Quarry Books, 2016).

37. Angel Jennings, Sarah Parvini, and Gary Robbins, "Recreational Pot Sales Roll Out in California, with Celebratory 'Blunts' and Big Crowds," *Los Angeles Times*, January 1, 2018, http://www.latimes.com/local/lanow/la-me-california-marijuana-sales-20180101-story.html.

38. Reid J. Epstein, "DOJ Won't Block Pot Legalization Laws," *Politico*, August 29, 2018, https://www.politico.com/story/2013/08/doj-marijuana-legalization-laws-096041.

39. Jefferson B. Sessions III, "Marijuana Enforcement" (memorandum to all US attorneys), January 4, 2018, https://www.politico.com/f/?id=00000160-c219-dcd4-a96b-f739f1ee0000.

40. US Department of Justice, "Justice Department Issues Memo on Marijuana Enforcement" (press release), January 4, 2018, https://www.justice.gov/opa/pr/justice-department-issues-memo-marijuana-enforcement.

41. "US Attorney for Colorado: No Changes on Marijuana Enforcement," *Associated Press/KDVR News*, January 5, 2018, http://kdvr.com/2018/01/04/u-s-attorney-for-colorado-status-quo-on-marijuana-prosecutions/.

42. Lisa Murkowski (@lisamurkowski), tweet, January 4, 2018, https://twitter.com/lisamurkowski?ref_src=twsrc%5Egoogle%7Ctwcamp%5Eserp%7Ctwgr%5Eauthor.

43. Cory Gardner (@SenCoryGardner), tweet, January 4, 2018, https://twitter.com/SenCoryGardner?ref_src=twsrc%5Egoogle%7Ctwcamp%5Eserp%7Ctwgr%5Eauthor.

44. Brandon Rittiman (@BrandonRittiman), tweet of July 29, 2016, interview, January 4, 2018, https://twitter.com/BrandonRittiman/status/948928646152044549.

45. Eric Katz, "VA Enables Vets to Discuss Marijuana Use with Doctors without Losing Benefits," GovExec.com, January 3, 2018, http://www.govexec.com/pay-benefits/2018/01/va-enables-vets-discuss-marijuana-use-doctors-without-losing-benefits/144927/?oref=river.

46. Fred Barnes, "The Resistance," *Weekly Standard*, March 3, 2014, https://www.weeklystandard.com/fred-barnes/the-resistance; Fred Barnes, "The Last Redoubt," *Weekly Standard*, July 22, 2013, https://www.weeklystandard.com/fred-barnes/the-last-redoubt.

47. Barnes, "The Resistance."

48. George F. Will, "Oklahoma Attorney General Scott Pruitt Is Lighting Fuses in Oklahoma," *Washington Post*, December 19, 2014, https://www.washingtonpost.com/opinions/george-will -lighting-fuses-in-oklahoma/2014/12/19/0629d37a-86ed-11e4-a702-fa31ff4ae98e_story.html ?utm_term=.a678fbc02c4c.

49. *Michigan v. Environmental Protection Agency*, 576 U.S. ____ (2015).

50. Elbert Lin, "States Suing the Federal Government: Protecting Liberty or Playing Politics?," *University of Richmond Law Review* 52:633 (2018).

51. Lin, "States Suing the Federal Government," 651, 652.

52. Paul Nolette, "Commandeering Federalism: The Rise of Activist State Attorneys General," *Liberty Law Forum*, September 5, 2016, https://www.lawliberty.org/liberty-forum /commandeering-federalism-the-rise-of-the-activist-state-attorneys-general/; see also Steven M. Teles, "Kludgeocracy in America," *National Affairs* 17 (Fall 2013), https://www.nationalaffairs .com/publications/detail/kludgeocracy-in-america.

Chapter 10. Madison's Invention Comes Undone

1. Aaron Wildavsky, "E Pluribus Unum: Plurality, Diversity, Variety, and Modesty," in *The Costs of Federalism: Essays in Honor of James W. Fesler*, ed. Robert T. Golembiewski and Aaron Wildavsky (New Brunswick, NJ: Transaction Books, 1984), 4, 5.

2. "Quote of the Day," *The Economist*, August 4, 2009, https://www.economist.com/blogs /freeexchange/2009/08/quote_of_the_day_10.

3. Wildavsky, "E Pluribus Unum," 17.

4. Quoted in Wildavsky, "E Pluribus Unum," 5.

5. Charles de Gaulle, 1951 speech; for variations, see "Cheese quote by Charles de Gaulle," http://listserv.linguistlist.org/pipermail/ads-l/2005-March/046740.html.

6. Theodore J. Lowi, "Why Is There No Socialism in the United States? A Federal Analysis," in Robert T. Golembiewski and Aaron Wildavsky, eds., *The Costs of Federalism: Essays in Honor of James W. Fesler* (New Brunswick, N.J.: Transaction Books, 1984), 45–46.

7. Deil S. Wright, *Understanding Intergovernmental Relations*, 3rd ed. (Pacific Grove, CA: Brooks-Cole, 1988); Robert Agranoff and Beryl A. Radin, "Deil Wright's Overlapping Model of Intergovernmental Relations: The Basis for Contemporary Intergovernmental Relationships," *Publius: The Journal of Federalism* 45:1 (2014), 139–59.

8. "Bringing Population Data to Life," University of Virginia, Weldon Cooper Center for Public Service, 2018, https://demographics.coopercenter.org/node/7143; "National Population Projections," University of Virginia, Weldon Cooper Center for Public Service, 2018, https:// demographics.coopercenter.org/national-population-projections.

9. Quoted in Philip Bump, "In about 20 Years, Half the Population Will Live in Eight States," *Washington Post*, July 12, 2018, https://www.washingtonpost.com/news/politics/wp/2018/07 /12/in-about-20-years-half-the-population-will-live-in-eight-states/?utm_term=.7e21209362fd.

10. Bill Bishop, *The Big Sort: Why the Clustering of Like-Minded America Is Tearing Us Apart* (Boston: Mariner Books, 2008).

11. For example, see *The Budget and Economic Outlook: 2018 to 2028*, US Congressional Budget Office, April 9, 2018, https://www.cbo.gov/publication/53651.

12. Jonathan Vespa, David M. Armstrong, and Lauren Medina, "Demographic Turning Points for the United States: Population Projections for 2020 to 2060," US Bureau of the Census, https://www.census.gov/content/dam/Census/newsroom/press-kits/2018/jsm/jsm-presentation-pop-projections.pdf.

13. "Budget and Economic Data: Long-Term Budget Projections," US Congressional Budget Office, June 2018, https://www.cbo.gov/about/products/budget-economic-data#1.

14. Bill Lucia, "Gap Grows between Well-Off and Troubled State Public Pension Plans," *Route-Fifty*, July 2, 2019, https://www.routefifty.com/finance/2019/07/pension-funding-states-pew/158183/.

15. Julia B. Isaacs, Cary Lou, Heather Hahn, Ashley Hong, Caleb Quakenbush, and C. Eugene Seurerle, *Kids' Share 2018: Report on Federal Expenditures on Children through 2017 and Future Projections*, Urban Institute, July 2018, https://www.urban.org/sites/default/files/publication/98725/kids_share_2018_0.pdf.

16. Boris Shor and Nolan McCarty, "Measuring American Legislatures," American Legislatures Project, 2018, https://americanlegislatures.com/data/; Boris Shor, "How US State Legislatures Are Polarized and Getting More Polarized (in 2 Graphs)," *Washington Post*, January 14, 2014, https://www.washingtonpost.com/news/monkey-cage/wp/2014/01/14/how-u-s-state-legislatures-are-polarized-and-getting-more-polarized-in-2-graphs/?utm_term=.339e0ec12511.

17. "State Legislative Policymaking in an Age of Political Polarization," National Conference of State Legislatures/Center for Legislative Strengthening, April 2017, http://www.ncsl.org/Portals/1/Documents/About_State_Legislatures/Partisanship_f04_web.pdf.

18. Daniel J. Hopkins, *The Increasingly United States* (Chicago: University of Chicago Press, 2018).

19. Lee Drutman, "America Has Local Political Institutions but Nationalized Politics. This Is a Problem," *Vox*, March 31, 2018, https://www.vox.com/polyarchy/2018/5/31/17406590/local-national-political-institutions-polarization-federalism; see also Jacob M. Grumbach, "From Backwaters to Major Policymakers: Policy Polarization in the States, 1970–2014," *Perspectives on Politics* 16:2 (2018), 416–35.

20. Hopkins, *The Increasingly United States*, 3.

21. James Fallows, "Eleven Signs a City Will Succeed," *Atlantic*, March 2016, https://www.theatlantic.com/magazine/archive/2016/03/eleven-signs-a-city-will-succeed/426885/.

22. William A. Niskanen, "On the Constitution of a Compound Republic," Cato Institute, 2001, 3, https://pdfs.semanticscholar.org/c820/5df7cec190f3bf281ad8639d15d8159e7449.pdf.

23. *National League of Cities v. Usery*, 426 U.S. 833 (1976).

24. *Garcia v. San Antonio Metropolitan Transit Authority*, 469 U.S. 528 (1985).

25. Wildavsky, "E Pluribus Unum," 6.

Chapter 11. Hamilton's Solution to Madison's Dilemma

1. Richard Brookhiser, *Alexander Hamilton: American* (New York: Free Press, 1999), 185.

2. Chernow, *Alexander Hamilton*, 266.

3. Chernow, *Alexander Hamilton*, 290.

4. Chernow, *Alexander Hamilton*, 600.

5. US Office of Management and Budget, *Budget of the United States Government: Historical Tables*, table 12.1, https://www.whitehouse.gov/omb/historical-tables/.

6. Stephen Goldsmith and Neil Kleiman, *A New City O/S: The Power of Open, Collaborative, and Distributed Governance* (Washington, DC: Brookings Institution, 2017).

7. "SXSW 2019: 2 Former Mayors Discuss the Future of Data," Governing (website), March 14, 2019, https://www.governing.com/topics/urban/gov-sxsw-omalley-podcast.html.

8. Chernow, *Alexander Hamilton*, 266.

9. Ruben Durante, Paolo Pinotti, and Andrea Tesei, "The Political Legacy of Entertainment TV," *American Economic Review* 109:7 (2019), 2497–2530.

10. John F. Harris, "Democrats Are Veering Left. It Might Just Work," *Politico* (July 30, 2019), https://www.politico.com/magazine/story/2019/07/30/democrats-left-2020-debates-227488.

INDEX

Abbott, Greg, 165–66

ACA. *See* Affordable Care Act

ACE. *See* Air, Climate, and Energy index

Adams, John, 23–24

Addams, Jane, 57

administration: compound republic, blurring of responsibilities in a, 175; federalism, crucial role in, 186–87; local governments as administrative agent for federal programs, 63, 75, 77; state governments as administrative agent for federal programs, 63, 75, 77, 153, 167–68, 171, 189

Affordable Care Act (ACA, a.k.a. "Obamacare"): battles fought within the states over, 15; enactment and structure of, 98–99; litigation by Republican state attorneys general against, 166; Medicaid expansion and, 99–102; political pragmatism spawns administrative complexity, 99–100; variation across states, 100–105; waivers for administering, 152; waivers for unwinding, 157

Air, Climate, and Energy (ACE) index, 119–22

Alabama, poverty in Lowndes county, 133–35

Alston, Philip, 133

American Lung Association, "State of the Air" report, 149

American Medical Association, 92

Anti-Federalists: Cato, 36–37; Madison's put-down of, 35; opposition to the proposed Constitution, 31, 36–37; "The Federal Farmer," 39

Arizona, Obamacare premiums in, 103–4

Arreguin, Jesse, 161

Articles of Confederation: as a collection of fatal vices, 26–29; failure of, 1–2; Hamilton's concerns about/criticism of, 19–20, 193; republican government, as a form of, 34; reserved powers clause in, 39; states, as rule by a confederation of, 31

balance between federal and state/local governments: challenges of striking a, 186; consequences of, 137–38 (*see also* federalism as a driver of inequality); in the Constitution, 30–31 (*see also* Constitution, United States; Fourteenth Amendment; Tenth Amendment); the constitutional convention, as the challenge at, 2–3; the Depression/New Deal and, 62–63, 66; emerging in the 1980s, 95–96; *The Federalist Papers*, addressed in, 32–36; Madison's dilemma/quest on (*see* Madison's dilemma/quest); the Progressives and, 59; questions of, 22, 24–26, 31; resetting in the twenty-first century, question of, 18, 173 (*see also* Fifth Generation of Federalism); in the Second Generation of Federalism, 55; self-correcting forces to maintain, 187–88; shifting over time, 6, 21, 137; states' rights, claims of, 49; in the Third Generation of Federalism, 76–77. *See also* federal government; federalism; local governments; state governments